Worn Condition
Noted -MVPL

MORENO VALLEY PUBLIC LIBRARY

P9-DTD-914

NO. AB.

APR 1 2 2019

MVFOL

VISUAL DICTIONARY

NEW EDITION

Written by Simon Beecroft, Jason Fry, and Simon Hugo

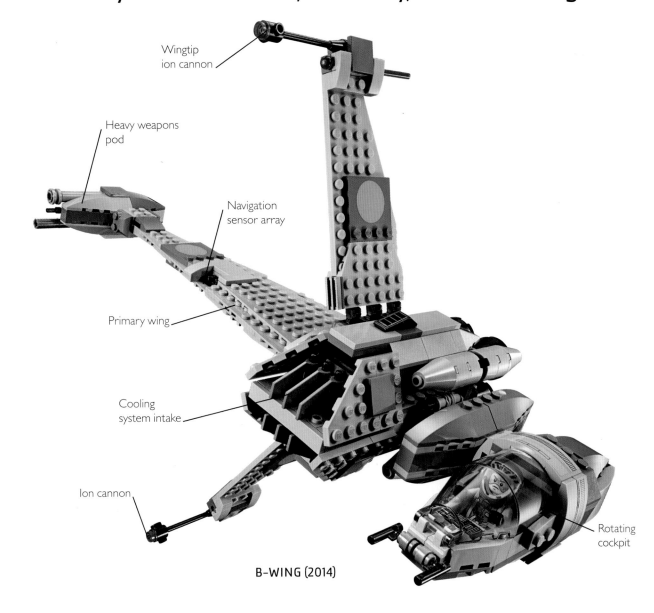

Wingtip
ion cannon

Heavy weapons
pod

Navigation
sensor array

Primary wing

Cooling
system intake

Ion cannon

Rotating
cockpit

B-WING (2014)

Moreno Valley Public Library

Contents

CHAPTER 3:
THE RISE OF THE FIRST ORDER

CHAPTER 4:
SPECIALIST SETS

CHAPTER 5:
BEYOND THE BRICK

Much to learn, you still have.

Introduction

The LEGO Group has been bringing the *Star Wars*™ galaxy into LEGO® form since 1999. Celebrate 20 years of this extraordinarily rich and detailed fantasy world—made entirely of LEGO bricks!

Delight in a wealth of movie-accurate details, from the steering vanes on a Tatooine skiff to the chin guns adorning the head of a lumbering AT-AT walker. Discover the endless creativity of the LEGO Group's designers as they use LEGO elements in surprising ways and make new elements especially for the sets.

Spot the differences between the movie originals and the LEGO versions, whether it's a change of color, a reconfigured interior, or a new feature. With LEGO® *Star Wars*™, curiosity is rewarded: headlights flip aside to reveal missile launchers, concealed compartments hide secret lightsabers, and Gungan subs sprout their own mini-subs in times of trouble.

Originally published in 2009, LEGO *Star Wars: The Visual Dictionary* has been thoroughly updated and expanded to celebrate the twentieth anniversary of the iconic and much-loved theme.

Dashing cape

Custom-made shirt

Detailed helmet

Blaster power cell container

Leg armor with knee protector plate

LANDO CALRISSIAN

STORMTROOPER

Ten years of LEGO designs have been added—yellow faces have become flesh-colored, starfighters and vehicles have been revised with even more detail and movie accuracy, and countless new *Star Wars* characters and sets have been translated into brick form.

Dive in and explore an ever-expanding galaxy of LEGO *Star Wars* sets, minifigures, and facts.

DATA BOXES

Throughout the book, LEGO *Star Wars* sets are identified with a data box, which lists the official name of the set, the year it was first released, the LEGO identification number of the set, the number of LEGO pieces or elements in the set, and the source that inspired the model.

Set name	Rey's Speeder	
Year	2015	Number 75099
Pieces	193	Source EP VII

Source abbreviations:
EP I–EP VIII—the Skywalker saga movies (for example EP I for *Star Wars: Episode I The Phantom Menace*)
R1—*Rogue One: A Star Wars Story*
Solo—*Solo: A Star Wars Story*
CW—*Star Wars: The Clone Wars* animated TV show and movie
Rebels—*Star Wars Rebels* animated TV series
TYC—LEGO *Star Wars: The Yoda Chronicles* animated TV series
TFA—LEGO *Star Wars: The Freemaker Adventures* animated TV series
Legends—*Star Wars* non-canon stories released prior to 2014

Toothy grin

Ammo bandolier

Multicolored hair

CHEWBACCA

Focused, determined expression

Loose, open-weave tabard

Leather and wool weapons belt

REY

20 Years of LEGO® *Star Wars*™

From the first simple playsets a long time ago, to far, far, and away the largest, most complex builds any LEGO® theme has ever seen— the LEGO® *Star Wars*™ galaxy has it all!

The first LEGO *Star Wars* sets go on sale. They showcase scenes and characters from the newly released *Star Wars: Episode I The Phantom Menace*.

The first LEGO models of the *Millennium Falcon* (set 7190) shown above and *Slave I* (set 7144) are released.

A unique, 1,868-piece bust of Darth Maul (set 10018) is released as part of the Ultimate Collector Series.

The first sets based on new movie *Star Wars: Episode II Attack of the Clones* include Republic Gunship (set 7163).

The first Jabba the Hutt minifigure features in Jabba's Palace (set 4480).

Lando Calrissian is the first LEGO *Star Wars* human character to have a non-yellow head.

1999   **2000**   **2001**   **2002**   **2003**

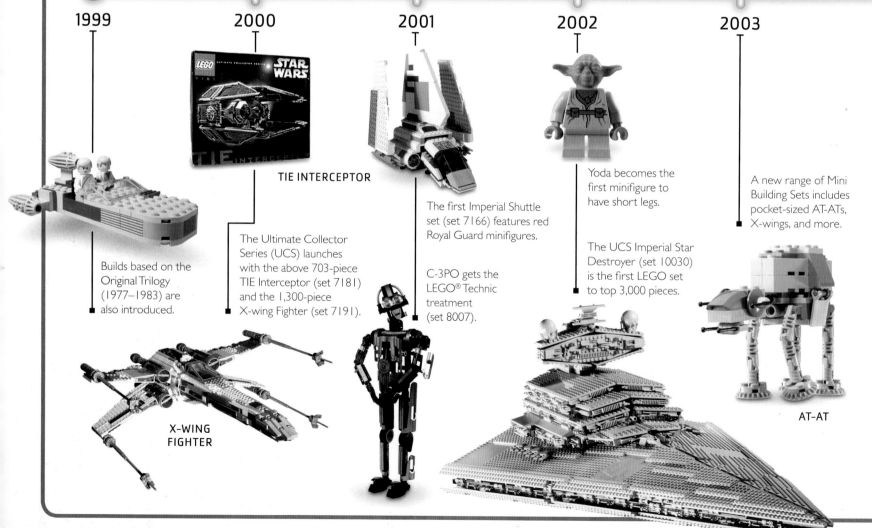

TIE INTERCEPTOR

Builds based on the Original Trilogy (1977–1983) are also introduced.

The Ultimate Collector Series (UCS) launches with the above 703-piece TIE Interceptor (set 7181) and the 1,300-piece X-wing Fighter (set 7191).

The first Imperial Shuttle set (set 7166) features red Royal Guard minifigures.

C-3PO gets the LEGO® Technic treatment (set 8007).

Yoda becomes the first minifigure to have short legs.

The UCS Imperial Star Destroyer (set 10030) is the first LEGO set to top 3,000 pieces.

A new range of Mini Building Sets includes pocket-sized AT-ATs, X-wings, and more.

X-WING FIGHTER

AT-AT

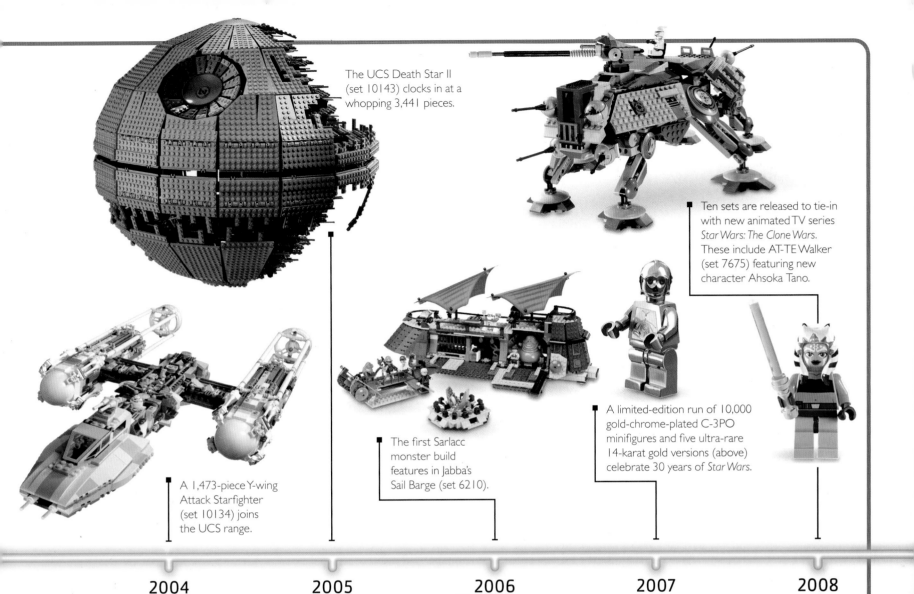

The UCS Death Star II (set 10143) clocks in at a whopping 3,441 pieces.

Ten sets are released to tie-in with new animated TV series *Star Wars: The Clone Wars*. These include AT-TE Walker (set 7675) featuring new character Ahsoka Tano.

The first Sarlacc monster build features in Jabba's Sail Barge (set 6210).

A limited-edition run of 10,000 gold-chrome-plated C-3PO minifigures and five ultra-rare 14-karat gold versions (above) celebrate 30 years of *Star Wars*.

A 1,473-piece Y-wing Attack Starfighter (set 10134) joins the UCS range.

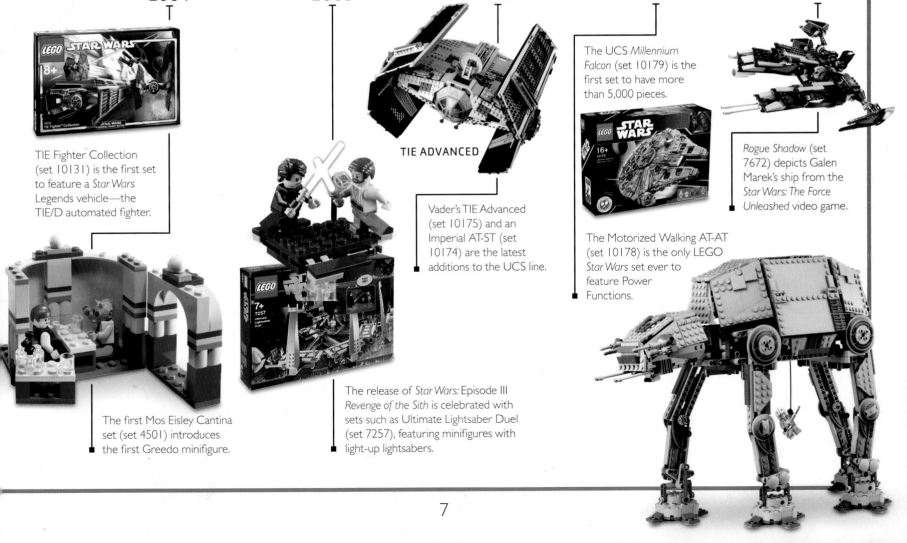

2004

2005

2006

2007

2008

TIE Fighter Collection (set 10131) is the first set to feature a *Star Wars* Legends vehicle—the TIE/D automated fighter.

TIE ADVANCED

The UCS *Millennium Falcon* (set 10179) is the first set to have more than 5,000 pieces.

Rogue Shadow (set 7672) depicts Galen Marek's ship from the *Star Wars: The Force Unleashed* video game.

Vader's TIE Advanced (set 10175) and an Imperial AT-ST (set 10174) are the latest additions to the UCS line.

The Motorized Walking AT-AT (set 10178) is the only LEGO *Star Wars* set ever to feature Power Functions.

The first Mos Eisley Cantina set (set 4501) introduces the first Greedo minifigure.

The release of *Star Wars: Episode III Revenge of the Sith* is celebrated with sets such as Ultimate Lightsaber Duel (set 7257), featuring minifigures with light-up lightsabers.

To mark the 10th anniversary of LEGO *Star Wars*, 10,000 chrome-effect Darth Vader minifigures are randomly inserted into sets.

New sets for *Star Wars: The Clone Wars* include Count Dooku's Solar Sailer (set 7752).

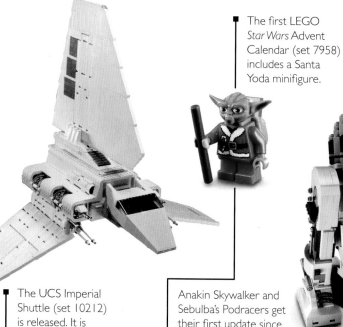

The UCS Imperial Shuttle (set 10212) is released. It is made from 2,503 pieces, most of which are white.

The first LEGO *Star Wars* Advent Calendar (set 7958) includes a Santa Yoda minifigure.

Anakin Skywalker and Sebulba's Podracers get their first update since 1999 (set 7962).

A UCS R2-D2 (set 10225) measures over 12 in (31 cm) tall.

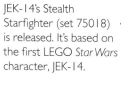

JEK-14's Stealth Starfighter (set 75018) is released. It's based on the first LEGO *Star Wars* character, JEK-14.

The Clone Wars version of Maul (with mechanical legs) makes his debut in Mandalorian Speeder (set 75022).

2009

The 1,758-piece Republic Dropship with AT-OT Walker (set 10195) is the largest LEGO *Star Wars* set outside of the UCS range.

2010

A new wampa figure features in Hoth Wampa Cave (set 8089).

2011

At close to 50 in (124 cm) long, UCS Super Star Destroyer (set 10221) becomes the longest ever LEGO set.

UCS SUPER STAR DESTROYER

2012

Two sets tie in with the *Star Wars: The Old Republic* video game, including the Sith *Fury*-class Interceptor (set 9500).

2013

New UCS sets include the elaborate Ewok Village (set 10236).

The UCS Sandcrawler (set 75059) has 3,296 pieces.

The Microfighters range launches with six sets, including the TIE Interceptor.

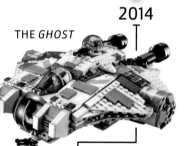

The theatrical release of Episode VII *The Force Awakens* heralds a whole new wave of LEGO *Star Wars* heroes, in sets such as Poe's X-Wing Fighter (set 75102).

Animated TV series LEGO *Star Wars: The Freemaker Adventures* launches, along with tie-in sets *StarScavenger* (set 75147) and *Eclipse Fighter* (set 75145).

STARSCAVENGER

As Episode VIII *The Last Jedi* soars into cinemas, LEGO *Star Wars* tracks its hyperdrive into stores with sets such as First Order Heavy Assault Walker (set 75189).

The Kessel Run *Millennium Falcon* (set 75212) is one of eight sets marking the theatrical release of *Solo: A Star Wars Story*, featuring a young Han Solo.

2014

THE *GHOST*

Animated TV series *Star Wars Rebels* blasts onto screens and into LEGO sets, starting with the *Ghost* (set 75053) and the *Phantom* (set 75048).

New buildable figures such as General Grievous (set 75112) allow for character battles on a whole new scale.

2015

2016

The UCS Death Star (set 75159) is updated to include more than 4,000 pieces.

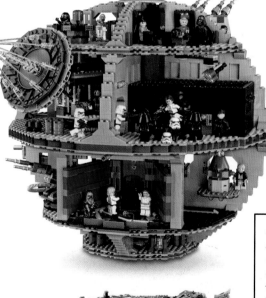

2017

A new UCS *Millennium Falcon* (set 75192) is the only LEGO set ever to have more than 7,000 pieces.

2018

Fifteen years after it was first made into a LEGO set, Cloud City gets the Master Builder Set treatment (set 75222).

Meanwhile, an old Luke Skywalker makes his LEGO debut in Ahch-To Island Training (set 75200).

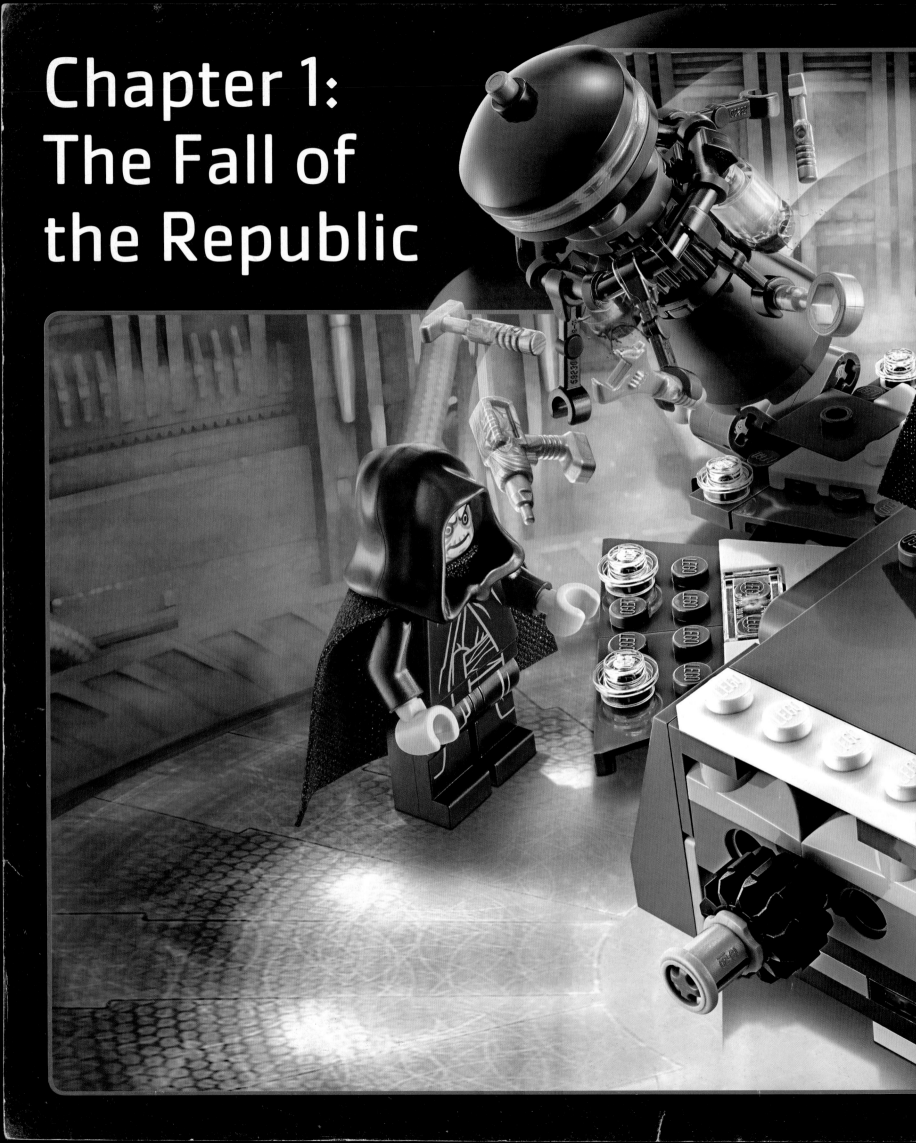

Chapter 1: The Fall of the Republic

Anakin Skywalker

Anakin's journey from a slave boy to perhaps the most capable and ambitious Jedi ever is filled with action and danger. Anakin has always been an incredible pilot and has flown everything from "borrowed" speeders to custom-designed Jedi starfighters during the Clone Wars. But Anakin's daring has its price: the loss of his hand in battle with Count Dooku starts a process of dehumanization that will end in the full body armor of Darth Vader.

ANAKIN (NABOO PILOT)
Anakin's Naboo Starfighter Microfighter minifigure (set 75223) is all set for action in a slave's tunic and helmet with flying goggles.

Naboo Starfighter

As a boy, Anakin flies a Naboo N-1 starfighter and blows up the Trade Federation's Droid Control Ship. He fits in the cockpit, boarding the fighter via a ladder included with this set. Spring-loaded shooters can be used to fire at battle droids and destroyer droids and a mechanism on the underside ejects R2-D2 from the droid socket in case of trouble.

Set name	Naboo Starfighter	
Year	2015	Number 75092
Pieces	442	Source EP I

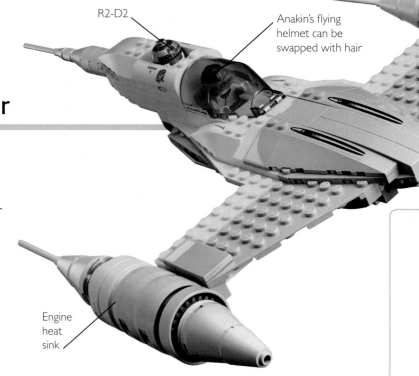

R2-D2

Anakin's flying helmet can be swapped with hair

Missile launcher

Engine heat sink

ANAKIN (PADAWAN)

YOUNG PADAWAN
Protecting Padmé Amidala, Anakin falls in love with the brave senator. He briefly wields a green lightsaber on Geonosis. This minifigure came with the Republic Gunship (set 75021).

Coruscant Airspeeder

Teenage Anakin is now a headstrong Padawan, training under Jedi Master Obi-Wan Kenobi. Anakin wears a Padawan braid (printed on his minifigure's shirt). He and Obi-Wan sit in this airspeeder with its exposed turbojets. The Jedi can store their lightsabers in a secret compartment. Can the Jedi catch up with assassin Zam Wesell's speeder, as they weave through the skyscrapers of the city planet, Coruscant?

Set name	Bounty Hunter Pursuit	
Year	2002	Number 7133
Pieces	253	Source EP II

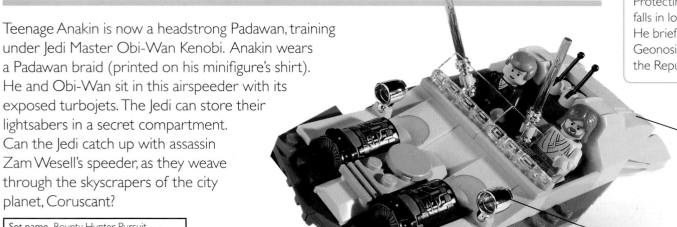

Trunk is at back of speeder

Turbojet engines

Headlights (used as cups in other LEGO® sets)

PADMÉ
(PEASANT
DISGUISE)

UNDERCOVER QUEEN
When Anakin first meets his future wife, Padmé Naberrie is disguised as a peasant for her trip to Tatooine. In Darth Maul's Sith Infiltrator (set 7961), Padmé has a natural skin tone.

▼ Swoop Bike

Padawan Anakin borrows Owen Lars's swoop bike to rescue his mother from the two Tusken Raiders included with this set. The bike has an engine compartment behind Anakin. Watch out for that moisture vaporator, Anakin! (The vaporator comes with the set and opens to reveal secret controls.)

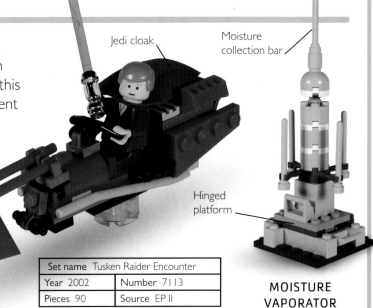

Jedi cloak

Moisture collection bar

Hinged platform

Steering vane

MOISTURE VAPORATOR

Set name	Tusken Raider Encounter	
Year	2002	Number 7113
Pieces	90	Source EP II

Large viewport

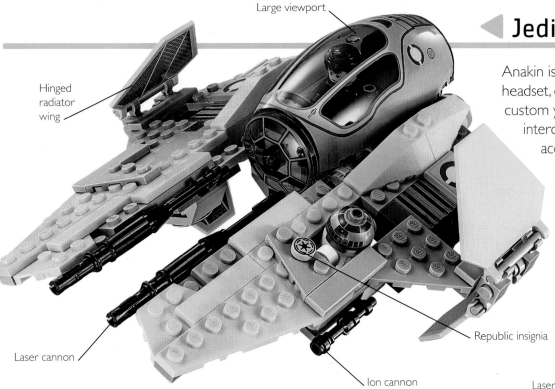

Hinged radiator wing

◀ Jedi Starfighter

Anakin is now a Jedi Knight, with a scarred face, pilot headset, cyborg hand, and black robe. He pilots a custom yellow starfighter (actually, an Eta-2 *Actis* interceptor) with movable wings and R2-D2's accompanying minifigure fully seated in the astromech socket. The original version in 2005 featured only R2-D2's headpiece.

Set name	Jedi Interceptor	
Year	2014	Number 75038
Pieces	223	Source EP III

Laser cannon

Republic insignia

Ion cannon

Laser turret

Deployable escape pod

Interior hold includes working two-cable winch

JEDI KNIGHT
After a lightsaber duel with Count Dooku, Anakin loses one of his hands, which is replaced with a cyborg one. Turn Anakin's head to reveal an angry expression. This minifigure came with the 2018 Anakin's Jedi Starfighter (set 75214).

**ANAKIN
(JEDI)**

▶ The *Twilight*

Anakin's personal starship in the Clone Wars is a battered Corellian G9 *Rigger*-class freighter, the *Twilight*. Anakin first "borrows" the damaged ship from a landing platform on Teth, when he and Ahsoka Tano are rescuing Jabba the Hutt's son, Rotta. Anakin has since repaired and upgraded its weapons and systems.

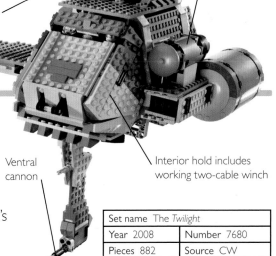

Ventral cannon

Set name	The *Twilight*	
Year	2008	Number 7680
Pieces	882	Source CW

Podracing

Ladies and gentlemen, Dugs and Hutts, please join us at the Boonta Eve Classic, the most keenly fought and downright dangerous podrace on Tatooine. Experienced racers Sebulba, Gasgano, and Aldar Beedo will power up their oversized podracers, while the human newcomer, nine-year-old Anakin Skywalker, climbs aboard his self-made machine, watched nervously by his supporters. The tension here is electric!

▼ **Starters' Box**

The podrace starts and finishes at the starters' box, with shaded towers for race officials and the press.

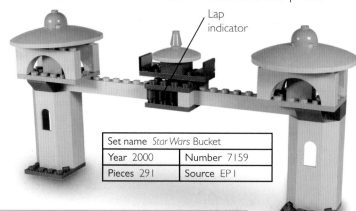

Lap indicator

Set name	*Star Wars* Bucket	
Year 2000		Number 7159
Pieces 291		Source EP1

▶ Sebulba's Podracer

SEBULBA

The dastardly Dug named Sebulba is determined to win the Boonta Eve Classic—and he doesn't care what dirty tricks he uses to do so. Sebulba's Podracer includes secret flip-up saws that the Dug uses to saw through his rival racers' machines.

SLAVE SPECTATOR
A Mos Espa slave, the Rodian Wald cheers on Anakin as he races in the Boonta Eve Classic. But Wald doubts Anakin can win the race—after all, he's never even managed to finish a competition before.

Control power generator

Afterburner

Combustion chamber

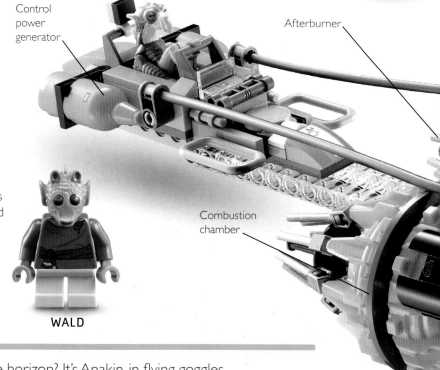

WALD

Set name	Anakin & Sebulba's Podracers	
Year 2011		Number 7962
Pieces 810		Source EP1

▼ Anakin's Podracer

What's that blur on the Tatooine horizon? It's Anakin, in flying goggles, piloting his super-fast podracer with "glowing" power couplings and hinged front air scoops, for additional control when cornering. Anakin built the pod himself, and relies on his Force-aided reflexes while racing. Padmé hopes Anakin will at least survive this dangerous enterprise.

Throttle lever

Control cable

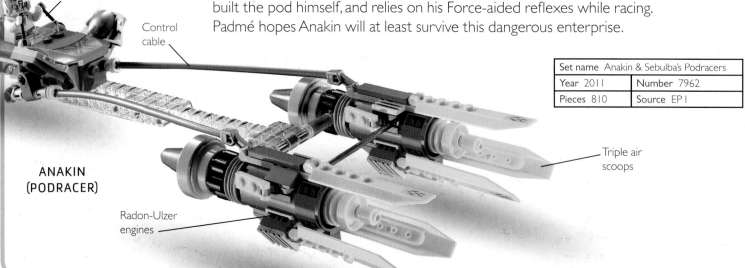

ANAKIN (PODRACER)

Radon-Ulzer engines

Triple air scoops

Set name	Anakin & Sebulba's Podracers	
Year 2011		Number 7962
Pieces 810		Source EP1

Boonta Eve Podracers

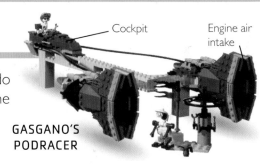

Cockpit

Engine air intake

GASGANO'S PODRACER

Tatooine podracer pilots such as Gasgano and Aldar Beedo rely on super-fast vehicles to stand a chance of winning the Boonta Eve Classic. Beedo looks for ways to make his Mark IV Flat-Twin Turbojet Podracer even faster, while Gasgano fine-tunes his Ord Pedrovia Podracer. Watto's junkyard is the place to find spare parts and custom accessories, or even to build a new craft. Perhaps parts from Mawhonic's GPE-3130 racer might prove useful—but both racers know that the winged Toydarian drives a hard bargain.

Set name	Mos Espa Podrace	
Year 1999	Number 7171	
Pieces 894	Source EP1	

Armored turbojet

Secondary thruster

MAWHONIC'S PODRACER

Set name	Watto's Junkyard	
Year 2001	Number 7186	
Pieces 466	Source EP1	

ALDAR BEEDO'S PODRACER

WATTO

JUNK DEALER
The Toydarian Watto is Anakin's master, and doesn't know that the boy has secretly built a podracer out of surplus parts. Watto loves to gamble, and usually bets heavily on the unscrupulous Sebulba.

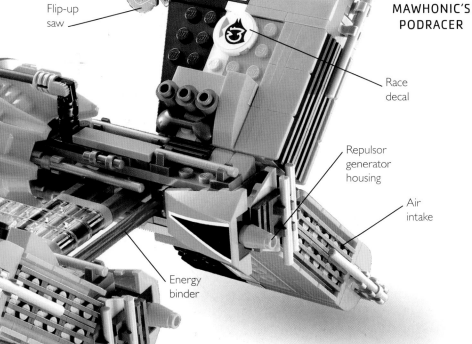

Flip-up saw

Race decal

Repulsor generator housing

Air intake

Energy binder

Coolant radiators

Split-X stabilizing vane

DROID MECHANIC
These pit droids are fast workers, but quite accident-prone. They see by using a single photoreceptor. This one belongs to Sebulba and appears in Mos Espa Podrace (set 7171).

PIT DROID

Other Podracers

Lined up and ready to race, simplified versions of Anakin's and Aldar Beedo's podracers rev up alongside Neva Kee's experimental machine, with its cockpit placed in front of the massive engines (which could be dangerous). Clegg Holdfast's Volvec KT9 Wasp Podracer has a winged protective canopy over its cockpit.

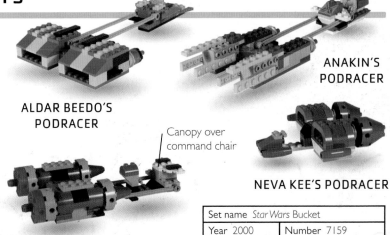

ANAKIN'S PODRACER

ALDAR BEEDO'S PODRACER

Canopy over command chair

NEVA KEE'S PODRACER

Set name	Star Wars Bucket	
Year 2000	Number 7159	
Pieces 291	Source EP1	

CLEGG HOLDFAST'S PODRACER

Obi-Wan Kenobi

For a Jedi who's not crazy about flying, Obi-Wan Kenobi pilots a starfighter a lot of the time—though he can't help losing them, too! Kenobi trains headstrong Anakin Skywalker, and goes on missions to far-flung planets including Utapau and Mustafar. Under the Empire, an exiled Obi-Wan meets Luke Skywalker and fights a final duel against his former Padawan, now known as Darth Vader.

Padawan braid

Utility belt

OBI-WAN (PADAWAN)

In *Star Wars*: Episode I *The Phantom Menace*, Obi-Wan is Qui-Gon Jinn's Padawan, and joins his master in trying to protect Queen Amidala from the Sith warrior Darth Maul. Swivel Obi-Wan's 2017 head to reveal a face with a fierce look—ready to enter into battle with his Sith opponent.

Shield projector module

Docking mechanism

Rotating engine

Ion acceleration pod

Opening cockpit

Deflector shield power hub

Stud shooters

Storage area for lightsaber under wing

R4-P17 astromech droid (dome only)

 ## Jedi Starfighter with Hyperdrive

Obi-Wan wears a headset when piloting his Delta-7 *Aethersprite* light interceptor. For a hyperdrive boost, the ship connects to a docking ring with two large engines. Supported by his trusty astromech, R4-P17, Kenobi duels with Jango Fett's *Slave 1*, blasting by the asteroids above rocky Geonosis.

Set name	Jedi Starfighter with Hyperdrive	
Year	2017	Number 75191
Pieces	825	Source EP II

TEACHER

As a Jedi Knight, Obi-Wan takes on an apprentice. Anakin proves to be a rebellious student, which may explain Obi-Wan's cross expression here. Until 2013, Episode II minifigures of Obi-Wan had yellow faces.

OBI-WAN (JEDI KNIGHT)

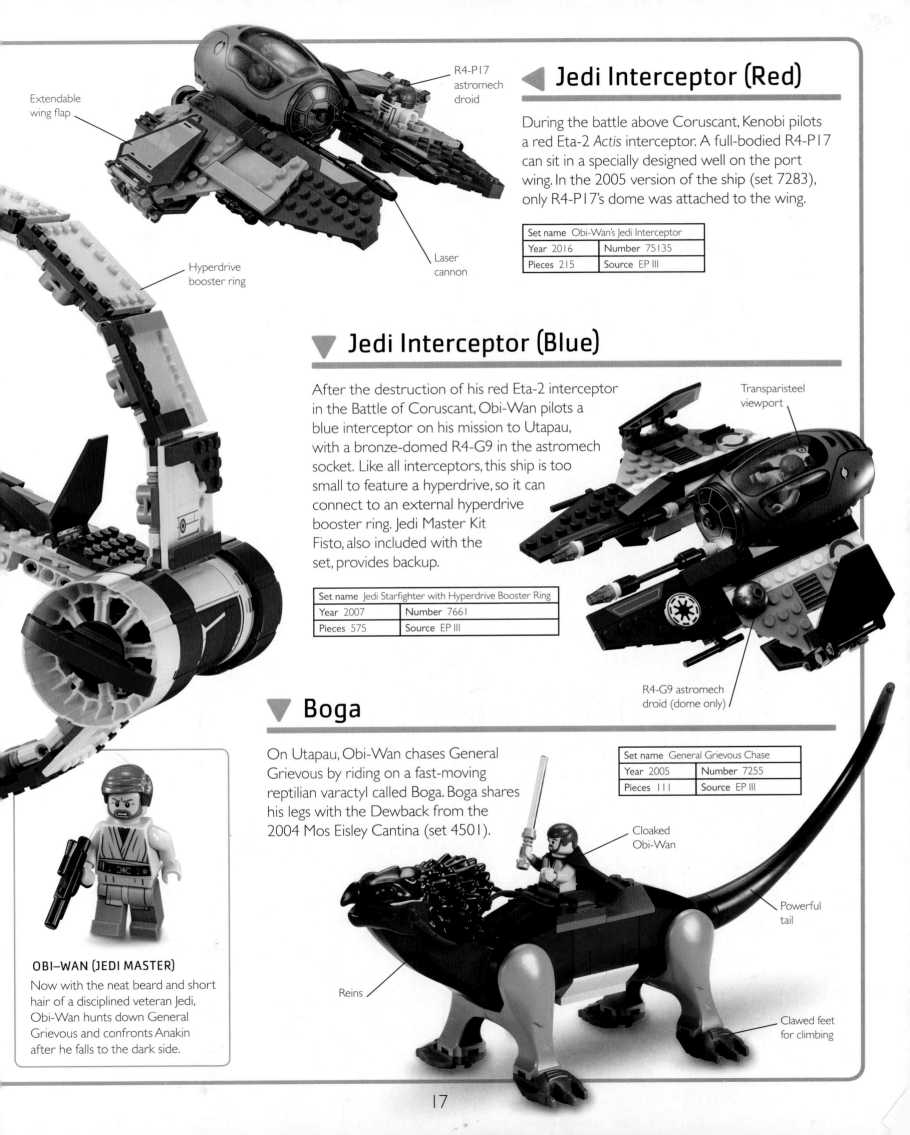

Extendable
wing flap

R4-P17
astromech
droid

Jedi Interceptor (Red)

During the battle above Coruscant, Kenobi pilots
a red Eta-2 *Actis* interceptor. A full-bodied R4-P17
can sit in a specially designed well on the port
wing. In the 2005 version of the ship (set 7283),
only R4-P17's dome was attached to the wing.

Hyperdrive
booster ring

Laser
cannon

Set name	Obi-Wan's Jedi Interceptor	
Year	2016	Number 75135
Pieces	215	Source EP III

Jedi Interceptor (Blue)

After the destruction of his red Eta-2 interceptor
in the Battle of Coruscant, Obi-Wan pilots a
blue interceptor on his mission to Utapau,
with a bronze-domed R4-G9 in the astromech
socket. Like all interceptors, this ship is too
small to feature a hyperdrive, so it can
connect to an external hyperdrive
booster ring. Jedi Master Kit
Fisto, also included with the
set, provides backup.

Transparisteel
viewport

Set name	Jedi Starfighter with Hyperdrive Booster Ring	
Year	2007	Number 7661
Pieces	575	Source EP III

R4-G9 astromech
droid (dome only)

Boga

On Utapau, Obi-Wan chases General
Grievous by riding on a fast-moving
reptilian varactyl called Boga. Boga shares
his legs with the Dewback from the
2004 Mos Eisley Cantina (set 4501).

Set name	General Grievous Chase	
Year	2005	Number 7255
Pieces	111	Source EP III

Cloaked
Obi-Wan

Powerful
tail

Reins

Clawed feet
for climbing

OBI–WAN (JEDI MASTER)

Now with the neat beard and short
hair of a disciplined veteran Jedi,
Obi-Wan hunts down General
Grievous and confronts Anakin
after he falls to the dark side.

Jedi Order

For millennia, the Jedi were the guardians of peace and justice in the galaxy. Within their massive temple on Coruscant, they trained children strong in the Force to become new generations of Padawans, Jedi Knights, and eventually Jedi Masters. During the Clone Wars, the Jedi became military leaders, fighting alongside clone troopers—but in vain. The Sith emerged victorious and destroyed the Jedi ranks as darkness engulfed the galaxy.

Sensitive ears

Short legs are unhinged

YODA
The title of Grand Master is given to the oldest and wisest member of the Jedi Order. Grand Master Yoda helped train Count Dooku before the Count abandoned the Jedi Order and joined the Sith. This 2019 minifigure, with its animation-style eye printing and head mold, looks like it could have jumped straight off the cinema screen.

▼ Jedi Masters

A Jedi who has trained a Padawan through to Jedi Knighthood earns the rank of Jedi Master. Twelve senior Jedi Masters form the Jedi Council, which makes decisions for the entire Jedi Order. The many species who make up the Jedi Order have expanded the varied collection of LEGO minifigures with weird and wonderful new head pieces.

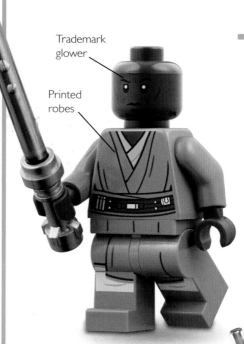

Trademark glower

Printed robes

Same leg piece as young Obi-Wan in set 75169

OBI-WAN KENOBI
Once Qui-Gon's Padawan, Obi-Wan is promoted to Jedi Knight. He takes on Anakin Skywalker as his apprentice.

Hair element unique to Qui-Gon

QUI-GON JINN
The esteemed Jedi Master has seven minifigure versions. This 2017 version includes gray hair details in the aging Jedi's beard.

▲ Mace Windu

A member of the Jedi Council, Mace is renowned for his skill with a lightsaber and his stern manner. His minifigure's saber blade is a unique purple. As a senior member of the Council, Mace commands great respect from younger Jedi, who rarely risk his wrath. Other minifigures with "bald" head pieces include Lobot, Asajj Ventress, Sugi, and Turk Falso.

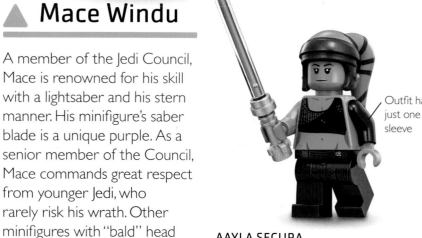

Outfit has just one sleeve

AAYLA SECURA
A Twi'lek Jedi Knight, Aayla's 2017 minifigure appears in set 75182. Her legs show a printed rycrit-hide belt.

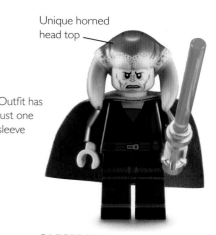

Unique horned head top

SAESEE TIIN
Saesee's second minifigure, from Palpatine's Arrest (set 9526) in 2012, has teeth bared for combat.

Oversized binary brain

KI-ADI-MUNDI
The Cerean Jedi Ki-Adi-Mundi's minifigure has a cone head top with creases and a ponytail.

Mirialan initiate's tattoos

Cape of rich fabric

▲ Barriss Offee

Barriss is a by-the-book Padawan. Her 2018 minifigure features a new black dress piece, instead of a leg piece, and a long cape. Her face has blue tattoos and comes with two expressions—calm and angry.

Ahsoka wields two green-colored lightsabers

Growing head-tails

▲ Ahsoka Tano

Young Ahsoka Tano is Anakin Skywalker's Jedi Padawan during the Clone Wars. She is a Togruta—a species with colorful skin and two long "head-tails." The 2013 version of the minifigure features brown legs with a printed purple sash.

MYSTERY JEDI
The end of the Clone Wars sees most Jedi killed and the Jedi Temple ransacked, with many records lost. All we know about this Jedi (whose name may have been Bob) is that he once flew on a Republic gunship (set 7163).

Gray tunic

JEDI BOB

Head top made of rubber

AGEN KOLAR

An Iridonian Zabrak, Agen Kolar's 2012 minifigure shares a head-top design with fellow Zabrak Eeth Koth.

Tholothian tendrils

STASS ALLIE

This Tholothian Jedi appears in Homing Spider Droid (set 75016), in 2013. Her headdress is unique.

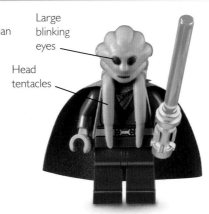

Large blinking eyes

Head tentacles

KIT FISTO

In 2007 Nautolan Jedi Kit Fisto was the first minifigure to have a rubber headpiece. His 2012 variant gained a cape.

Headdress piece is also found on the Jedi Consular minifigure

LUMINARA UNDULI

The Mirialan Jedi is one of the last survivors of Order 66. This third version from 2016 has a dark-brown color scheme.

Full-grown head-tails

SHAAK TI

Shaak Ti's 2011 minifigure comes with a unique rubber head piece with head-tails at front and back.

Eye lost in combat

EVEN PIELL

A scarred Lannik Jedi, Even appeared with the Jedi fighter of his friend Saesee Tiin in 2012.

Head crest

COLEMAN TREBOR

A hulking Vurk Jedi, Coleman fights alongside Mace Windu in the 2013 AT-TE set (75019).

Fighting expression

QUINLAN VOS

Unconventional Jedi Vos's 2016 minifigure includes a big hair piece to represent his long locks.

Jedi Fleet

The Jedi Knights' many missions on behalf of the Republic take them across the galaxy in a variety of transports, including the diplomatic cruisers called "Coruscant reds" and agile shuttles such as the T-6. With the arrival of the Clone Wars, the Jedi take to the spacelanes in starfighters specially made for them, becoming aces in dogfights against Separatist droid fighters and other enemies.

The T-6 shuttle's cockpit is designed to remain upright during flight maneuvers, with the wings rotating around it. Thanks to LEGO designers, Anakin Skywalker, Obi-Wan Kenobi, Shaak Ti, and Saesee Tiin can use the cockpit as an escape pod—it detaches from the shuttle in case the craft takes too much of a beating in combat.

Set name	T-6 Jedi Shuttle	
Year 2011	Number 7931	
Pieces 389	Source CW	

▶ Yoda's Jedi Starfighter

Jedi Master Yoda uses a modified Jedi Starfighter on a mission to the mysterious planet of Dagobah. The LEGO set includes astromech droid R2-D2, who accompanies Yoda. The fighter features Yoda's personal crest and spring-loaded shooters for fending off enemy ships during mission flights.

Set name	Yoda's Jedi Starfighter	
Year 2017	Number 75168	
Pieces 262	Source CW	

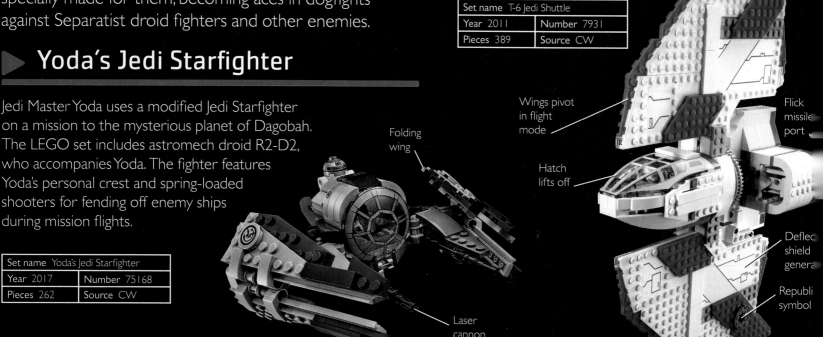

Wings pivot in flight mode

Flick missile port

Hatch lifts off

Deflec shield genera

Republi symbol

Folding wing

Laser cannon

▼ Republic Cruiser

The red Republic cruiser *Radiant VII* carries Qui-Gon Jinn and Obi-Wan Kenobi to their diplomatic mission on Naboo. The ship also accommodates the Republic captain and pilot minifigures, with seats for the Jedi in the detachable salon pod. The ship has hidden blaster cannons, detachable landing gear, storage for guns and electrobinoculars, and a space speeder mini-vehicle. An R2-R7 droid provides inflight backup.

Set name	Republic Cruiser	
Year 2007	Number 7665	
Pieces 919	Source EP1	

SALON POD
An oversized escape pod below the Republic Cruiser's bridge allows Qui-Gon and Obi-Wan to flee and activate a beacon to summon help.

Attachment point

Pod sensors

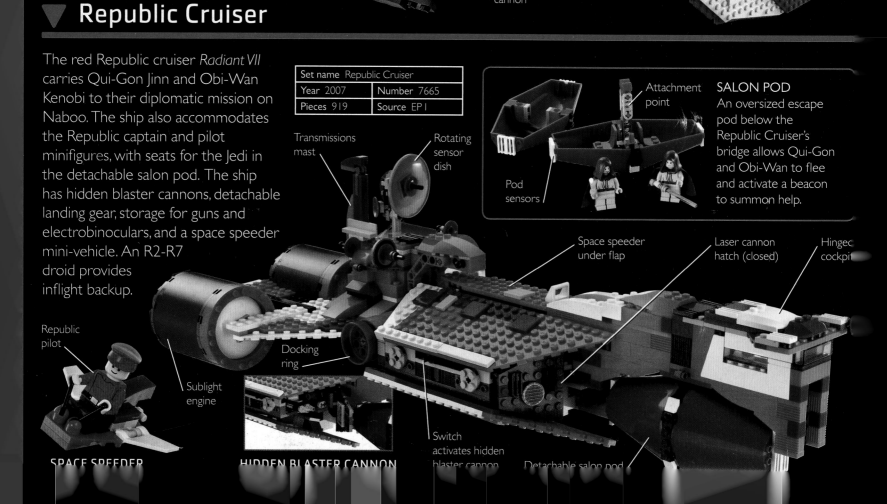

Transmissions mast

Rotating sensor dish

Space speeder under flap

Laser cannon hatch (closed)

Hinged cockpit

Republic pilot

Sublight engine

Docking ring

Switch activates hidden blaster cannon

Detachable salon pod

SPACE SPEEDER

HIDDEN BLASTER CANNON

During the Clone Wars, the Jedi train on Delta-7B *Aethersprite*-class interceptors. These are innovative strike fighters built to respond to the lightning-fast reflexes of Force-wielding Jedi. Each fighter is tailored for its pilot and has its own quirks in both the galaxy far, far away and the LEGO world. Anakin's fighter has retractable landing gear, Ahsoka Tano and Mace Windu's ships can fire multiple missiles, Plo Koon's cockpit has an ejection seat, and Saesee Tiin's cockpit breaks away as an escape pod.

Radar eye

R7-D4 **R3-D5**

Hologram projector

R8-B7 **R4-P44**

Linkage/repair arms

R4-P17 **R7-A7**

ASTROMECHS

Astromech droids help the Jedi plot safe courses through hyperspace, repair damage to their fighters, and handle the routines of spaceflight. Some develop personalities and a rapport with their Jedi partners. Most astromechs are variants of the same standard mold, but their varied color schemes and printed

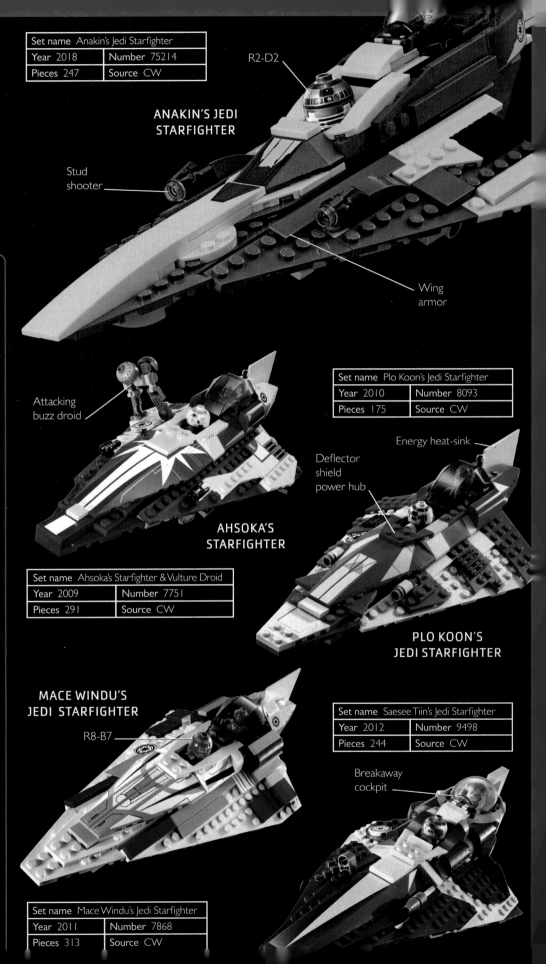

Set name	Anakin's Jedi Starfighter	
Year 2018	Number 75214	
Pieces 247	Source CW	

R2-D2

ANAKIN'S JEDI STARFIGHTER

Stud shooter

Wing armor

Attacking buzz droid

Set name	Plo Koon's Jedi Starfighter	
Year 2010	Number 8093	
Pieces 175	Source CW	

Energy heat-sink

Deflector shield power hub

AHSOKA'S STARFIGHTER

Set name	Ahsoka's Starfighter & Vulture Droid	
Year 2009	Number 7751	
Pieces 291	Source CW	

PLO KOON'S JEDI STARFIGHTER

MACE WINDU'S JEDI STARFIGHTER

R8-B7

Set name	Saesee Tiin's Jedi Starfighter	
Year 2012	Number 9498	
Pieces 244	Source CW	

Breakaway cockpit

Set name	Mace Windu's Jedi Starfighter	
Year 2011	Number 7868	
Pieces 313	Source CW	

Chancellor Palpatine

Once a Senator from remote Naboo, Palpatine has cunningly risen to become Chancellor of the Republic. He has agreed to stay in office while the Republic battles the Separatists in the Clone Wars. What no one knows is that he secretly leads both sides in the conflict, and he is the hidden mastermind of the war. His true identity is Darth Sidious, the Sith Lord who seeks to destroy the Jedi and control the galaxy.

Rotate head to see Sith eyes

Robes of office

Venator-Class Republic Attack Cruiser

The precursor to the Imperial Star Destroyer, the *Venator*-class attack cruiser has enough firepower to blast through Separatist battleships with ease. The interior hangar carries Supreme Chancellor Palpatine and two Senate commandos, while the crew comprises a clone pilot and a clone gunner.

Set name	*Venator*-Class Republic Attack Cruiser	
Year 2009	Number 8039	
Pieces 1,170	Source CW	

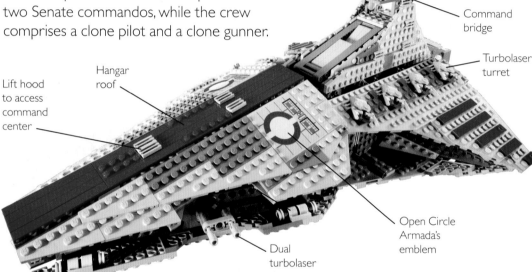

Lift hood to access command center

Hangar roof

Command bridge

Turbolaser turret

Open Circle Armada's emblem

Dual turbolaser

PALPATINE'S ARREST

There are two minifigures of Palpatine in his red Chancellor robes. This 2012 version has him brandishing a secret Sith lightsaber that he uses when the Jedi arrive in his office in Palpatine's Arrest (set 9526).

Wing projects deflector shield

Cockpit hood

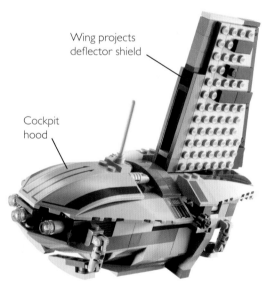

CAPTIVE LEADER

General Grievous seems to raid Coruscant and capture the Chancellor, carrying him off to his Separatist flagship.

Handcuffs

PALPATINE (KIDNAPPED)

Palpatine's Shuttle

Now Emperor, Palpatine races across the galaxy in his speedy *Theta*-class shuttle to rescue a badly injured Anakin, following Anakin's duel with Obi-Wan Kenobi on Mustafar. A clone pilot accompanies the Emperor, while a 2-1B medical droid stands ready to transform Anakin into Darth Vader.

Set name	Emperor Palpatine's Shuttle	
Year 2010	Number 8096	
Pieces 592	Source EP III	

Shield generator

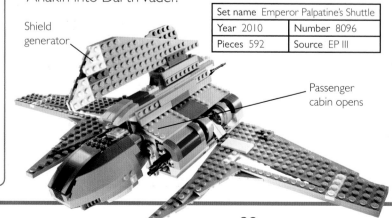

Passenger cabin opens

▲ Separatist Shuttle

Palpatine secretly commands the wealthy Trade Federation. Neimoidian puppet leader Nute Gunray travels in a *Sheathipede*-class shuttle flown by a battle droid pilot, with two battle droids for security (Neimoidians are cowardly).

Set name	Separatist Shuttle	
Year 2009	Number 8036	
Pieces 259	Source CW	

Count Dooku

The lethal Sith Lord Count Dooku was once a Jedi, but he lost his faith in the Jedi Order and abandoned it, eventually becoming the political leader of the Separatists. In secret, Dooku is the apprentice of Darth Sidious, and is called Darth Tyrannus. He works to advance Sidious's plot to defeat the Jedi, not suspecting that his master plans to replace him with a younger, more powerful apprentice.

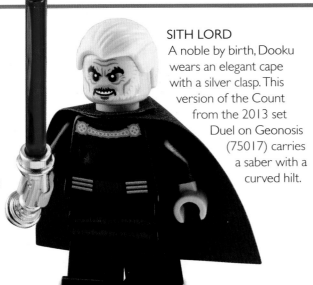

SITH LORD
A noble by birth, Dooku wears an elegant cape with a silver clasp. This version of the Count from the 2013 set Duel on Geonosis (75017) carries a saber with a curved hilt.

▼ Duel on Geonosis

Dooku flees the fight on Geonosis, seeking to escape with the secret plans for the Death Star. He duels with Yoda in an abandoned factory that serves as a hangar for the Count's Solar Sailer. Connected to a LEGO® Technic pole, Yoda's minifigure proves a nimble, acrobatic opponent— just watch out for falling columns!

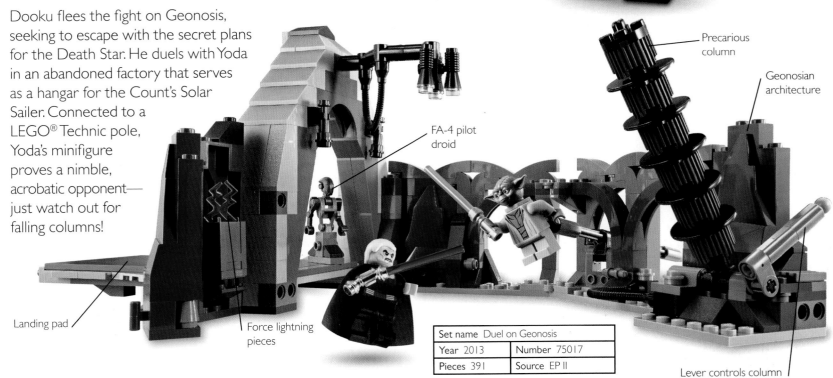

Precarious column

Geonosian architecture

FA-4 pilot droid

Landing pad

Force lightning pieces

Lever controls column

Set name	Duel on Geonosis	
Year 2013	Number 75017	
Pieces 391	Source EP II	

▼ Dooku's Speeder Bike

Dooku's open-cockpit Flitknot speeder bike enables the Sith Lord to escape the Republic's forces on Geonosis. He flees Yoda in 2002 on a blue version and later, on a brown, more streamlined, version.

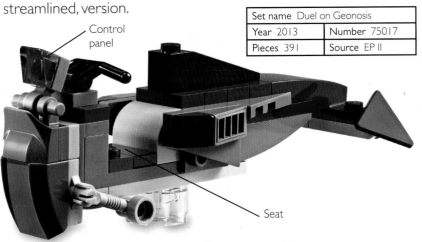

Control panel

Set name	Duel on Geonosis	
Year 2013	Number 75017	
Pieces 391	Source EP II	

Seat

▼ Solar Sailer

Count Dooku's personal starship is an elegant Geonosian Solar Sailer, piloted by a FA-4 droid. Dooku and two MagnaGuards travel to battlefields, where Dooku then uses his speeder bike to meet Separatist leaders.

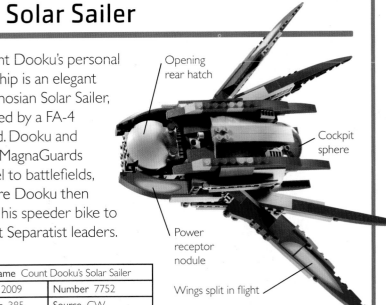

Opening rear hatch

Cockpit sphere

Power receptor nodule

Wings split in flight

Set name	Count Dooku's Solar Sailer	
Year 2009	Number 7752	
Pieces 385	Source CW	

Sith Followers

"Always two there are. A Master and an apprentice." Yoda explains that, for millennia, the secret Sith Order has preserved itself by passing down teachings while waiting for the right time to overthrow the Jedi and seize galactic control. But the Sith are deceitful by nature, with apprentices always plotting against their masters. And masters recruit beyond their apprentice to find other followers to do their bidding.

▼ Sith Infiltrator

Darth Maul is Darth Sidious's apprentice. His Sith Infiltrator appears for the first time on Tatooine in search of Padmé Amidala. There are four versions of the ship, each with its own version of Maul's speeder bike. This ship has a large compartment in the center for the bike, and storage for Maul's probe droids.

Set name	Sith Infiltrator	
Year	2015	Number 75096
Pieces	662	Source EP I

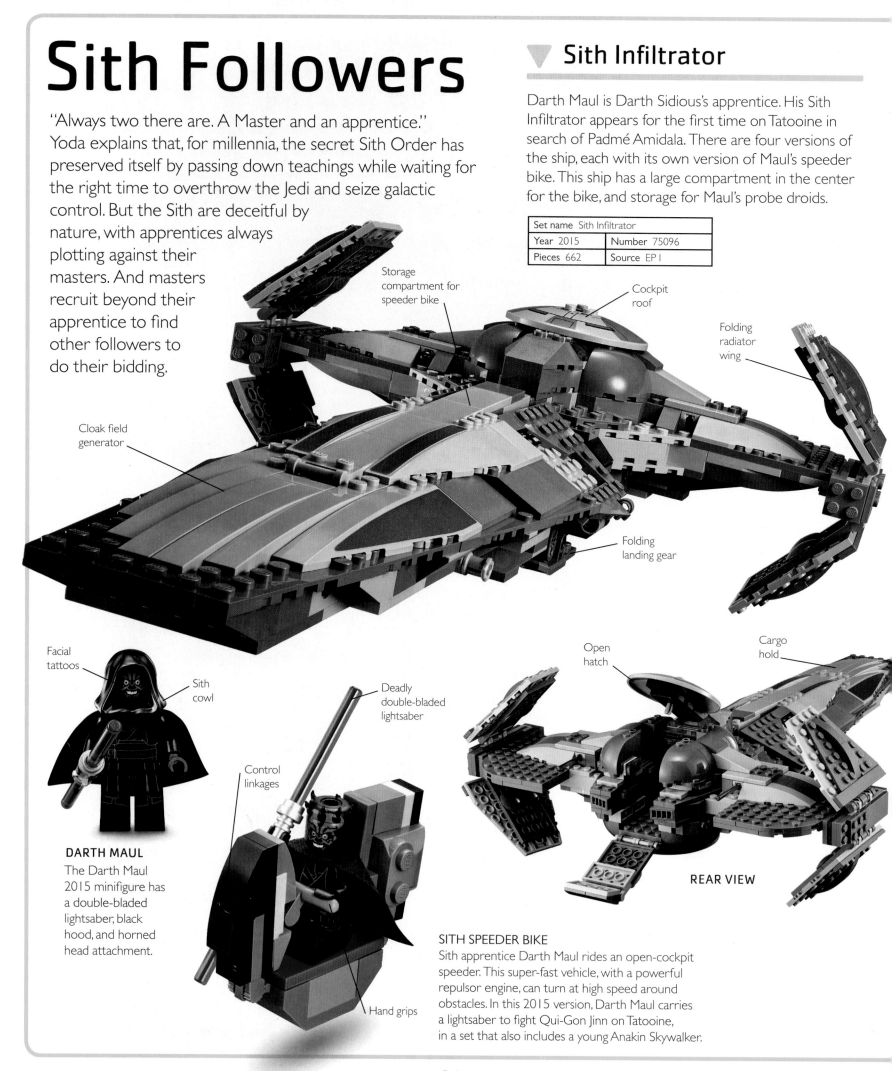

Storage compartment for speeder bike

Cockpit roof

Folding radiator wing

Cloak field generator

Folding landing gear

Facial tattoos

Sith cowl

DARTH MAUL
The Darth Maul 2015 minifigure has a double-bladed lightsaber, black hood, and horned head attachment.

Deadly double-bladed lightsaber

Control linkages

Hand grips

Open hatch

Cargo hold

REAR VIEW

SITH SPEEDER BIKE
Sith apprentice Darth Maul rides an open-cockpit speeder. This super-fast vehicle, with a powerful repulsor engine, can turn at high speed around obstacles. In this 2015 version, Darth Maul carries a lightsaber to fight Qui-Gon Jinn on Tatooine, in a set that also includes a young Anakin Skywalker.

Sith Nightspeeder

The Dathomirian Asajj Ventress rides a fearsome speeder bike with a spiked hull while on a mission for the Nightsisters, witches who rule her home world of Dathomir. In battle, Asajj's bike and its sidecar can split off from the hulking portside engine pod, which can launch missiles at enemies. Asajj returns aboard the nightspeeder with Savage Opress—a warrior who will serve Count Dooku, but remain secretly loyal to the Nightsisters, who seek revenge on Dooku for his betrayal of Asajj.

Set name	Sith Nightspeeder	
Year	2011	Number 7957
Pieces	213	Source CW

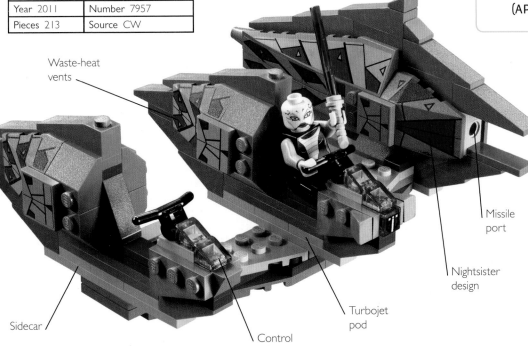

Waste-heat vents

Sidecar

Control linkages

Turbojet pod

Missile port

Nightsister design

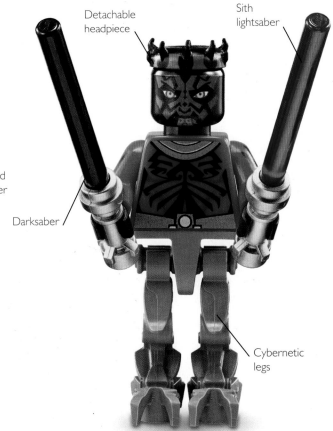

SITH APPRENTICE
Darth Sidious trained Maul from infancy, using cruelty and trickery to turn the young Zabrak into a ruthless warrior who would be an instrument of his will. As Sidious's sinister agent, Maul struck without warning against his Master's enemies. This minifigure, with Zabrak horns and a tattooed face and torso, was released with the Sith Infiltrator Microfighter (75224) in 2019.

DARTH MAUL (APPRENTICE)

Darth Maul

Maul somehow survived being cut in half by Obi-Wan Kenobi, fleeing into the Outer Rim, but losing his sanity in exile. After Savage Opress found him, the Nightsisters' magic healed his mind and created cybernetic legs for him. Joined by Savage, Maul tried to take over the galactic underworld. This intimidating 2013 minifigure with unique leg pieces is from the Mandalorian Speeder (set 75022).

Detachable headpiece

Sith lightsaber

Darksaber

Cybernetic legs

Facial tattoos

One of two sabers

Zabrak horns

Double-bladed saber

Enchanted Nightsister blade

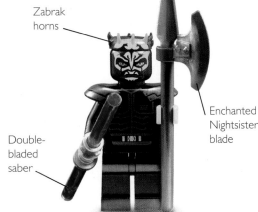

ASAJJ VENTRESS
Asajj once trained as a Jedi, but turned to the dark side after the death of her Master, becoming Dooku's servant. She fights using twin lightsabers. The 2015 minifigure represents Asajj from the original *Star Wars: The Clone Wars* animated TV series (2003).

SAVAGE OPRESS
A Nightbrother from Dathomir, Savage was transformed into a deadly warrior by dark-side magic. Infuriated by Dooku's training and the Nightsisters' scheming, he fled in search of his lost brother, Darth Maul, who became his new teacher.

Republic Army

For generations, the Republic had no army, relying only on the Jedi Knights to maintain peace and justice in the galaxy. But the vast Separatist Droid Army forced Republic leaders to take decisive action. The Republic quickly amassed one of the largest armies ever seen, with millions of clone troopers led by Jedi generals and diverse, specialized vehicles designed for missions on the ground.

▼ AT-AP Walker

The All Terrain Attack Pod (AT-AP) is a two-legged walker. Like the previous two LEGO AT-APs, this version has a third retractable stabilizer leg for extra stability. It is equipped with a massive blaster cannon and the roof and side doors open to reveal an interior cabin.

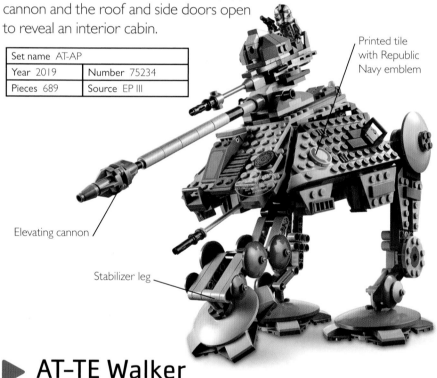

Set name	AT-AP	
Year 2019	Number 75234	
Pieces 689	Source EP III	

Printed tile with Republic Navy emblem

Elevating cannon

Stabilizer leg

▶ AT-TE Walker

The six-legged All Terrain Tactical Enforcer, or AT-TE Walker, blasts ground or air targets with massive cannon, while six laser cannon turrets focus on smaller targets. This set features four minifigures: two battle droids, a clone commander, and Jedi Coleman Trebor.

Set name	AT-TE	
Year 2013	Number 75019	
Pieces 794	Source EP II	

▼ AT-RT Walker

The All Terrain Recon Transport (AT-RT), or scout walker, is an open-cockpit recon vehicle. Heavily armed, it's also a swift opponent in battle. The 2013 set has a swiveling laser cannon.

Repeating blaster

Set name	AT-RT	
Year 2013	Number 75002	
Pieces 222	Source CW	

▼ AV-7 Anti-Vehicle Cannon

These artillery units reposition themselves by shuffling on their four heavy legs, then spreading their feet to take the shock of blasts from the cannon barrel. They are effective against both enemy ground units and aircraft.

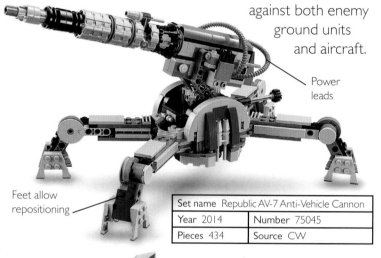

Power leads

Feet allow repositioning

Set name	Republic AV-7 Anti-Vehicle Cannon	
Year 2014	Number 75045	
Pieces 434	Source CW	

Gunner's station

Laser cannon turret

Heavy projectile cannon

Hinged roof lifts up

Bar step access to cabin

Servomotor disk

Cabin slides out

Terrain sensors

Clone Turbo Tank

Stud shooters

Sides fold
down to
release AT-RT

The Clone Turbo Tank, properly called the HAV A6 Juggernaut, or more simply the "rolling slab," is the stuff of legend. Its armor is nearly impenetrable, its weapons are devastating, and its ten wheels crush droids under them. A folded AT-RT Walker and extra ammo are stored in the cargo bay.

Set name	Clone Turbo Tank	
Year 2016	Number 75151	
Pieces 903	Source EP III	

Sturdy
wheel
suspension

Huge rolling
wheel

► BARC Speeder

This one-person Biker Advanced Recon Commando (BARC) speeder often escorts other ships but is also used for scouting missions. Clone troopers rode it during the Battle of Saleucami. The 75037 model includes a spring-loaded shooter.

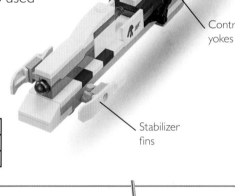

Control
yokes

Stabilizer
fins

Set name	Battle on Saleucami	
Year 2014	Number 75037	
Pieces 178	Source CW	

Space for
16 troops

PILOT TO GUNNER
A 2013 variant model of the BARC Speeder includes a sidecar, allowing a gunner to shoot down enemies while the pilot flies (set 75012).

Obi-Wan's
lightsaber

SPEEDER WITH SIDECAR

Foot
armor

Cabin
splits open

▲ AT-OT Walker

Open-topped All Terrain Open Transports (AT-OTs) are not designed to be tanks, but to transport troops and cargo within safe zones.

Set name	Republic Dropship with AT-OT Walker	
Year 2009	Number 10195	
Pieces 1,758	Source CW	

▼ Swamp Speeder

Formally known as an Infantry Support Platform, or ISP, the Swamp Speeder uses its giant turbofan and repulsorlifts to race through marshy terrain.

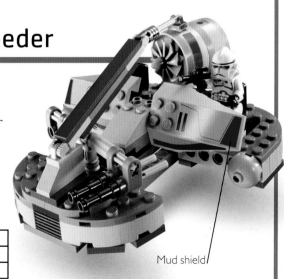

Set name	Republic Swamp Speeder	
Year 2010	Number 8091	
Pieces 176	Source EP III	

Mud shield

Set name	Republic Attack Shuttle	
Year 2009	Number 8019	
Pieces 636	Source CW	

Bombs reload through top

Clone pilot

Missiles launch via LEGO® Technic lever

Fold-down wings

Republic Attack Shuttle

The *Nu*-class attack shuttle is a fast, long-range gunship with heavy armor, powerful shields, and a range of laser weaponry, though this model is also equipped to drop missiles from a bomb hatch on the underside. A clone pilot flies the ship, which carries Mace Windu and a clone trooper into battle.

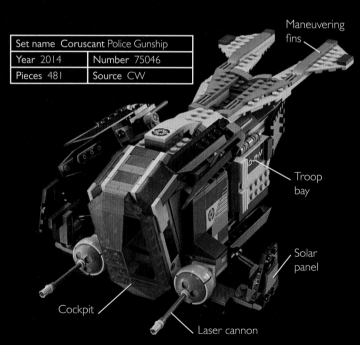

Set name	Coruscant Police Gunship	
Year 2014	Number 75046	
Pieces 481	Source CW	

Maneuvering fins

Troop bay

Solar panel

Cockpit

Laser cannon

Police Gunship

Fast and maneuverable, police gunships respond to trouble on the Republic capital of Coruscant. They are less heavily armed than attack gunships, as avoiding damage to crowded city blocks is more important than the ability to unleash a heavy bombardment. Clone troopers sometimes command these craft for military missions.

Republic Navy

The Republic defends its spacelanes and millions of worlds with a massive navy composed of giant warships; smaller transports and gunships; and sleek, speedy starfighters. Navy personnel include both clone officers and non-clones drawn from many species. These brave beings clash with Count Dooku's Separatist starships above countless planets as the Clone Wars rage.

▼ Z-95 Headhunter

Clones serving Jedi General Pong Krell pilot Z-95s in the Battle of Umbara. The LEGO version flies into battle with retractable landing gear, a weapons locker, and a LEGO Technic missile.

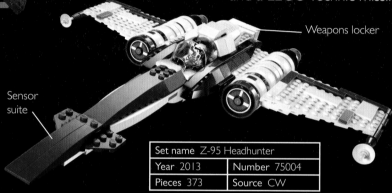

Weapons locker

Sensor suite

Set name	Z-95 Headhunter	
Year 2013	Number 75004	
Pieces 373	Source CW	

▼ Republic Frigate

Most Republic frigates were originally consular ships used by ambassadors and diplomats for galaxy-wide missions. With the galaxy torn apart by war, the Republic upgraded these vessels for battle. This ship comes with flick-fire missiles, a mechanism for dropping three further missiles in bombing raids, gun turrets, and a detachable escape pod.

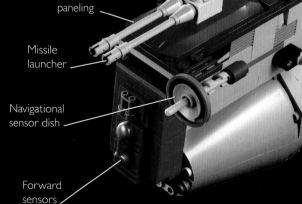

Hatch under paneling

Missile launcher

Navigational sensor dish

Detachable escape pod

Forward sensors

Set name	Republic Frigate	
Year 2011	Number 7964	
Pieces 1,015	Source CW	

ARC-170 Starfighter

The Aggressive ReConnaissance (ARC-170) fighter is hyperdrive-equipped for long-range missions. The 2010 ship's crew consists of Kit Fisto, Captain Jag, a clone pilot, and an R4 astromech. The ship's wings unfold when in flight, while mines can be dropped from the underside.

Wing-mounted laser cannon

Red styling

Heat sinks and cooling radiator panels on split wings

Set name	ARC-170 Starfighter	
Year	2010	Number 8088
Pieces	396	Source CW

CAPTAIN JAG

Clone pilots such as Jag are chosen early in the training cycle after demonstrating superior eyesight, reflexes, and spatial awareness. Jag serves Jedi Plo Koon as a wingman.

Dropship

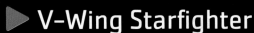

Turbine

LEGO Technic carry pin for AT-OT

Nose art (choice of stickers)

Low Altitude Assault Transport/carriers (LAAT/c or dropships) carry tanks into battle zones. This 2009 ship can lift and carry the AT-OT (see p27) from this set with the use of LEGO Technic mechanisms.

Set name	Republic Dropship with AT-OT	
Year	2009	Number 10195
Pieces	1,758	Source CW

Laser cannon

Concussion missile launcher

Powerful thruster

Ventral aerofoil

V-19 Torrent Starfighter

Communications antenna

Radiator panel wing

Sublight engine

This fast, agile assault fighter features wing-mounted laser cannon and concussion missile launchers. The wings extend in flight and close for landing, allowing the clone pilot access to the cockpit via a sliding hatch.

Set name	V-19 Torrent	
Year	2008	Number 7674
Pieces	471	Source CW

Ignition chamber

Portside guns

Bomb chamber

EETH KOTH

Eeth Koth (set 7964) is a Zabrak Jedi Master and member of the Jedi High Council during the final years of the Galactic Republic.

V-Wing Starfighter

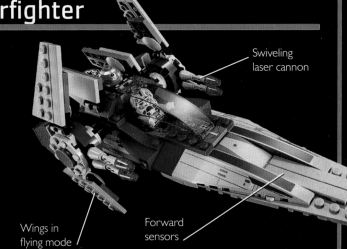

Clone troopers pilot agile V-wing fighters, with spherical Q7 astromechs as copilots. The wings unfold in flight and the laser cannon are powerful and deadly.

Swiveling laser cannon

Set name	V-Wing Starfighter	
Year	2014	Number 75039
Pieces	201	Source CW

Wings in flying mode

Forward sensors

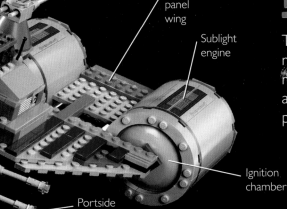

Republic Gunship

Formally known as the Low Altitude Assault Transport/infantry (LAAT/i), the Republic gunship ferries clone troopers into battle and gives deadly air-to-air and air-to-ground support, raking targets with missiles and blaster fire. The Republic first used this versatile attack craft at the Battle of Geonosis, where they dropped off the surprise delivery of clone troopers that turned the tide of the battle.

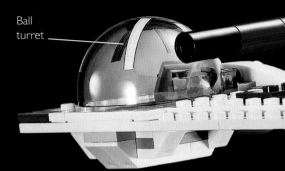

Ball turret

Engine nacelle

Swoop-bike ramp (closed during flight)

REAR VIEW

Sticker details on control panels

Obi-Wan Kenobi as co-pilot/gunner

Clone pilot with Episode II markings on helmet

SWOOP BIKE
A ramp at the gunship's rear folds down to reveal a swoop bike. Once the gunship lands, it takes just seconds to deploy a clone trooper for a reconnaissance mission.

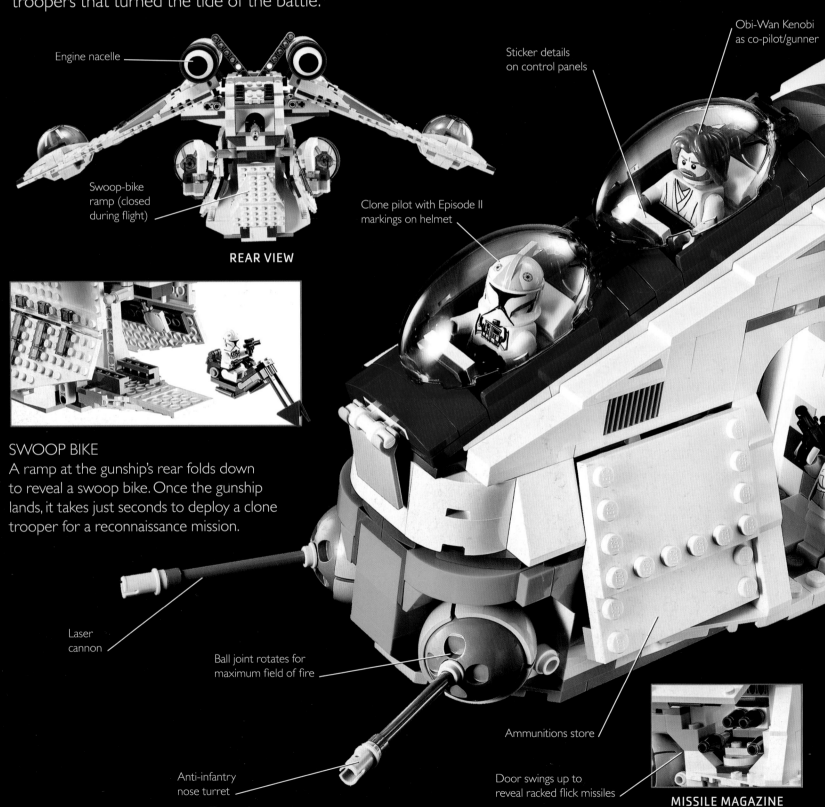

Laser cannon

Ball joint rotates for maximum field of fire

Anti-infantry nose turret

Ammunitions store

Door swings up to reveal racked flick missiles

MISSILE MAGAZINE

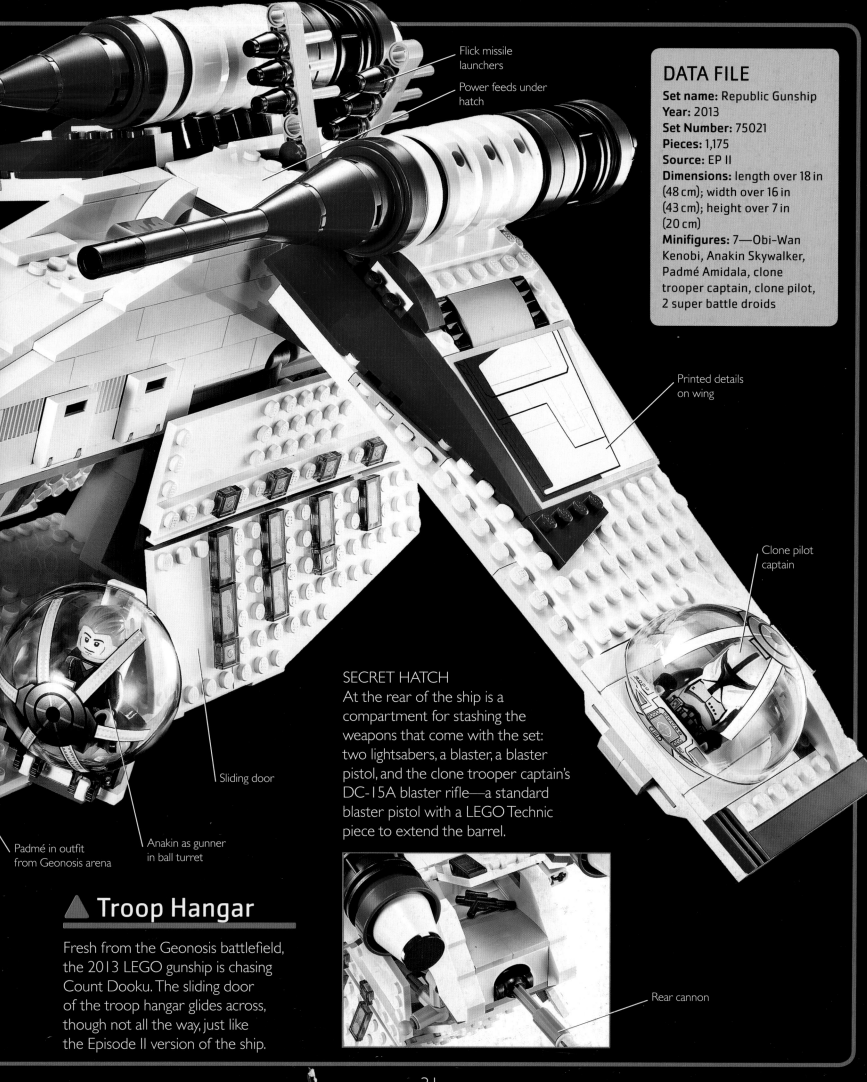

Flick missile launchers

Power feeds under hatch

DATA FILE

Set name: Republic Gunship
Year: 2013
Set Number: 75021
Pieces: 1,175
Source: EP II
Dimensions: length over 18 in (48 cm); width over 16 in (43 cm); height over 7 in (20 cm)
Minifigures: 7—Obi-Wan Kenobi, Anakin Skywalker, Padmé Amidala, clone trooper captain, clone pilot, 2 super battle droids

Printed details on wing

Clone pilot captain

SECRET HATCH
At the rear of the ship is a compartment for stashing the weapons that come with the set: two lightsabers, a blaster, a blaster pistol, and the clone trooper captain's DC-15A blaster rifle—a standard blaster pistol with a LEGO Technic piece to extend the barrel.

Sliding door

Padmé in outfit from Geonosis arena

Anakin as gunner in ball turret

▲ Troop Hangar

Fresh from the Geonosis battlefield, the 2013 LEGO gunship is chasing Count Dooku. The sliding door of the troop hangar glides across, though not all the way, just like the Episode II version of the ship.

Rear cannon

Clone Troopers

At the start of the Clone Wars, clone troopers wear Phase I armor, which is loosely based on Jango Fett's Mandalorian shock trooper armor. Informally called "the body bucket," this armor is heavy and often uncomfortable. Colored stripes denote rank. During the later part of the Clone Wars, Phase II armor mainly replaces Phase I armor. Phase II armor is stronger, lighter, and more adaptable than the earlier type, with many specialist variations. Color now denotes unit affiliation rather than rank.

CLONE TROOPER (PHASE I)

Phase I clone trooper minifigures wear basic white armor with white helmets. The printed legs are new for 2018.

"T" visor derived from Mandalorian design

Printed minifigure legs

▶ Phase I Clone Troopers

Early Phase I clones had a faceless black head piece and carried a LEGO loudhailer piece for a weapon. In 2008, a new version of the Phase I clone minifigure gave them flesh-colored heads and bespoke blasters.

DC-15 rifle

CLONE CAPTAIN

Yellow pilot stripes

CLONE PILOT

Specially reinforced helmet

BOMB SQUAD TROOPER

Dots indicate rank

CLONE SERGEANT

Blue markings denote lieutenant rank

CLONE LIEUTENANT

ANATOMY OF A CLONE TROOPER

"Explode" this ARC trooper from Elite Clone Trooper and Commando Droid Battle Pack (set 9488) and you see just how complex a simple minifigure can get!

Rangefinder

Visor

Phase II helmet

Determined expression

Backpack mount

Backpack

Kama (a flexible, anti-blast skirt)

Unique printed legs

Pauldron armor

Ammo pouch

DC-17 commando blasters

ELITE ARC TROOPER

▶ Phase I Clone Commanders

Promising clones are discovered early on in their production and are given special training, with more individuality than the troops they command. Commanders such as Wolffe, Fox, and Cody work closely with Jedi generals in the fight against the Separatists.

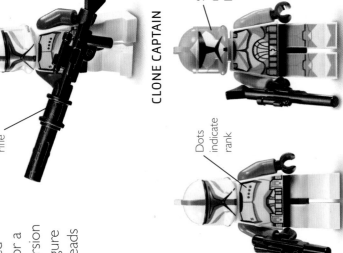

Rangefinder

COMMANDER (HORN COMPANY)

COMMANDER WOLFFE

COMMANDER FOX

Visor shield unique to LEGO commanders

COMMANDER CODY

▶ Phase II Clone Troopers

Later in the Clone Wars, the Republic created more sophisticated Phase II armor. As well as improved breath filters, it allows for greater agility in combat situations. Camouflage is also sometimes used on Phase II armor.

SHOCKTROOPER

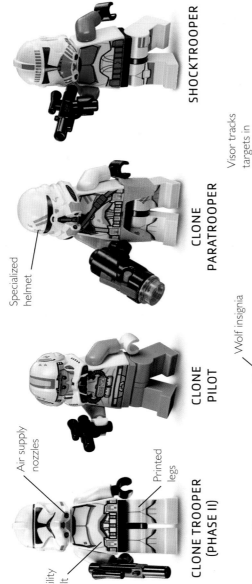

Specialized helmet

CLONE PARATROOPER

Air supply nozzles

Printed legs

CLONE PILOT

CLONE TROOPER (PHASE II)

Utility belt

Visor tracks targets in jungle terrain

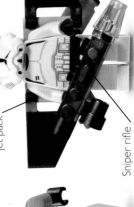

KASHYYYK CLONE TROOPER

Camouflage armor

GEONOSIS CLONE TROOPER

Wolf insignia

WOLF PACK TROOPER

Chest plate protects from weapon recoil

CLONE GUNNER

Winged jet pack

Sniper rifle

AERIAL TROOPER

Color indicates legion affiliation

212TH TROOPER

501ST TROOPER

Heat dispersion vent

STAR CORPS TROOPER

ELITE CLONE TROOPERS

As clone troopers pursue specialized missions, the Republic develops new helmets and armor for these units. Advanced Recon Force troopers are trained for stealth, with infrared cameras built into their helmets. A variant ARF trooper LEGO minifigure has white shoulder and forearm armor and green helmet markings.

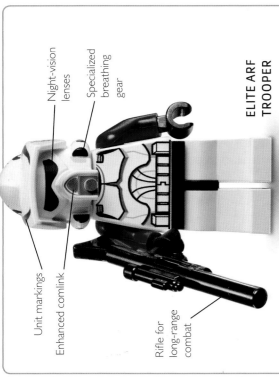

Night-vision lenses

Specialized breathing gear

ELITE ARF TROOPER

Unit markings

Enhanced comlink

Rifle for long-range combat

▶ Phase II Clone Commanders

By the end of the Clone Wars, many clone commanders are veterans of years of battle and have formed close relationships with their Jedi generals. When Chancellor Palpatine issues Order 66 these friendships mean nothing: obeying their insidious conditioning and training, clone commanders turn their guns on the Jedi they have served on so many missions.

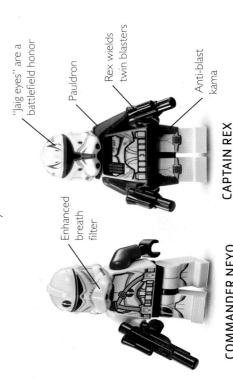

"Jaig eyes" are a battlefield honor

Pauldron

Rex wields twin blasters

Anti-blast kama

CAPTAIN REX

Enhanced breath filter

COMMANDER NEYO

Separatist Army

Although mass armies are illegal at the start of the Clone Wars, many wealthy commercial bodies use private forces to enforce payments and collect debts. These forces are pooled to create the Separatist war machine, under the command of Count Dooku. Consisting of huge numbers of deadly droids backed by attack vehicles, the Separatist army assaults Republic worlds from one side of the galaxy to the other.

▼ Droid Speeder

The commando droid on this speeder chases Obi-Wan and Captain Rex in 2013. The earlier 2011 version of the bike is used by a TX-20 tactical droid to ambush Mace Windu's Jedi starfighter.

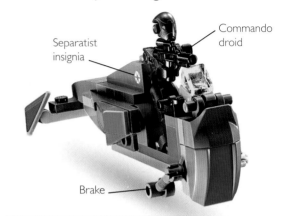

Separatist insignia

Commando droid

Brake

Set name BARC Speeder with Sidecar	
Year 2013	Number 75012
Pieces 226	Source CW

▼ Armored AAT

The 2015 AAT glides into battle armed with laser weapons and two battle droids, which can fit inside the opening cockpit. Jar Jar Binks and his fellow Gungans do everything they can to stop the Trade Federation's battle tanks from taking control of their home world, Naboo.

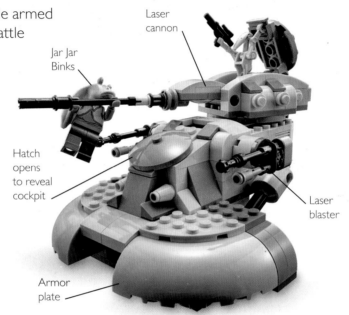

Laser cannon

Jar Jar Binks

Hatch opens to reveal cockpit

Laser blaster

Armor plate

Set name AAT	
Year 2015	Number 75080
Pieces 251	Source EP1

MECHANICAL MARVEL
Programmed to think up ideal strategies for the battlefield, tactical droids assist the flesh-and-blood generals of the Separatist cause.

TACTICAL DROID

▼ MTT

The updated MTT carries eight battle droids. Turning the side gear deploys the droid storage rack, while various exterior panels are hinged to allow access to the interior. Hidden wheels allow the set to roll smoothly for the rapid transport of battle-ready droids. The set includes seven battle droids, one battle droid pilot, a PK-4 droid, a Naboo security guard, Obi-Wan Kenobi, and Qui-Gon Jinn.

Front hatch

Access to cockpit

Storage area for Single Trooper Aerial Platform

Battle droids

Troop deployment rack

Twin blaster cannons

Panel opens to reveal gun rack

Set name MTT	
Year 2014	Number 75058
Pieces 954	Source EP1

Infantry Battle Droid

Infantry battle droids make up the majority of the Separatist land troops. Early versions of the minifigure have two identical hands. From 2007 onward, battle droid minifigures have had a turned hand in order to properly hold a blaster.

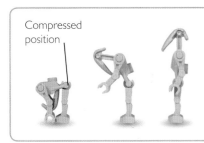

Compressed position

COLLAPSIBLE SOLDIERS
Battle droid minifigures fold up for efficient storage in deployment racks in MTTs and other carriers.

STAP

Battle droids pilot repulsorlift gun platforms called STAPs (Single Trooper Aerial Platforms). Brown and blue LEGO versions of the vehicles have been created.

One of two blasters

Power cell housing

Clear piece for "floating" action

Set name	Battle on Saleucami	
Year	2014	Number 75037
Pieces	178	Source CW

SUPER BATTLE DROIDS
Super battle droids are larger, stronger versions of regular battle droids. They are also equipped with tougher armor. There are three versions of the minifigure in different colors; one with a specially molded blaster arm.

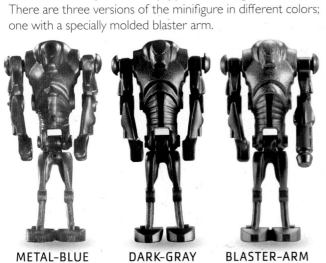

METAL-BLUE (2002)   DARK-GRAY (2007)   BLASTER-ARM (2009)

Droid Transports

Separatist troop carriers ferry battle droids to the battlefield more quickly than bulky MTT transports. Two battle-droid pilots control the troop carrier, deploying 12 battle droids. This model of troop carrier can carry weapons, but is unarmed, relying on its speed to escape Gungan warriors and other enemies.

Each compartment can hold six droids

Pilot battle droid

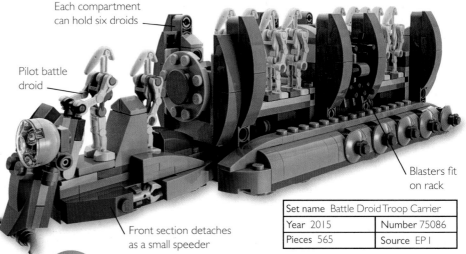

Blasters fit on rack

Front section detaches as a small speeder

Set name	Battle Droid Troop Carrier	
Year	2015	Number 75086
Pieces	565	Source EP1

Octuptarra Droid

Missile

Multiple photoreceptors and blasters give these stilt-legged droids the ability to detect and target enemies on all sides of them, making them tough opponents. Octuptarras defended General Grievous's headquarters against the Republic's clone troopers on Utapau.

Hydraulic limb

Set name	Utapau Troopers	
Year	2014	Number 75036
Pieces	83	Source CW

Separatist Cannon

Proton cannons use their powerful legs to shift position on the battlefield. Controlled by a battle-droid gunner, they launch powerful explosive shells that are a threat to far-off transports and Republic airborne gunships. The cannon's bright red eyes are made from a versatile LEGO piece that has served as a headlight, a spotlight, and a segment of a medical droid!

High-velocity muzzle

Operator's station

Set name	Battle for Geonosis	
Year	2011	Number 7869
Pieces	331	Source CW

Droideka

Destroyer droids, or droidekas, roll into battle, uncurl, and then deploy built-in blasters to deadly effect. So far, droideka models have battled clones in eight LEGO sets, with the droids looking more and more like their on-screen counterparts.

Set name	Naboo Starfighter	
Year	2015	Number 75092
Pieces	442	Source EP I

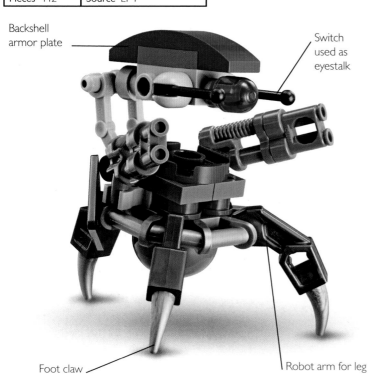

Backshell armor plate

Switch used as eyestalk

Foot claw

Robot arm for leg

Battlefield Droids

For years, the galaxy's wealthy, unsavory corporations enforced their will on customers with menacing weaponized droids designed to collect debts, force labor settlements, and eliminate rivals. When those corporations join together to form the Separatist Alliance, their droids become the muscle of the armies sent to invade Republic worlds, with Separatist factories working overtime to turn out new models.

Dwarf Spider Droid

Dwarf spider droids are mobile laser cannon turrets that walk into battle in advance of battle droids. While not very smart, these droids sometimes refuse to advance when badly outnumbered by enemies.

Set name	Homing Spider Droid	
Year	2016	Number 75142
Pieces	310	Source EP III

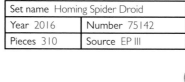

Tracing antenna

Infrared photoreceptor

Hinged knee joint

Clawed feet

Wheels are printed radar dishes

Missile pod

Spring-loaded dart

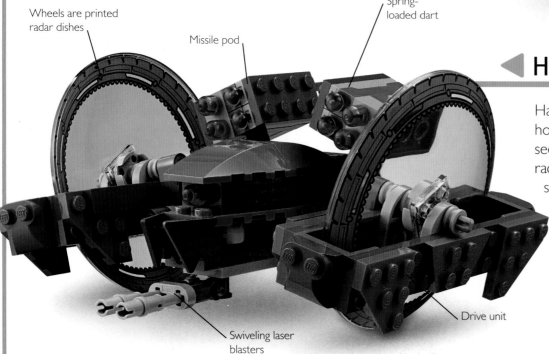

Hailfire Droid

Hailfire droids roll into battle on giant hoop wheels while firing deadly heat-seeking missiles from two top-mounted racks. The Hailfire's red photoreceptor sees in the infrared spectrum, determines range to a target, and then feeds that data to the systems controlling its weapons.

Set name	Hailfire Droid	
Year	2015	Number 75085
Pieces	163	Source EP II

Swiveling laser blasters

Drive unit

Tank Droid

Amphibious NR-N99 tank droids roll into battle on high-traction caterpillar treads. Three LEGO versions of the tank have been deployed: on Kashyyyk in 2005, one for the new *Clone Wars* movie in 2009, and this one on Geonossis in 2013. Deployed side by side, they form an unstoppable wall of armor, obliterating everything in their path.

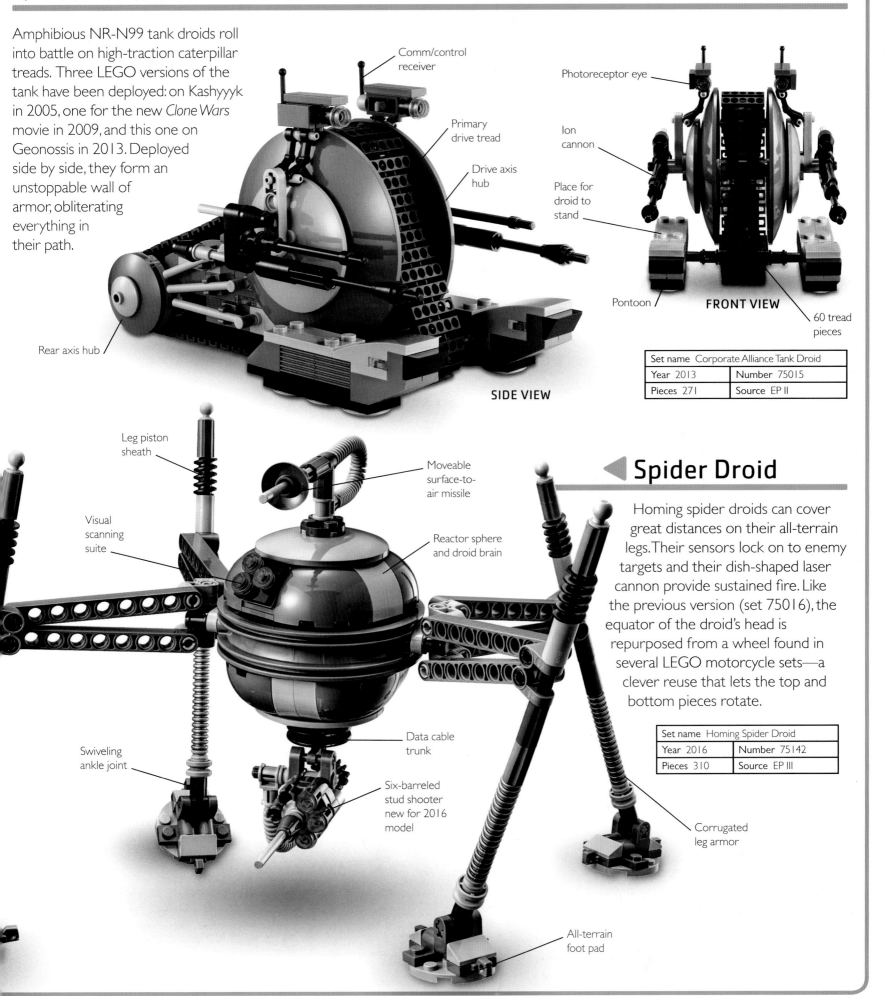

Comm/control receiver

Primary drive tread

Drive axis hub

Rear axis hub

SIDE VIEW

Photoreceptor eye

Ion cannon

Place for droid to stand

Pontoon

FRONT VIEW

60 tread pieces

Set name	Corporate Alliance Tank Droid	
Year	2013	Number 75015
Pieces	271	Source EP II

Leg piston sheath

Moveable surface-to-air missile

Visual scanning suite

Reactor sphere and droid brain

Swiveling ankle joint

Data cable trunk

Six-barreled stud shooter new for 2016 model

Corrugated leg armor

All-terrain foot pad

◀ Spider Droid

Homing spider droids can cover great distances on their all-terrain legs. Their sensors lock on to enemy targets and their dish-shaped laser cannon provide sustained fire. Like the previous version (set 75016), the equator of the droid's head is repurposed from a wheel found in several LEGO motorcycle sets—a clever reuse that lets the top and bottom pieces rotate.

Set name	Homing Spider Droid	
Year	2016	Number 75142
Pieces	310	Source EP III

Separatist Navy

After their first success at the Battle of Geonosis, Separatist forces plot and scheme even greater exploits. The gigantic space battle above Coruscant, in which General Grievous attempts to kidnap Supreme Chancellor Palpatine, sees the use of a deadly range of specialized droid fighters. Other Separatist units batter enemy ground forces and civilian targets on contested planets such as Kashyyyk and Ryloth.

▼ Droid Gunship

Droid gunships are well-shielded heavy missile platforms (HMPs) designed for sub-orbital air strikes. They are relatively slow to maneuver, but their firepower is devastating. Droid brains usually control the gunships, but some modified versions include a cockpit for a battle droid pilot.

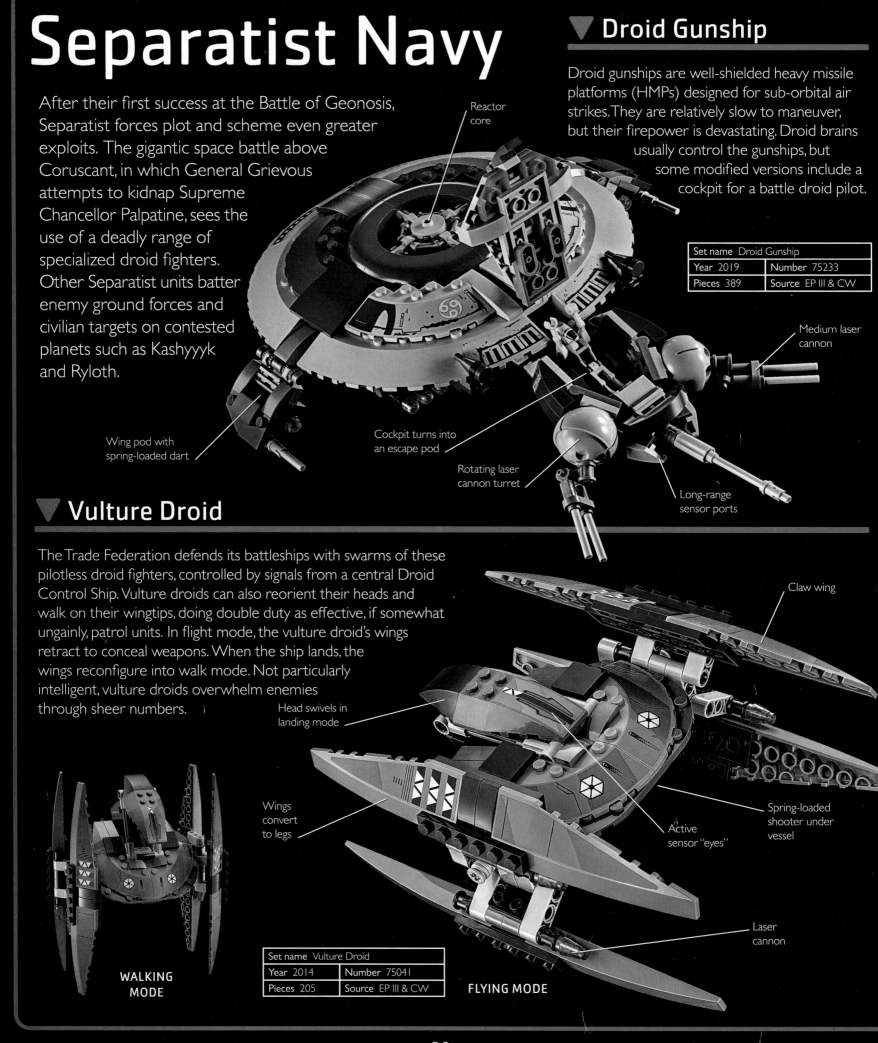

Reactor core

Set name	Droid Gunship	
Year 2019	Number 75233	
Pieces 389	Source EP III & CW	

Medium laser cannon

Wing pod with spring-loaded dart

Cockpit turns into an escape pod

Rotating laser cannon turret

Long-range sensor ports

▼ Vulture Droid

The Trade Federation defends its battleships with swarms of these pilotless droid fighters, controlled by signals from a central Droid Control Ship. Vulture droids can also reorient their heads and walk on their wingtips, doing double duty as effective, if somewhat ungainly, patrol units. In flight mode, the vulture droid's wings retract to conceal weapons. When the ship lands, the wings reconfigure into walk mode. Not particularly intelligent, vulture droids overwhelm enemies through sheer numbers.

Head swivels in landing mode

Claw wing

Wings convert to legs

Active sensor "eyes"

Spring-loaded shooter under vessel

Laser cannon

WALKING MODE

Set name	Vulture Droid	
Year 2014	Number 75041	
Pieces 205	Source EP III & CW	

FLYING MODE

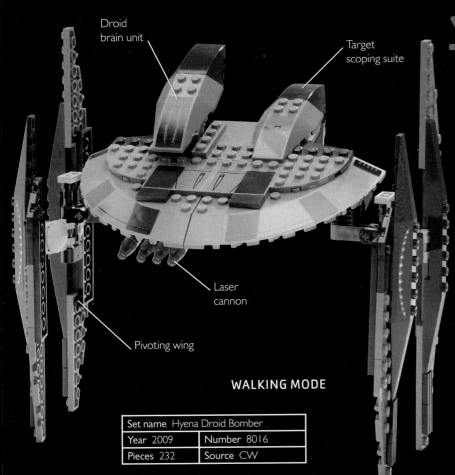

Droid brain unit

Target scoping suite

Laser cannon

Pivoting wing

WALKING MODE

Set name	Hyena Droid Bomber	
Year 2009	Number 8016	
Pieces 232	Source CW	

▼ Hyena Droid Bomber

Hyena-class droid bombers are modified vulture fighters, with a secondary cockpit sensor "head" for improved target scoping and upgraded weapons systems, including concussion missile launchers. Notoriously, hyena droid bombers performed carpet-bombing raids on Twi'lek cities during the Battle of Ryloth.

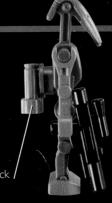

Jetpack

ROCKET BATTLE DROID

Torpedo channel

Concussion missiles drop from underneath

FLYING MODE

▼ Droid Tri-Fighter

With a nose-mounted laser cannon and three light laser cannon, droid tri-fighters are deadlier than vulture droids. These agile, fast droids excel at dogfights with Republic starfighters. Some modified tri-fighters are piloted by battle droids that sit in their central spheres.

Set name	Droid Tri-Fighter	
Year 2014	Number 75044	
Pieces 262	Source EP II & III	

Swivelling wing blaster

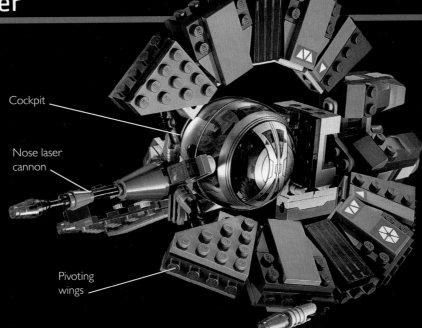

Cockpit

Nose laser cannon

Pivoting wings

ROCKET BATTLE DROIDS
These modified B1 battle droids are designed for scouting missions deep in space. They hunt down and destroy enemies fleeing in escape pods. Commanders are recognizable by a yellow marking on their head.

Color indicates rank

ROCKET BATTLE DROID COMMANDER

SPRING-LOADED MISSILE LAUNCHER

BUZZ DROID
Separatist fighters launch swarms of buzz droids as guided missiles. They hunt for enemy ships, slip through shields, and wreak havoc with their saws and graspers.

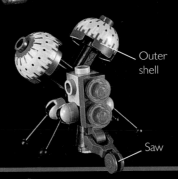

Outer shell

Saw

General Grievous

The Supreme Commander of the Droid Armies is a villainous cyborg called General Grievous. Grievous does not consider himself a droid, however—and reacts savagely to anyone who calls him one. His hatred of the Jedi Knights in particular is long-standing and all-consuming. His only pleasure is defeating Jedi in battle and collecting their lightsabers as trophies.

Carved skull mask

Clawed feet

GENERAL GRIEVOUS

The first two Grievous minifigures used mostly battle droid parts. In 2010, a more specialized minifigure was created in tan, which was then released in white in 2014.

▼ Malevolence

General Grievous's flagship, the *Malevolence*, is one of the largest warships ever built. It strikes terror into Republic worlds, with no fleet able to stand up to its massive twin ion cannon, backed up with turbolasers. The *Subjugator*-class heavy cruiser has an internal transport train and the top of the LEGO model lifts off to reveal the inner ship.

Set name *Malevolence*	
Year 2012	Number 9515
Pieces 1,092	Source CW

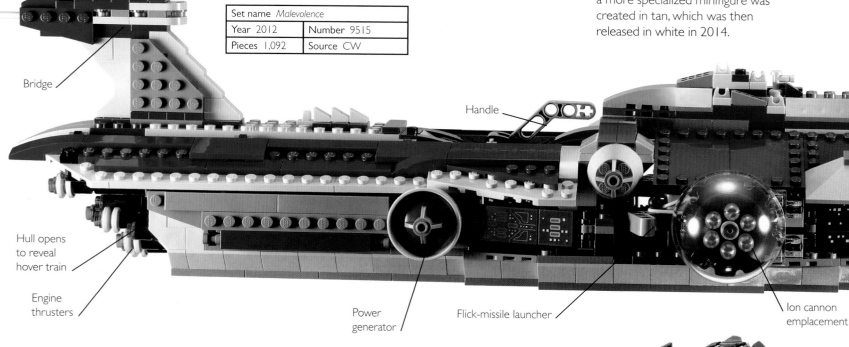

Bridge

Hull opens to reveal hover train

Engine thrusters

Power generator

Handle

Flick-missile launcher

Ion cannon emplacement

▶ Wheel Bike

On Utapau, General Grievous rides a wheel bike, designed to achieve intimidatingly high speeds across hard terrain. If obstacles block its path, no problem—its two pairs of legs just walk over them! When Grievous flees clone troops on Utapau, Obi-Wan Kenobi gives chase on Boga, a brave varactyl.

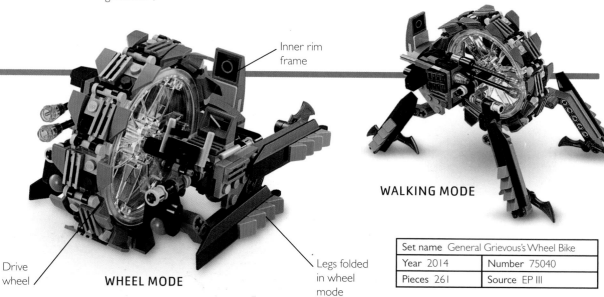

Inner rim frame

WALKING MODE

Drive wheel

WHEEL MODE

Legs folded in wheel mode

Set name General Grievous's Wheel Bike	
Year 2014	Number 75040
Pieces 261	Source EP III

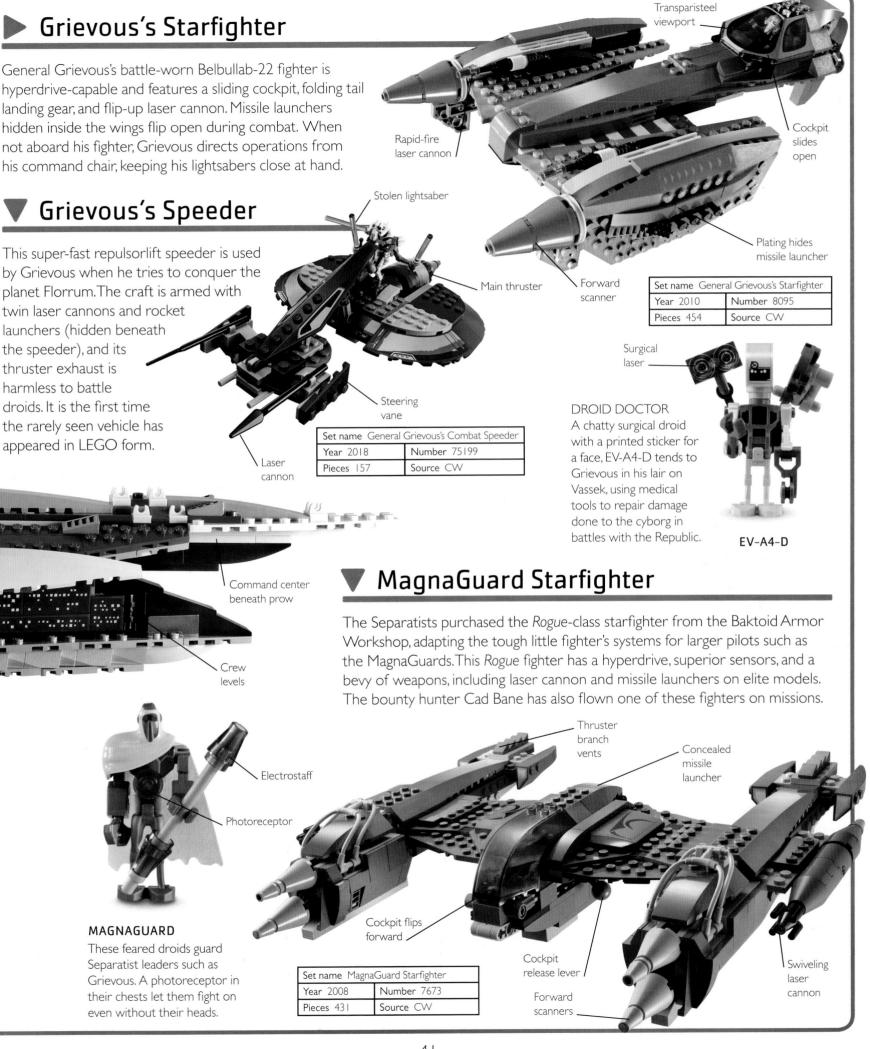

▶ Grievous's Starfighter

General Grievous's battle-worn Belbullab-22 fighter is hyperdrive-capable and features a sliding cockpit, folding tail landing gear, and flip-up laser cannon. Missile launchers hidden inside the wings flip open during combat. When not aboard his fighter, Grievous directs operations from his command chair, keeping his lightsabers close at hand.

Transparisteel viewport

Rapid-fire laser cannon

Cockpit slides open

Plating hides missile launcher

▼ Grievous's Speeder

This super-fast repulsorlift speeder is used by Grievous when he tries to conquer the planet Florrum. The craft is armed with twin laser cannons and rocket launchers (hidden beneath the speeder), and its thruster exhaust is harmless to battle droids. It is the first time the rarely seen vehicle has appeared in LEGO form.

Stolen lightsaber

Main thruster

Forward scanner

Set name	General Grievous's Starfighter	
Year 2010	Number 8095	
Pieces 454	Source CW	

Steering vane

Laser cannon

Set name	General Grievous's Combat Speeder	
Year 2018	Number 75199	
Pieces 157	Source CW	

Surgical laser

DROID DOCTOR
A chatty surgical droid with a printed sticker for a face, EV-A4-D tends to Grievous in his lair on Vassek, using medical tools to repair damage done to the cyborg in battles with the Republic.

EV-A4-D

Command center beneath prow

Crew levels

▼ MagnaGuard Starfighter

The Separatists purchased the *Rogue*-class starfighter from the Baktoid Armor Workshop, adapting the tough little fighter's systems for larger pilots such as the MagnaGuards. This *Rogue* fighter has a hyperdrive, superior sensors, and a bevy of weapons, including laser cannon and missile launchers on elite models. The bounty hunter Cad Bane has also flown one of these fighters on missions.

Electrostaff

Photoreceptor

MAGNAGUARD
These feared droids guard Separatist leaders such as Grievous. A photoreceptor in their chests let them fight on even without their heads.

Thruster branch vents

Concealed missile launcher

Cockpit flips forward

Cockpit release lever

Forward scanners

Swiveling laser cannon

Set name	MagnaGuard Starfighter	
Year 2008	Number 7673	
Pieces 431	Source CW	

Geonosians

During the Clone Wars, the hive-dwelling Geonosians are notorious for their huge factories that endlessly churn out battle droids for the Separatist Army. A winged elite class rules over this savage, caste-based society, with wingless drones doing all the work. Geonosian soldiers carry exotic sonic weapons and fly twin-pronged fighter ships.

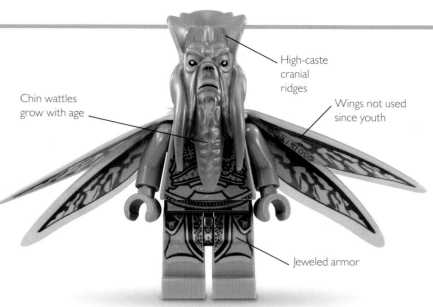

Chin wattles grow with age

High-caste cranial ridges

Wings not used since youth

Jeweled armor

POGGLE THE LESSER

A key Separatist leader, Poggle the Lesser takes his orders from Karina the Great, the hidden Queen of Geonosis, who dwells in a subterranean lair. Poggle's minifigure, with its impressive quadruple wings, appears in the Duel on Geonosis (set 75017) from 2013.

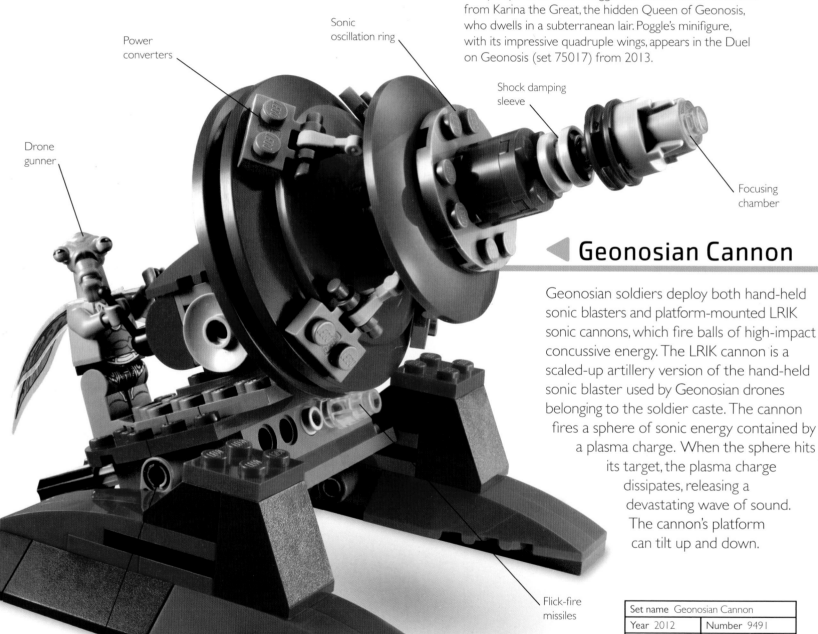

Power converters

Sonic oscillation ring

Drone gunner

Shock damping sleeve

Focusing chamber

Geonosian Cannon

Geonosian soldiers deploy both hand-held sonic blasters and platform-mounted LRIK sonic cannons, which fire balls of high-impact concussive energy. The LRIK cannon is a scaled-up artillery version of the hand-held sonic blaster used by Geonosian drones belonging to the soldier caste. The cannon fires a sphere of sonic energy contained by a plasma charge. When the sphere hits its target, the plasma charge dissipates, releasing a devastating wave of sound. The cannon's platform can tilt up and down.

Flick-fire missiles

Platform pivots

Shock-absorbing legs

Set name	Geonosian Cannon	
Year	2012	Number 9491
Pieces	132	Source CW

Geonosian Fighter

Thousands of deadly *Nantex*-class starfighters are launched against Republic forces at the Battle of Geonosis. These ships are specially designed to accommodate the anatomy of Geonosian pilots, and include a lifting cockpit hatch, swiveling laser cannon, and a hidden proton torpedo.

Set name	Geonosian Starfighter	
Year	2011	Number 7959
Pieces	155	Source CW

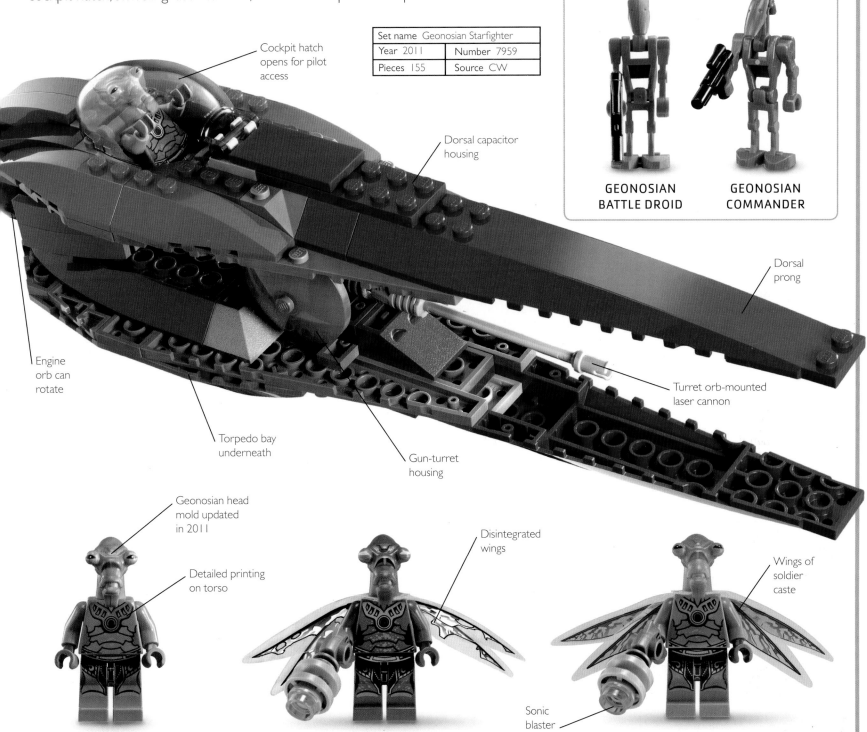

GEONOSIAN BATTLE DROIDS
The Geonosians designed the Separatists' battle droids as robot versions of themselves. These reddish-brown variants are camouflaged for battle on the desert surface of Geonosis.

GEONOSIAN BATTLE DROID

GEONOSIAN COMMANDER

Cockpit hatch opens for pilot access

Dorsal capacitor housing

Dorsal prong

Engine orb can rotate

Turret orb-mounted laser cannon

Torpedo bay underneath

Gun-turret housing

Geonosian head mold updated in 2011

Detailed printing on torso

Disintegrated wings

Wings of soldier caste

Sonic blaster

GEONOSIAN PILOT

Ironically, Geonosian pilots lack wings. They receive orders through scent messages pumped into their starfighters' cockpits. The 2003 minifigure was dark gray; this 2011 redesign is light brown.

GEONOSIAN ZOMBIE

"Zombie" soldiers (actually exoskeletons controlled by brain-worm parasites) are captured in LEGO form by being muted gray and having tattered wings.

GEONOSIAN WARRIOR

Only Geonosian soldiers have functional wings. This 2012 minifigure, from the Geonosian Cannon set (9491), offers a more-detailed head mold than its 2003 predecessor.

Naboo and Gungans

It takes an invasion by the villainous Trade Federation to propel peaceful Naboo to consider war. Its inhabitants—human Naboo and amphibious Gungans—must band together and work with their Jedi protectors to repel the hordes of merciless battle droids.

▼ Naboo Swamp

Jedi Qui-Gon Jinn and Obi-Wan Kenobi land on Naboo to help its inhabitants. In the Naboo swamp, Qui-Gon Jinn uses his lightsaber to deflect blaster fire from battle droids on STAPs (Single Trooper Aerial Platforms) and shield his Gungan guide, Jar Jar Binks. The STAPs come with "invisible" stands to make them hover.

Set name	Naboo Swamp	
Year	1999	Number 7121
Pieces	81	Source EP1

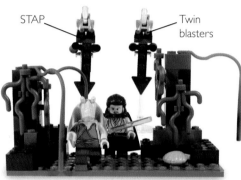

STAP

Twin blasters

Set name	Gungan Sub	
Year	2012	Number 9499
Pieces	465	Source EP1

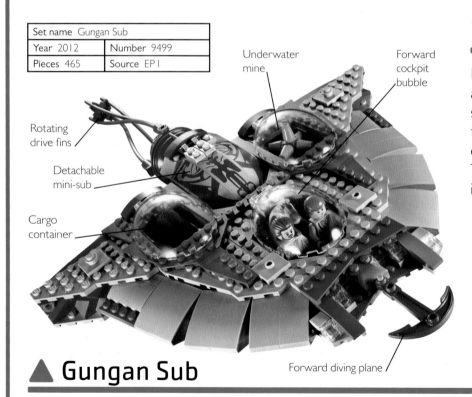

Underwater mine

Forward cockpit bubble

Rotating drive fins

Detachable mini-sub

Cargo container

Forward diving plane

▲ Gungan Sub

Qui-Gon, Obi-Wan, and Jar Jar Binks travel to Theed from the underwater city of Otoh Gunga in a bongo, or Gungan sub. Naboo's watery depths are home to dangerous monsters. The 2012 set has bongo defenses not shown on-screen: a mine to scare off attackers, flick-fire missiles, and a detachable mini-sub for a quick getaway. It was also the first LEGO set to feature a Queen Amidala minifigure in all her royal garb.

Set name	Gungan Patrol	
Year	2000	Number 7115
Pieces	77	Source EP1

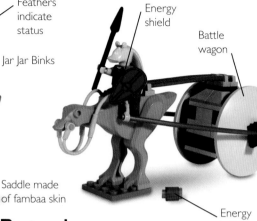

Feathers indicate status

Jar Jar Binks

Energy shield

Battle wagon

Billed snout

Saddle made of fambaa skin

Energy ball

▲ Gungan Patrol

Gungans ride large, flightless kaadu. These amphibious animals are fast and agile. Many kaadu are used as beasts of burden, though larger four-legged falumpasets are also popular. One of these kaadu is ridden by a Gungan soldier and is pulling a wagon carrying energy-ball ammunition into battle against the droid army. The energy balls roll out of the back of the wagon.

▼ Flash Speeder

Repulsorlift flash speeders are normally piloted by Naboo security officers. They are used for patrols in peacetime, but employed in the defense of Theed Palace during the invasion of Naboo.

Set name	Flash Speeder	
Year	2015	Number 75091
Pieces	312	Source EP1

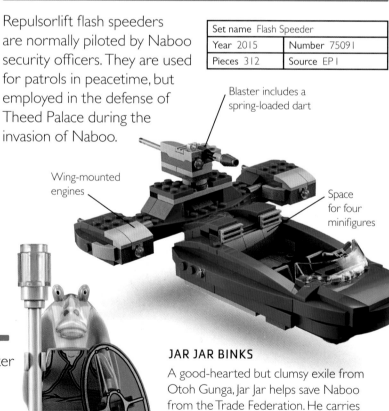

Blaster includes a spring-loaded dart

Wing-mounted engines

Space for four minifigures

JAR JAR BINKS

A good-hearted but clumsy exile from Otoh Gunga, Jar Jar helps save Naboo from the Trade Federation. He carries an energy shield and a plasma spear, known as a cesta, into battle. Back in 1999, his minifigure was the first to have a unique head sculpt.

Umbarans and Mandalorians

The Republic faces many perils in the galaxy's Outer Rim as the Clone Wars grind on. The shadowy world of Umbara is home to Separatist-allied soldiers whose technology rivals anything in the Republic. Mandalore is a neutral world, but ruthless warriors known as the Death Watch will stop at nothing to overthrow its ruler, the pacifist Duchess Satine.

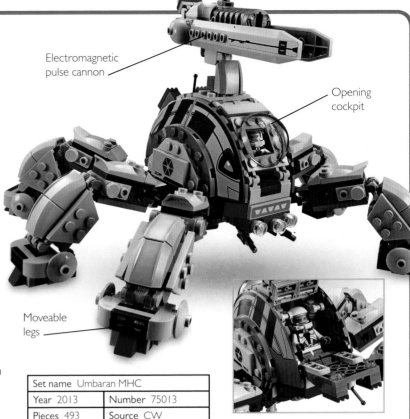

Electromagnetic pulse cannon

Opening cockpit

Moveable legs

REAR COCKPIT

▼ The Death Watch

Duchess Satine insists Mandalore has left its warlike past behind. But a secretive band of armored warriors, the Death Watch, has allied itself with the Separatists. Well-armed and deadly, they seek to take over the planet.

SPEEDER

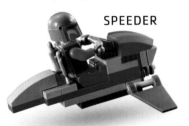

Sniper rifle

MANDALORIAN ASSASSIN

Swiveling cannon

GUN TURRET

Set name	Mandalorian Battle Pack	
Year 2011	Number 7914	
Pieces 68	Source CW	

Set name Umbaran MHC	
Year 2013	Number 75013
Pieces 493	Source CW

▲ Umbaran Cannon

On Umbara, one of the toughest opponents for the clones is the juggernaut or Mobile Heavy Cannon. A blast from this six-legged tank can wipe out an entire Republic platoon. This 2013 Umbaran MHC comes with Ahsoka Tano, a 212th Attack Battalion clone trooper and two Umbaran soldiers.

UMBARAN SOLDIER

MANDALORIANS
The Death Watch's Mandalorian super commandos are led by Pre Vizsla, who wields the Darksaber: an ancient lightsaber with a black blade. After Darth Maul takes over Death Watch, the super commandos repaint their armor red and black in his honor.

Maul's colors

Darksaber

MANDALORIAN SUPER COMMANDO

PRE VIZSLA

▼ Mandalorian Speeder

When Maul and Death Watch take over Mandalore, they patrol its skies in these fast, powerful police speeders. The craft is full of surprises: its front hatch hides a missile emplacement, while its gun turret is built atop a secret weapons locker.

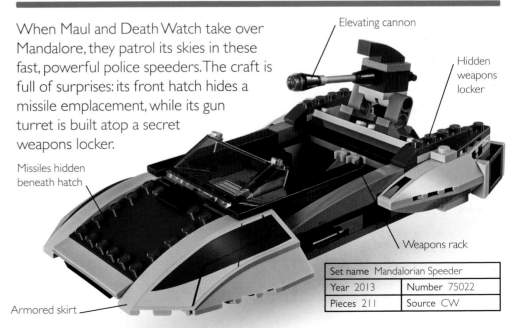

Elevating cannon

Hidden weapons locker

Missiles hidden beneath hatch

Weapons rack

Armored skirt

Set name Mandalorian Speeder	
Year 2013	Number 75022
Pieces 211	Source CW

Bounty Hunters

Bounty hunters track down and capture people in order to collect a fee, or bounty. These ruthless, capable hunters prefer to work alone, but occasionally they hire fellow professionals such as assassin Zam Wesell. One of the most legendary bounty hunters in the galaxy is Jango Fett.

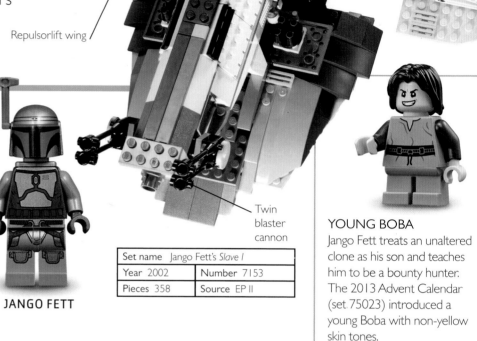

Repulsorlift wing

▶ Jango Fett's *Slave I*

Jango Fett's *Firespray*-class patrol and attack ship, *Slave I*, is bristling with weapons, many of which are hidden in order to deliver devastating surprise assaults. The armaments consist of two four-barrel fold-out blaster cannon, twin rotating laser cannon, two concealed heat-seeking rocket launchers, and three drop-bombs, as well as a removable prisoner cage. A smuggling box can be magnetically attached to the underside of the ship. When the repulsorlift wings swivel, they rotate the cockpit from landing to flight mode.

Twin blaster cannon

JANGO FETT

Set name	Jango Fett's *Slave I*	
Year	2002	Number 7153
Pieces	358	Source EP II

YOUNG BOBA
Jango Fett treats an unaltered clone as his son and teaches him to be a bounty hunter. The 2013 Advent Calendar (set 75023) introduced a young Boba with non-yellow skin tones.

▼ HH-87 Starhopper

HH-87 Starhoppers are tough little gunships favored by lawless organizations in the shadowy corners of the galaxy, such as Zygerrian slavers, pirates, and the Hutt clans. While on the Hutt home world of Nal Hutta, HH-87s piloted by Hutt servants hunt down a ship carrying the bounty hunter Cad Bane, who has fled to Nal Hutta with a disguised Obi-Wan.

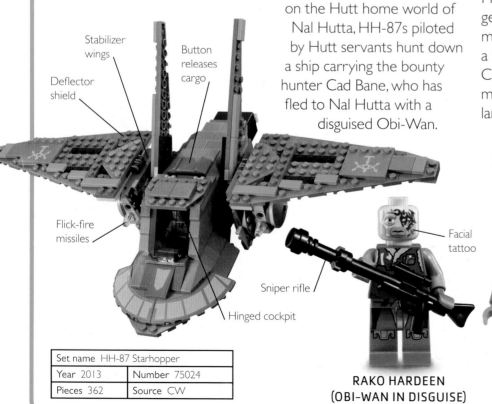

Stabilizer wings

Button releases cargo

Deflector shield

Flick-fire missiles

Sniper rifle

Hinged cockpit

Set name	HH-87 Starhopper	
Year	2013	Number 75024
Pieces	362	Source CW

Facial tattoo

RAKO HARDEEN (OBI-WAN IN DISGUISE)

▼ Zam Wesell's Airspeeder

Hired assassin Zam Wesell flies an airspeeder for quick getaways on risky missions. It is streamlined and fast, which makes it difficult for Anakin and Obi-Wan to give chase in a borrowed airspeeder through the towering spires of Coruscant. Zam's cockpit screen is hinged, and a hidden mechanism makes the wings fall off, re-creating the crash-landing at the end of the high-speed chase in the film.

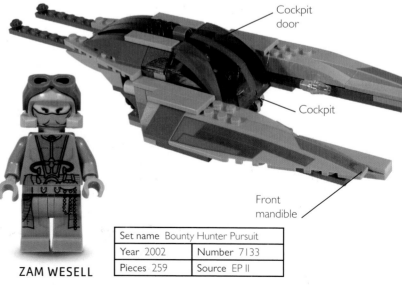

Cockpit door

Cockpit

Front mandible

ZAM WESELL

Set name	Bounty Hunter Pursuit	
Year	2002	Number 7133
Pieces	259	Source EP II

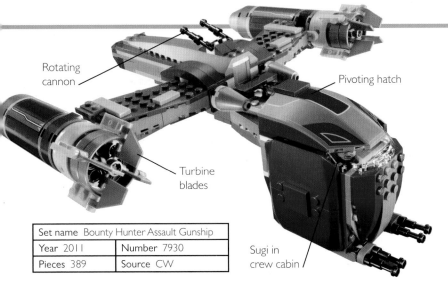

Rotating cannon

Pivoting hatch

Turbine blades

Sugi in crew cabin

Set name	Bounty Hunter Assault Gunship	
Year	2011	Number 7930
Pieces	389	Source CW

Bounty Hunter Assault Ship

During the Clone Wars, the Zabrak bounty hunter Sugi is captain of a gunship called the *Halo*. The craft was originally built for military strikes, but Sugi refitted it with a crew cabin and hold, making it suitable for longer-term missions. Sliding the top of the hull pivots the wings and allows access to a hidden compartment for stashing valuable cargo. The set comes with these three exclusive bounty-hunter minifigures—Aurra Sing, Embo, and Sugi.

AURRA SING

EMBO

SUGI

Pirate Tank

Led by Hondo Ohnaka, Weequay pirates on the planet Florrum use starships, speeder bikes, and tanks to defend their base. For ground operations, Hondo depends on his WLO-5 tanks, which boast thick armor and heavy guns.

TURK FALSO

Anti-personnel armor

Ancient pistols

Turbine engine

Steering vane

Pop-up mechanism opens hatch doors

Missile launcher

Set name	Pirate Tank	
Year	2009	Number 7753
Pieces	372	Source CW

Cad Bane's Speeder

Cad Bane and his crew favor these repulsorlift vehicles for their high speeds and agility. In one of his most daring raids, Bane and a gang of hired thugs attack the Senate Building in the heart of Coruscant, taking a group of Senators hostage and demanding that the Republic free crime lord Ziro the Hutt in exchange for the captives. Bane and his hunters, including Shahan Alama and an assassin droid, then flee the Senate.

Beloved fedora

CAD BANE
A Duros bounty hunter, Cad Bane is infamous across the galaxy for his ruthlessness and successful methods. He often works for the Sith Lord Darth Sidious.

Set name	Cad Bane's Speeder	
Year	2010	Number 8128
Pieces	318	Source CW

Bow hatch

Headlights hide missiles

Hidden storage compartment

Fancy stolen coat

HONDO OHNAKA
Hondo Ohnaka believes in grog, loot, and good times, though he is not without a sense of honor. He shares his black epaulets with the bounty hunter Embo and a LEGO space officer.

Anakin Skywalker— Fallen Jedi

Tormented by visions of Padmé Amidala coming to harm, Anakin turns to Chancellor Palpatine, who hints that there is more to the Force than Jedi teachings. He also reveals his true identity: he is the Sith Lord Darth Sidious! Desperate to save Padmé, Anakin falls to the dark side, leading Sidious's assault on the Jedi and crossing lightsabers with his old master Obi-Wan Kenobi on the lava planet Mustafar.

▼ Palpatine's Arrest

Mace Windu assembles a party of Jedi to arrest Chancellor Palpatine, but the Sith Lord proves full of tricks and his office has many surprises: will Mace fall victim to the hidden locker of dark-side weapons, or get flung out of the set's breakaway window? Anakin docks his airspeeder and rushes into the fray, where he must choose between his loyalty to the Jedi and his hunger to learn the dark side's secrets.

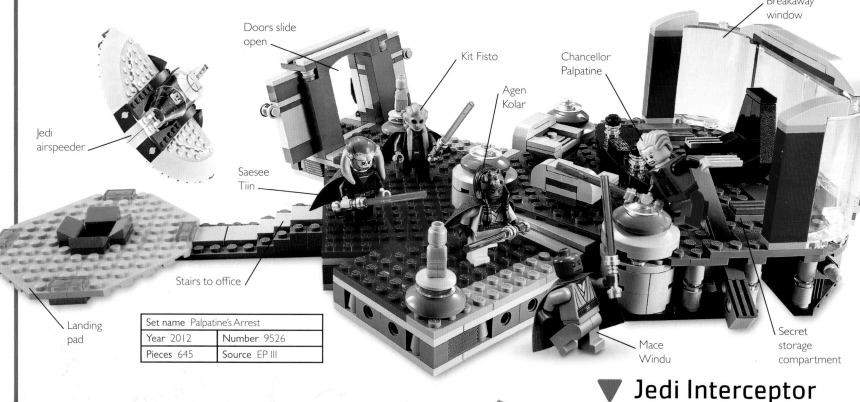

Doors slide open

Kit Fisto

Agen Kolar

Chancellor Palpatine

Breakaway window

Jedi airspeeder

Saesee Tiin

Stairs to office

Landing pad

Mace Windu

Secret storage compartment

Set name	Palpatine's Arrest	
Year	2012	Number 9526
Pieces	645	Source EP III

▼ Jedi Interceptor

ALTERNATIVE FACE

SITH ANAKIN

The strain of the Clone Wars shows on the face of Anakin's Episode III minifigure. His alternative face has yellow Sith eyes.

Hinged cockpit

R2-D2

Wings unfold in flight mode

Ion cannon

Laser cannon

After swearing allegiance to Darth Sidious, Anakin becomes his apprentice. He attacks the Jedi Temple, and says goodbye to Padmé. Boarding his Jedi interceptor, Anakin travels to Mustafar to eliminate the Separatist leaders. But Padmé and Obi-Wan follow him, leading to a fateful duel and tragic consequences. This 2012 set comes with five minifigures, including Nute Gunray and a battle droid.

Set name	Anakin's Jedi Interceptor	
Year	2012	Number 9494
Pieces	300	Source EP III

Duel on Mustafar

Teetering on service platforms above the red-hot lava of Mustafar, Obi-Wan fights his former Padawan, Anakin Skywalker, now recruited to the Sith and renamed Darth Vader. They are moved on long rods and their lightsabers glow. Meanwhile the pillars could come crashing down at any time!

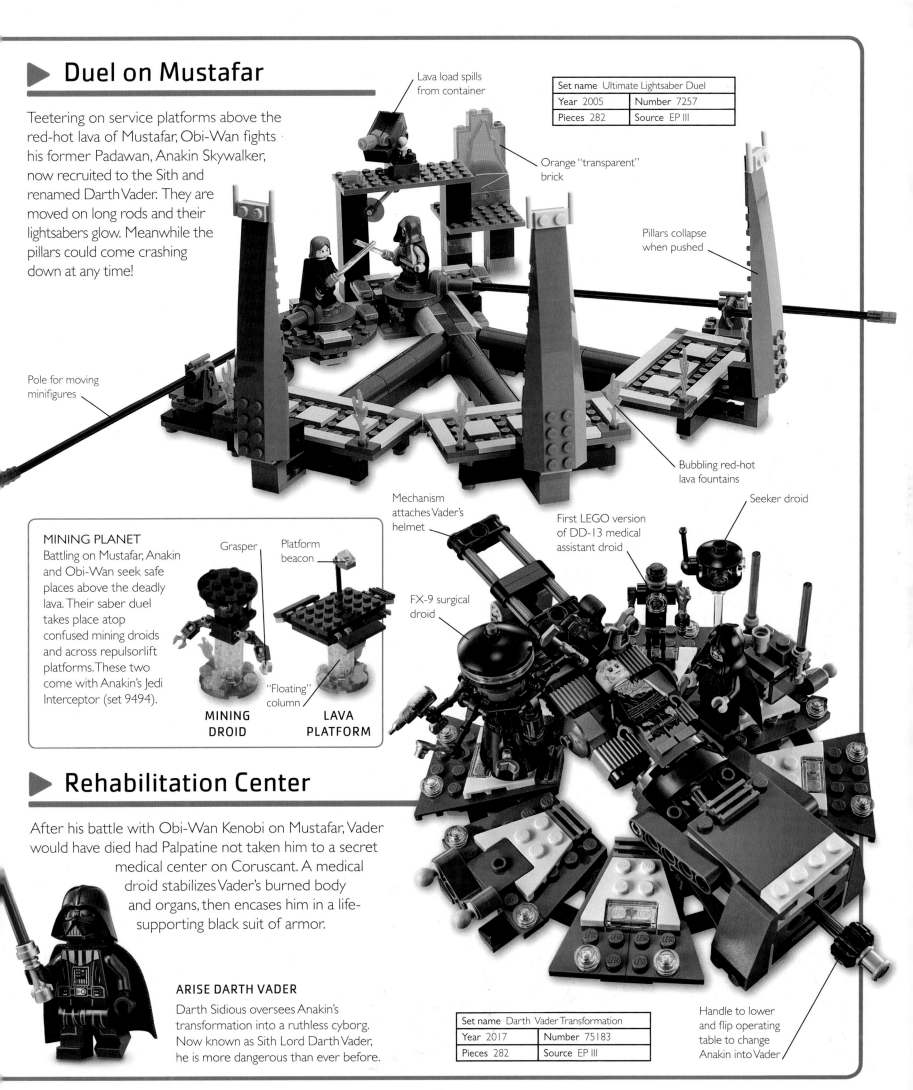

Lava load spills from container

Set name Ultimate Lightsaber Duel	
Year 2005	Number 7257
Pieces 282	Source EP III

Orange "transparent" brick

Pillars collapse when pushed

Pole for moving minifigures

Bubbling red-hot lava fountains

MINING PLANET

Battling on Mustafar, Anakin and Obi-Wan seek safe places above the deadly lava. Their saber duel takes place atop confused mining droids and across repulsorlift platforms. These two come with Anakin's Jedi Interceptor (set 9494).

Grasper

Platform beacon

"Floating" column

MINING DROID

LAVA PLATFORM

Mechanism attaches Vader's helmet

First LEGO version of DD-13 medical assistant droid

Seeker droid

FX-9 surgical droid

Rehabilitation Center

After his battle with Obi-Wan Kenobi on Mustafar, Vader would have died had Palpatine not taken him to a secret medical center on Coruscant. A medical droid stabilizes Vader's burned body and organs, then encases him in a life-supporting black suit of armor.

ARISE DARTH VADER

Darth Sidious oversees Anakin's transformation into a ruthless cyborg. Now known as Sith Lord Darth Vader, he is more dangerous than ever before.

Set name Darth Vader Transformation	
Year 2017	Number 75183
Pieces 282	Source EP III

Handle to lower and flip operating table to change Anakin into Vader

Wookiees

During the Clone Wars, an epic battle takes place on Kashyyyk, home planet of the Wookiees. Droid armies face fierce resistance from well-armed and proud Wookiee warriors, led by the chieftain Tarfful, and including Chewbacca. Wookiees use traditional wood-framed vehicles, many of which are unarmed, but the Wookiees' knowledge of the swamps and forests of their planet gives them an advantage over the ruthless droids.

On Kashyyyk, Separatist battle droids, spider droids, and tank droids launch a massive attack. The Wookiees fight bravely in their ornithopters, catamarans, and other vehicles, supported by Republic clone troops led by Jedi generals.

Radiator grille

Pressure release vents

Laser cannon tail-gun

Maneuverable flight wings

Power generator

◀ Ornithopter

Wookiee ornithopters, also known as fluttercraft, are lightweight, two-seated fliers used to patrol the swamps of Kashyyyk. During the Battle of Kashyyyk, Wookiee pilots and gunners fly these open-cockpit craft, many retrofitted with tail-mounted laser cannon, relying on speed and agility to avoid incoming fire.

Wooden frame

Primary control nexus

Set name	Wookiee Attack	
Year	2005	Number 7258
Pieces	366	Source EP III

Steering vanes

Stabilizing flaps

CLONE LEADER
Like the 41st Elite Corps troopers he commands, Gree's 2014 minifigure is dirty and battle-scarred. This seasoned clone leader carries a blaster weapon and specialist macrobinoculars.

CLONE COMMANDER GREE

▶ Kashyyyk Troopers

Camouflaged to blend in on lush, jungle planets, the 41st Elite Corps come to the Wookiees' defense on Kashyyyk. The troopers' minifigure armor is printed to look scratched and battle-worn after lengthy duty in hostile terrains.

Phase II helmet

Scout trooper helmet

Stud is propelled by blaster

KASHYYYK CLONE TROOPER

41ST ELITE CORPS TROOPER

Kashyyyk long-gun

Clan pectoral

WOOKIEE WARRIOR
An old friend of Chewbacca's, the clan chieftain Tarfful fights alongside the Republic's clones on Kashyyyk. Then he helps rescue Yoda when the clone troopers mysteriously turn their guns on their Jedi generals. Tarfful fights with a long-barreled rifle and wears a bandolier displaying his clan emblem on a pectoral.

CHIEF TARFFUL

▼ Catamaran

Slim, twin-hulled Wookiee catamarans skim over the waters of Kashyyyk at great speeds. During the Battle of Kashyyyk, Chewbacca joins forces with Yoda and Luminara Unduli on board a catamaran to make a raid on Separatist lines. Usually unarmed, this retrofitted catamaran features a centrally mounted heavy missile cannon and several bombs (dropped from each hull). Catamarans are lifted by repulsors and propelled by jet engines or, as here, a propeller pod.

Propeller pod

Set name	Wookiee Catamaran	
Year	2005	Number 7260
Pieces	376	Source EP III

Exhaust vent

Propeller

Stabilizing spar

Engine

Rudder

Heater liquefies fuel

Wookiee warrior

Streamlined prow

Luminara Unduli

Wooden hull

Teeth bared

▶ Chewbacca

Small and skinny for a Wookiee, Chewbacca fights against the Separatists' battle droids on Kashyyyk, firing energy bolts from his bowcaster. This 2014 version of Chewie's minifigure has a new mold, with visible teeth and new details in his multicolored fur and eyes. His bowcaster is now black. He's found in Droid Gunship (set 75042).

Bowcaster

Bandolier

CHEWBACCA (REDDISH-BROWN)

BRICK FACTS
Reddish-brown Chewbacca appears in several Imperial-era sets: Death Star (set 10188), *Millennium Falcon* (set 4504) and the Ultimate Collector *Millennium Falcon* (set 10179), and X-Wing Fighter (set 6212). A brown Chewbacca appears in Imperial AT-ST (set 7127), *Millennium Falcon* (set 7190), and the minifigure pack *Star Wars #3* (set 3342).

Chapter 2: The Galactic Civil War

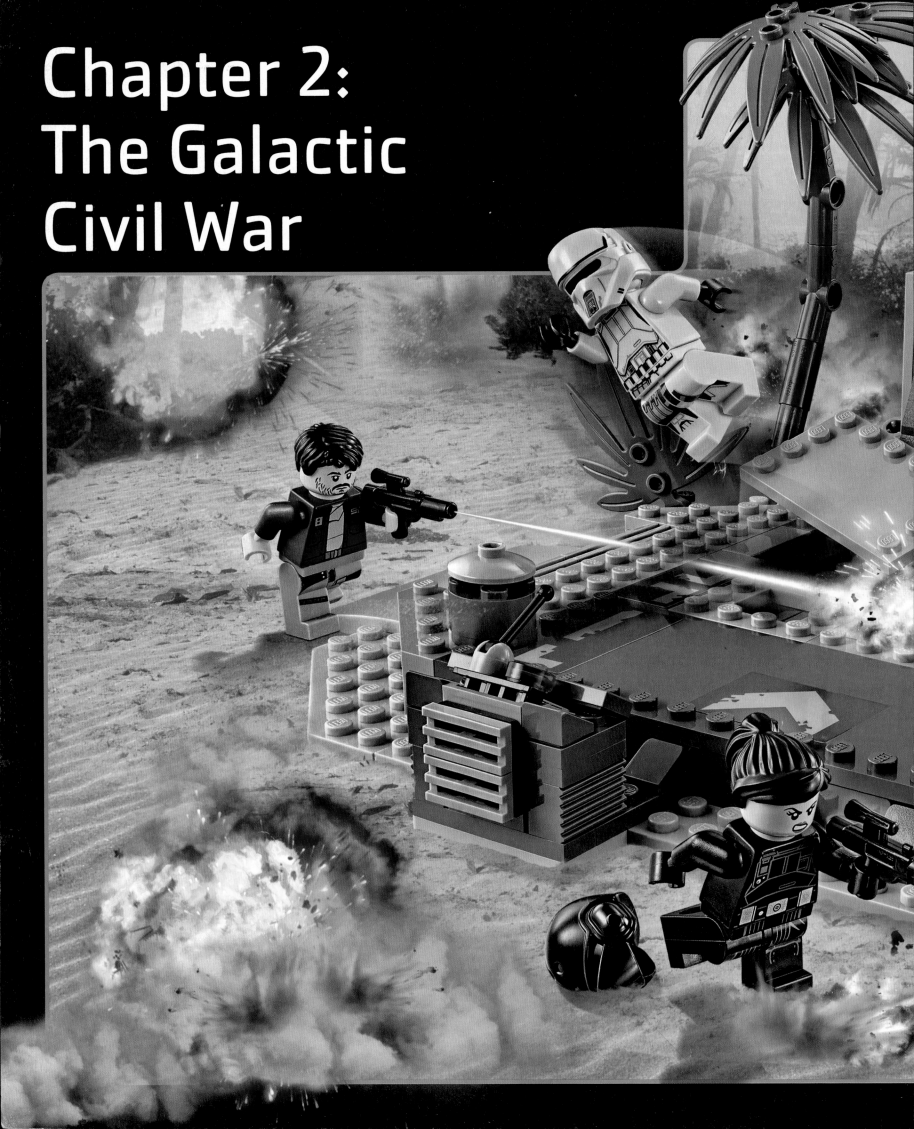

Han Solo

Han Solo is a hero of the Rebellion, but at one point he worked for the Empire! He didn't make a very good Imperial soldier, though, so he became a smuggler instead. The key to his success as a thief and a scoundrel is down to two things: his super-fast ship, the *Millennium Falcon*, and his brave co-pilot and best friend Chewbacca. Han and Chewie are happy being small-time crooks, but fate has a way of involving them in the galaxy's greatest struggles.

GUNSLINGING HAN
In this 2018 minifigure, Han wears a gunslinger's belt and a holster that allows for a quick draw.

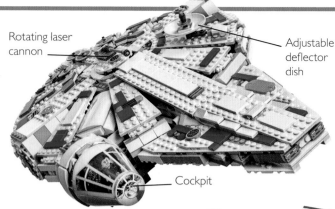
Rotating laser cannon
Adjustable deflector dish
Cockpit
FLYING MODE

▶ *Millennium Falcon*

When Han Solo first flies the *Millennium Falcon*, it belongs to another smuggler, Lando Calrissian. Lando has turned the cargo freighter into a gleaming white sports ship, and Han pushes it to its limits by piloting it through the hazardous Kessel Run in just over 12 parsecs. Later, he challenges Lando to a card game for ownership of the vessel, and he wins the *Falcon* fair and square.

Set name	Kessel Run *Millennium Falcon*	
Year	2018	Number 75212
Pieces	1,414	Source *Solo*

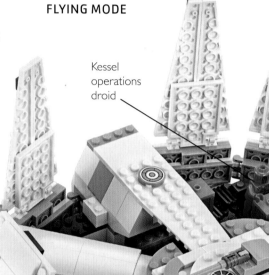
Kessel operations droid

Detachable escape craft
DD-BD droid
Dejarik table

NOT QUITE SOLO
Han and Chewie team up with a rag-tag bunch of crooks and scoundrels for their first smuggling jobs, from the flamboyant Lando to the four-armed Rio Durant.

RIO DURANT   **LANDO CALRISSIAN**   **VAL**   **TOBIAS BECKETT**   **QI'RA**

Han and Qi'ra

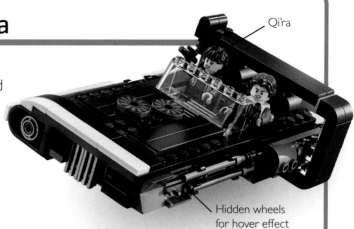

Qi'ra

Hidden wheels for hover effect

Han was born on Corellia, and grew up wishing he could get away from its Imperial factories and criminal gangs. He eventually steals an M-68 landspeeder in the hope of escaping the planet with his girlfriend, Qi'ra.

Set name	Han Solo's Landspeeder	
Year	2018	Number 75209
Pieces	345	Source *Solo*

FAITHFUL FURBALL

The Wookiee Chewbacca swears his loyalty to Han after they team up to escape an Imperial prison cell. A veteran of the Clone Wars, Chewie is an expert shot with a bowcaster and wears ammunition across his huge, hairy chest.

CHEWBACCA

Moloch and the White Worms

Hinged hull section

Moloch

On Corellia, Han and Qi'ra work for the criminal gang called the White Worms. Its other members include a worm-like Grindalid called Moloch who chases the pair when they try to escape. His A-A4B speeder is bigger and more powerful than Han's.

Rapid-fire stud shooter

Drink bar

Corellian Hound

Set name	Moloch's Landspeeder	
Year	2018	Number 75210
Pieces	464	Source *Solo*

BRICK FACTS

DK's LEGO® *Star Wars*™ *Character Encyclopedia* (2011) included this exclusive Han minifigure. He wears the medal he earned by helping to destroy the first Death Star.

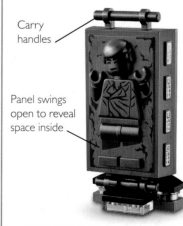

CELEBRATION HAN

SOLIDIFIED SOLO

A Han Solo minifigure fits inside this special piece, which has appeared in four sets to date. It depicts Han after he was frozen in carbonite and given to Jabba the Hutt as a gift!

Carry handles

Panel swings open to reveal space inside

HAN SOLO IN CARBONITE

Full disguise includes a helmet

Standard blaster

Head has a smiling face printed on reverse side

Classic LEGO hair piece

Camouflage coat

HELPING HAN

Han donned a stormtrooper disguise to help rescue rebel leader Leia from the Death Star. He liked Leia so much that he swiftly joined the Rebellion!

HOTH HAN

Han wore cold-weather gear on the icy world of Hoth when he ventured out to find Luke Skywalker, who had gone missing in the snow.

HAN WITH A PLAN

General Solo was a vital part of the plan to destroy the second Death Star, and his efforts on Endor helped to end the Empire once and for all.

Millennium Falcon

According to its captain, Han Solo, the *Millennium Falcon* "may not look like much, but she's got it where it counts." It's fast and well-equipped, though prone to malfunctions. Han and its previous captains have tinkered with its systems over the years, adding Imperial military-grade armor, quad laser cannon, an outsized sensor dish, and many other customized features—all of which require frequent repairs!

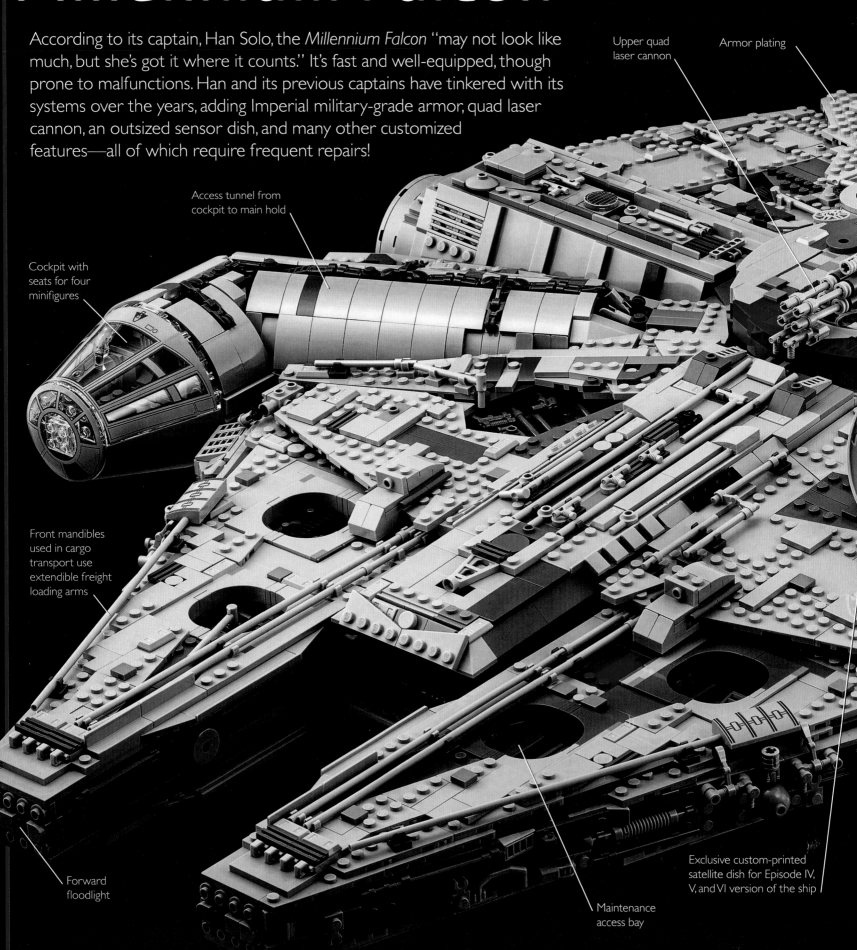

Upper quad laser cannon

Armor plating

Access tunnel from cockpit to main hold

Cockpit with seats for four minifigures

Front mandibles used in cargo transport use extendible freight loading arms

Forward floodlight

Maintenance access bay

Exclusive custom-printed satellite dish for Episode IV, V, and VI version of the ship

Engines

Moving at sublight speed, the *Falcon* relies on two heavily modified Girodyne SRB42 engines that emit glowing blue exhaust gases when fired up. Sublight drives propel starships within star systems or far enough away from planets so they can safely jump to hyperspace.

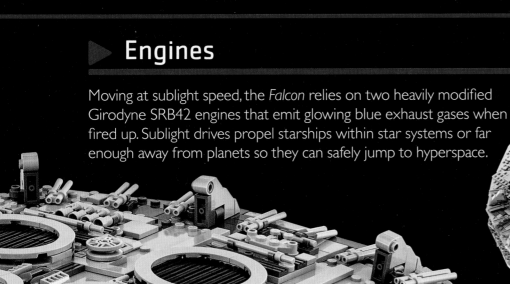

REAR VIEW

Heat exhaust vent

Engine exhausts

Port docking ring

BRICK FACTS

On its release in 2017, UCS *Millennium Falcon* was the largest LEGO set ever, with more than 7,500 bricks and a 494-page instruction manual.

The set includes features, such as an interchangeable satellite, that allow builders to convert the original ship to the version flown in episodes VII and VIII.

BOARDING RAMP
The *Falcon*'s crew enter via a retractable boarding ramp that lowers from behind the starboard docking ring. Han and Leia are all set to board!

DATA FILE

Set name: *Millennium Falcon*
Year: 2017   **Set Number:** 75192
Pieces: 7,541   **Source:** EP IV–VIII
Dimensions:
length over 33 in (84 cm)
width over 8¹/₂ in (22 cm)
height over 8 in (21 cm)
Minifigures: 8—C-3PO, Chewbacca, Finn, Han Solo (young), Han Solo (older), Princess Leia, Rey, BB-8

Luke Skywalker

Yearning for adventure, farm boy Luke Skywalker grows up on a remote planet named Tatooine. When he meets Obi-Wan Kenobi, Luke begins to learn the truth of his origins as the secret son of Anakin Skywalker. Luke's journey transforms him into a pilot for the Rebel Alliance and a Jedi Knight—and ends in a reconciliation with his father and freedom from Imperial rule for the galaxy.

LUKE ON TATOOINE

On the desolate planet Tatooine, Luke wears a simple farm tunic, a utility belt for his tools, and leg bindings to keep out the planet's sand.

BRICK FACTS

In 2009, the LEGO Group made an exclusive Luke Skywalker minifigure for DK's LEGO® *Star Wars*™: *The Visual Dictionary*. Because the 2009 edition of the book celebrates 10 years of LEGO *Star Wars*, Luke is dressed for the celebration scene at the end of *Star Wars: Episode IV A New Hope*.

CELEBRATION LUKE

▶ T-16 Skyhopper

With the demise of podracing on Tatooine, teenagers take to racing skyhoppers through narrow ravines, blasting womp rats with front-mounted rifles. Luke owns an Incom T-16 skyhopper (though his Uncle Owen disapproves of it). The 2003 variant featured an open cockpit, but the 2015 model has been upgraded with an angled cockpit canopy. Both models feature an unnamed pilot—they are two of just a few sets to feature an unnamed main minifigure.

Set name	T-16 Skyhopper	
Year	2015	Number 75081
Pieces	247	Source EP II, IV & VI

Upper aerofoil

Cockpit

Movable lower aerofoil

Navigation light

Spring-loaded missiles under wing

Primary laser cannon

Dorsal turbine hides secret compartment

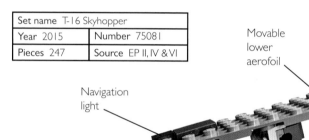

◀ Luke's Landspeeder

Luke and his new friends travel around the desert terrain of his home world in his battered X-34 landspeeder. Its low-power repulsors make it hover off the ground, while triple turbines provide thrust. Speeders are a common sight on Tatooine, though heat and sand make maintenance a constant headache.

Set name	Luke's Landspeeder	
Year	2017	Number 75173
Pieces	149	Source EP IV

Communications receiver

Turbine engine

Repulsor vent

Battered front

X-Wing Starfighter

Luke flies an X-wing as "Red Five" in the rebel attack on the first Death Star. The 2018 fighter has a hinged cockpit canopy, an astromech droid socket, functional landing gear, and a lever behind the cockpit to move the wings between cruise and attack modes. It can also be customized as Luke's fighter or as Biggs Darklighter's craft. The set includes minifigures of Luke, Biggs, R2-D2, and R2-Q2.

Set name	X-Wing Starfighter	
Year	2018	Number 75218
Pieces	730	Source EP IV & VI

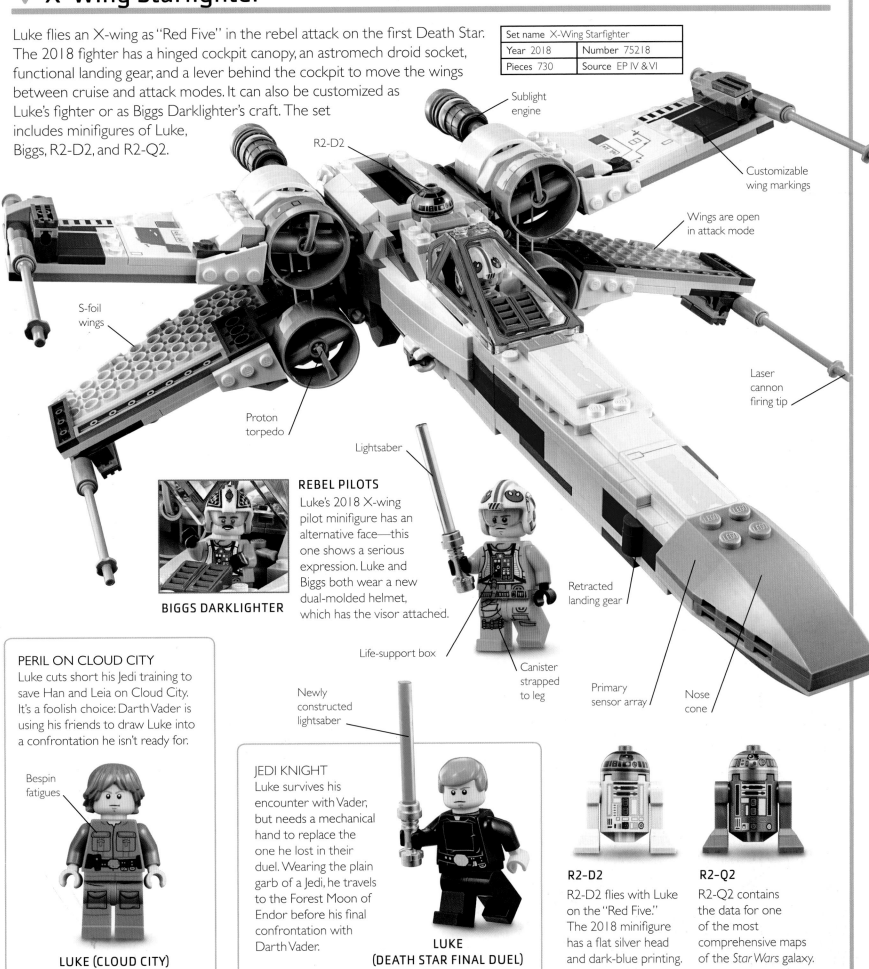

Sublight engine

R2-D2

Customizable wing markings

Wings are open in attack mode

S-foil wings

Laser cannon firing tip

Proton torpedo

Lightsaber

Retracted landing gear

Primary sensor array

Nose cone

Life-support box

Canister strapped to leg

REBEL PILOTS
Luke's 2018 X-wing pilot minifigure has an alternative face—this one shows a serious expression. Luke and Biggs both wear a new dual-molded helmet, which has the visor attached.

BIGGS DARKLIGHTER

PERIL ON CLOUD CITY
Luke cuts short his Jedi training to save Han and Leia on Cloud City. It's a foolish choice: Darth Vader is using his friends to draw Luke into a confrontation he isn't ready for.

Bespin fatigues

LUKE (CLOUD CITY)

Newly constructed lightsaber

JEDI KNIGHT
Luke survives his encounter with Vader, but needs a mechanical hand to replace the one he lost in their duel. Wearing the plain garb of a Jedi, he travels to the Forest Moon of Endor before his final confrontation with Darth Vader.

LUKE (DEATH STAR FINAL DUEL)

R2-D2
R2-D2 flies with Luke on the "Red Five." The 2018 minifigure has a flat silver head and dark-blue printing.

R2-Q2
R2-Q2 contains the data for one of the most comprehensive maps of the *Star Wars* galaxy.

▼ Escape Pod

C-3PO and R2-D2 slip into a small escape pod to avoid being caught by Darth Vader when he seizes the rebel blockade runner. After the droids crash-land on Tatooine, Jawas capture them and sell them to Owen Lars.

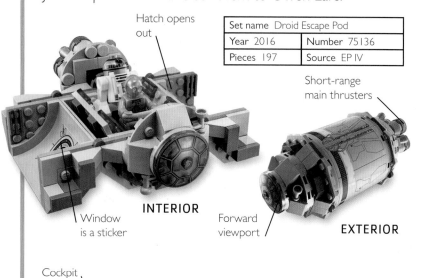

Hatch opens out

Short-range main thrusters

Forward viewport

Window is a sticker

INTERIOR

EXTERIOR

Set name	Droid Escape Pod	
Year	2016	Number 75136
Pieces	197	Source EP IV

Tatooine

The barren desert planet of Tatooine is a dangerous, lawless world. The galaxy's most wretched hive of villainy has become a port of call for smugglers, pirates and gangsters. Life is tough for its inhabitants, who face water shortages, ferocious sandstorms and extreme heat. Fierce Tusken Raiders and scavenging Jawas have found ways to survive. Jawas patrol the deserts and wastelands in large sandcrawlers in search of salvage from spaceship crashes.

▼ Sandcrawler

Jawas have repurposed these old mining vehicles to round up stray droid junked vehicles, scrap metal or minerals that can be used or sold. Each sandcrawler is home to an entire clan of Jawas, and serves as transport, workshop, travelling store—and protection from predators, such as rampaging Sand People.

Set name	Sandcrawler	
Year	2018	Number 75220
Pieces	1,239	Source EP IV

OPEN COCKPIT

Cockpit

Weather-beaten hull

Side-loading hatch

Main cargo hold

Ramp opens to deploy vehicles and cargo

R5-A2

Steerable treads

Medical droid

JAWA
The small, hooded Jawas use scrap parts to mend broken equipment or droids. After a sale, they move on quickly, as their patched-up goods rarely remain working for long.

Tusken Raider Attack

Hostile Tusken Raiders—or Sand People—attack Jawas and other settlers on Tatooine. The Jawas defend themselves and their service vehicle with their ion blasters. The small vehicle cleverly uses LEGO® Technic beams as treads.

Tap piece connects to top of droid

Articulated crane

Mask keeps out sand and retains moisture

Gaffi stick

TUSKEN RAIDER

Sand People dress to survive Tatooine's harsh climate. They wrap themselves in cloth to protect against the blazing sun and sandstorms. There are two variants of the Tusken Raider minifigure. The latest has a specially moulded head and mask piece with mouth grilles and eye coverings.

Set name	Tatooine Battle Pack	
Year	2018	Number 75198
Pieces	97	Source EP IV

Mos Eisley Cantina

The Cantina is a perilous den of smugglers, misfits and renegade pilots. Han's tense encounter with a battle-ready Greedo can be recreated in this third LEGO version of the raucous watering hole, with both seats featuring flipping mechanisms. This is the first set to include a model of the Ubrikkian 9000 landspeeder parked outside, and a minifigure of Wuher the bartender.

Opening cockpit

Ubrikkian landspeeder

Viewport

Traditional Tatooine architecture

Entrance with sliding door

Drinks are piped from the cellar

Wuher's latest concoction

Sandtrooper watches for trouble

Glowing table light

Set name	Mos Eisley Cantina	
Year	2018	Number 75205
Pieces	378	Source EP IV

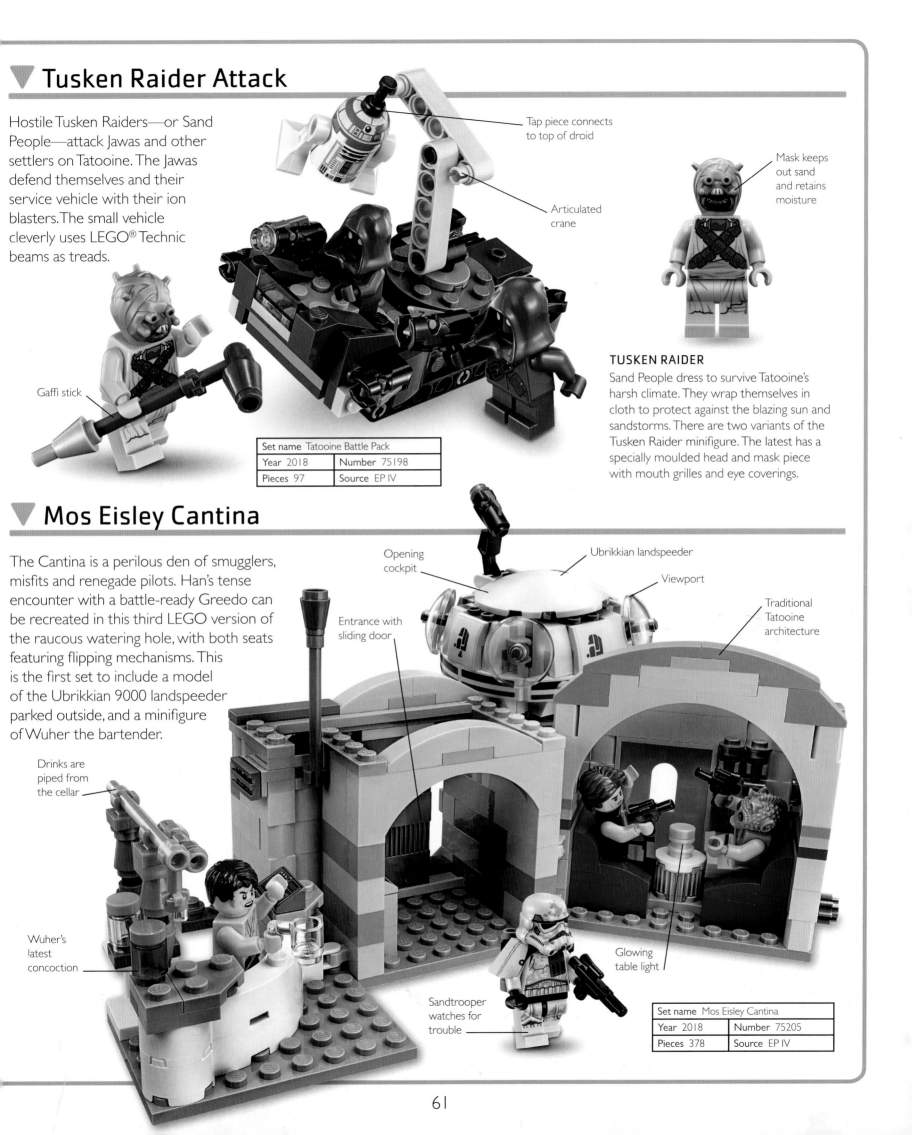

Imperial Leaders

Feared Sith Lord Emperor Palpatine rules as dictator over the most oppressive regime the galaxy has ever known. His apprentice, once known as Anakin Skywalker, was one of the most celebrated Jedi before he fell to the dark side and became Darth Vader. Vader now travels the Empire to enforce his Master's dark will. But Palpatine is never content with the extent of his rule. His focus turns to replacing his apprentice with Vader's own son, powerful Jedi Luke Skywalker.

Force lightning shoots from hands

EMPEROR PALPATINE

Sith Lord Emperor Palpatine's face is distorted by dark side energies and his sulfurous eyes betray his inner anger. Rarely seen even by his own officers, Palpatine wears a black robe to hide his face.

▼ Palpatine's Throne Room

On board the second Death Star, the Emperor commands the stars from his throne room tower. It is here that Darth Vader steps in to save his son from the deadly Force lightning that the Emperor lashes out at Luke Skywalker.

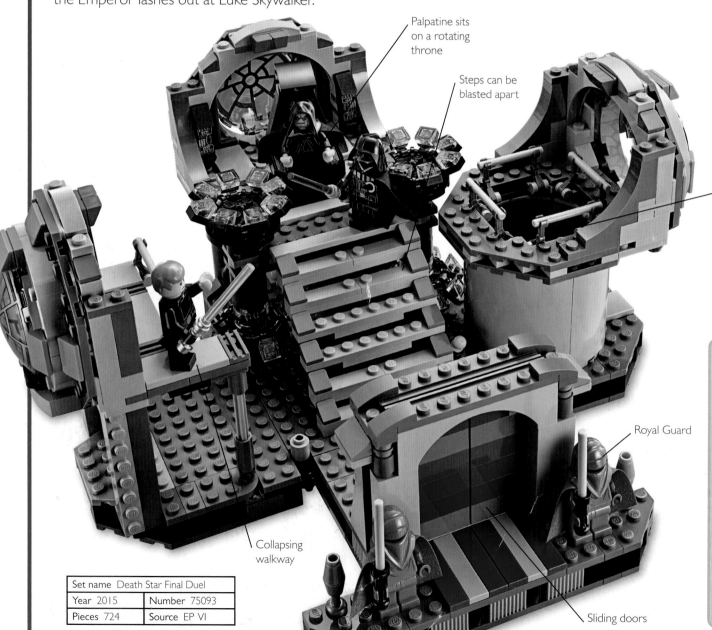

Palpatine sits on a rotating throne

Steps can be blasted apart

Reactor shaft where the Emperor tumbles to his doom

Royal Guard

Collapsing walkway

Sliding doors

Set name	Death Star Final Duel	
Year	2015	Number 75093
Pieces	724	Source EP VI

BRICK FACTS

The Imperial Star Destroyer (set 6211), released in 2006, included a room below decks where Vader communicates with a hologram of Emperor Palpatine—achieved by a sticker on a translucent brick.

DARTH VADER

Horribly wounded on Mustafar, Vader now lives encased in a terrifying breath mask and black armor. The minifigure of the merciless Sith apprentice has a scarred face beneath the helmet.

SERVING THE EMPIRE

The Emperor's will is enforced by a number of high-ranking officials who carry out his and Darth Vader's orders. Only the most cunning and ambitious can survive.

TARKIN	**KRENNIC**	**YULAREN**	**THRAWN**	**THE INQUISITOR**
Grand Moff Tarkin is ruthless and intimidating in his role as Imperial Governor.	Director Krennic runs the Death Star—until Grand Moff Tarkin pulls rank.	Admiral Yularen serves as a senior officer aboard the Death Star.	Thrawn is one of a few nonhuman officers to have risen through the ranks.	Taking his orders from Vader, the highest-ranking Inquisitor hunts for Jedi in hiding.

▼ Darth Vader's TIE Advanced

Darth Vader is a gifted pilot so he has his own high-tech starfighter called the TIE Advanced. The 2016 edition of the craft is the most detailed minifigure-scale model to date. The laser cannons beneath the cockpit are spring-loaded missiles operated by a trigger behind the top hatch.

EVOLUTION OF AN ICON

The original Darth Vader minifigure from 1999 has a simplified torso design compared with later versions, but the iconic black mask was there from the start.

Removable helmet

Control function panel

Flowing cape

DARTH VADER (1999)

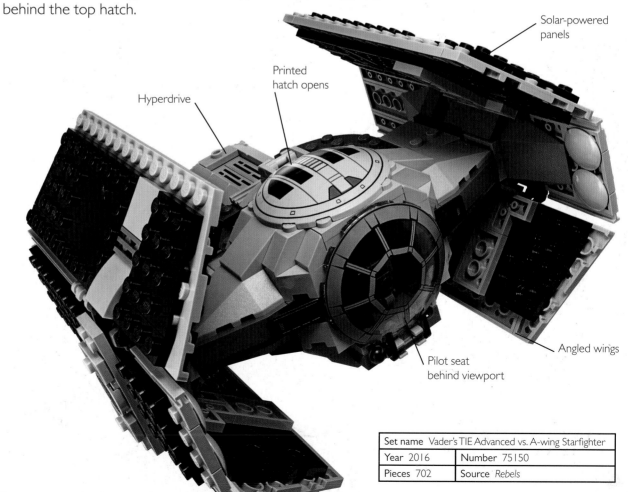

Solar-powered panels

Printed hatch opens

Hyperdrive

Angled wings

Pilot seat behind viewport

Set name	Vader's TIE Advanced vs. A-wing Starfighter	
Year	2016	Number 75150
Pieces	702	Source *Rebels*

Darth Vader's Castle

Darth Vader's menacing castle is on the volcanic planet of Mustafar, the site of his worst defeat. It's here that his former self, Anakin Skywalker, lost his lightsaber duel with Obi-Wan Kenobi, cementing his status as a Dark Lord. At his castle, Darth Vader meditates on the dark side of the Force and meets with his Imperial leaders.

Transport pilot on lookout

▲ Darth Vader's Castle

The central stronghold of the castle is made of obsidian. It has high tuning towers that transmit dark powers. Red-hot magma flows beneath its foundations. The set features a brick-built lava flow and a circular area at the top with a defensive stud-shooter cannon operated by an Imperial transport pilot.

EXTERIOR VIEW

Castle sits on cliff edge

TRANSPORT PILOTS

Imperial transport pilots were first visualized in *Star Wars: Secrets of the Empire* in 2017. In this hyper-reality experience, players wear a virtual reality headset and goggles and take on the role of rebels in a mission to steal a powerful weapon from an Imperial facility on Mustafar.

Blaster pistol

ROYAL GUARDS

The Royal Guards are formed from the most skilled soldiers in the Imperial military. They are known for their strength, intelligence, and loyalty—and their sinister crimson uniforms. Royal Guard minifigures carry a baton and wear long robes with a special hood element.

▲ Interior chambers

At the base of the castle is an underground hangar with a mouse droid and a docking station for a TIE Advanced fighter. Within the tower there is an ancient Sith shrine with a holocron, racks for ammunition, and a secret compartment hiding a lightsaber. There is also a bacta tank and a meditation chamber for Darth Vader, with a holographic communication unit.

Set name	Darth Vader's Castle	
Year	2018	Number 75251
Pieces	1060	Source R1

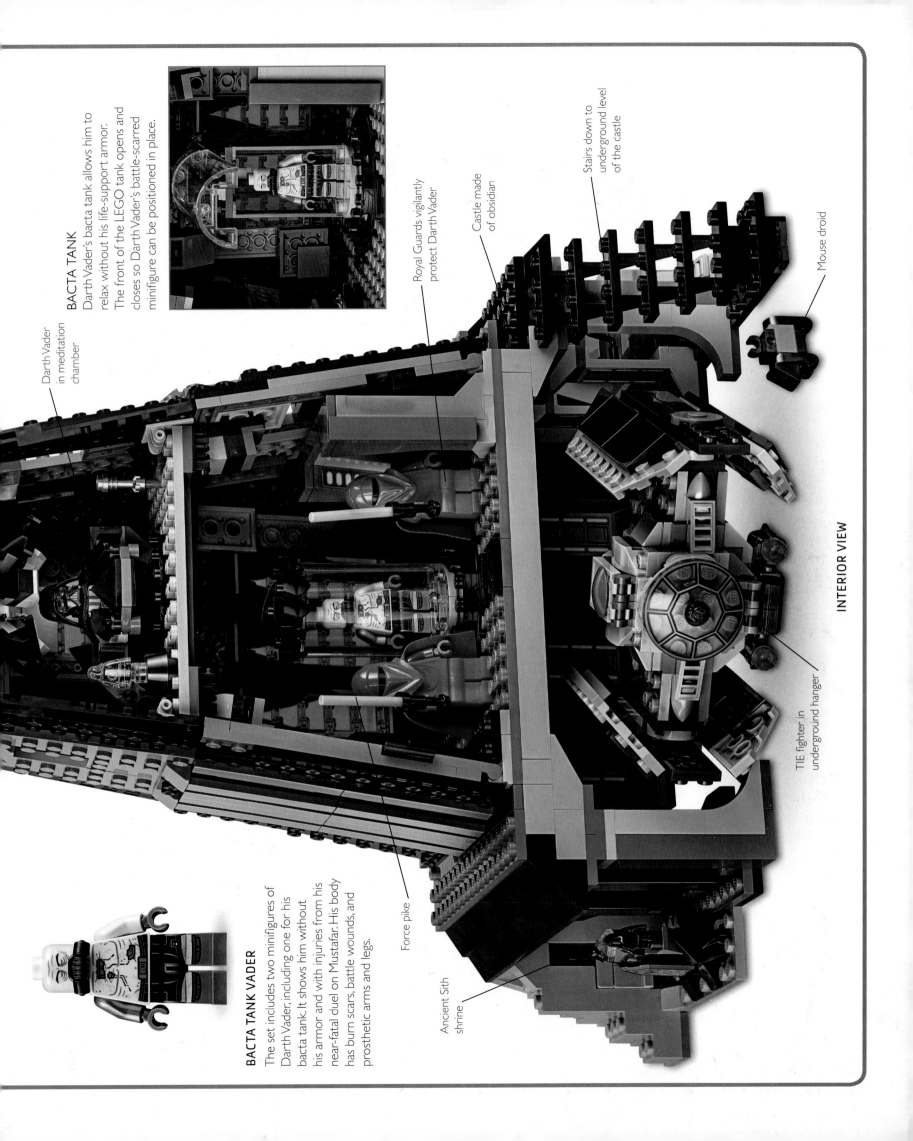

BACTA TANK

Darth Vader's bacta tank allows him to relax without his life-support armor. The front of the LEGO tank opens and closes so Darth Vader's battle-scarred minifigure can be positioned in place.

Darth Vader in meditation chamber

Royal Guards vigilantly protect Darth Vader

Castle made of obsidian

Stairs down to underground level of the castle

Mouse droid

BACTA TANK VADER

The set includes two minifigures of Darth Vader, including one for his bacta tank. It shows him without his armor and with injuries from his near-fatal duel on Mustafar. His body has burn scars, battle wounds, and prosthetic arms and legs.

Force pike

Ancient Sith shrine

TIE fighter in underground hanger

INTERIOR VIEW

Death Star

The Imperial battle station known as the Death Star is designed to quash potential dissent through displays of great force. The first Death Star uses its superweapon to obliterate Princess Leia's home planet, Alderaan. The second Death Star, though seemingly incomplete, is actually fully operational—and is intended to lure the rebels to their doom.

TIE ADVANCED
The mini-sized TIE Advanced is unique to this set. It can be flown into the hangar and docked on a slide-out TIE fighter rack. The cockpit viewscreen opens to allow Vader to take the controls.

Opening cockpit

Mechanism controls central turbolift

Death Star droid on work bench

Imperial astromech

Stormtrooper helmet

TIE docking rack

TIE Advanced

Redesigned hangar bay elevator

Imperial Navy officer

Winch handle raises and lowers pilot lift

Loading bay

Cargo crane is operated by stormtrooper

Cargo crate

Mouse droid in storage bay

Central turbolift shaft

Updated rotating turbolaser turret

Turbolaser turning mechanism

Emperor Palpatine's throne

Collapsing catwalk

Vader duels with Luke

Railing

Air duct

Air shaft

Luke and Leia swing across chasm

DATA FILE
Set name: Death Star
Year: 2016
Set Number: 75159
Pieces: 4,016
Source: EP IV & VI
Dimensions: length over 16 in (41 cm); width over 16 in (41 cm); height over 15¾ in (40 cm)
Minifigures: 28—Luke Skywalker (in regular outfit, Stormtrooper disguise, and Jedi Knight outfit), Han Solo (in regular outfit and Stormtrooper disguise), Obi-Wan Kenobi, Princess Leia, Chewbacca, Imperial astromech droid, Emperor Palpatine, Darth Vader, Grand Moff Tarkin, Imperial officer, 2 Royal Guards, 2 stormtroopers, 2 Death Star troopers, Death Star droid, 2 Imperial gunners, Imperial Navy officer, C-3PO, R2-D2, dianoga, interrogation droid, and mouse droid.

MOVIE ACTION
More than a dozen different scenes can be recreated within the playset, including the iconic duel between old enemies Obi-Wan and Vader.

Two Death Stars in One

The Death Star set combines aspects of the first and second Death Stars. Luke, for example, appears three times: in stormtrooper uniform to rescue Leia, in his regular outfit to swing across the air shaft, and as a Jedi Knight to battle Darth Vader.

DETENTION CELL
In her detention cell, Princess Leia refuses to give Vader the location of the rebel base. She even stands firm against the interrogator droid's ultrasonic and electroshock devices. Finally Luke and Han arrive to rescue her—and they all dive into a filthy trash compactor!

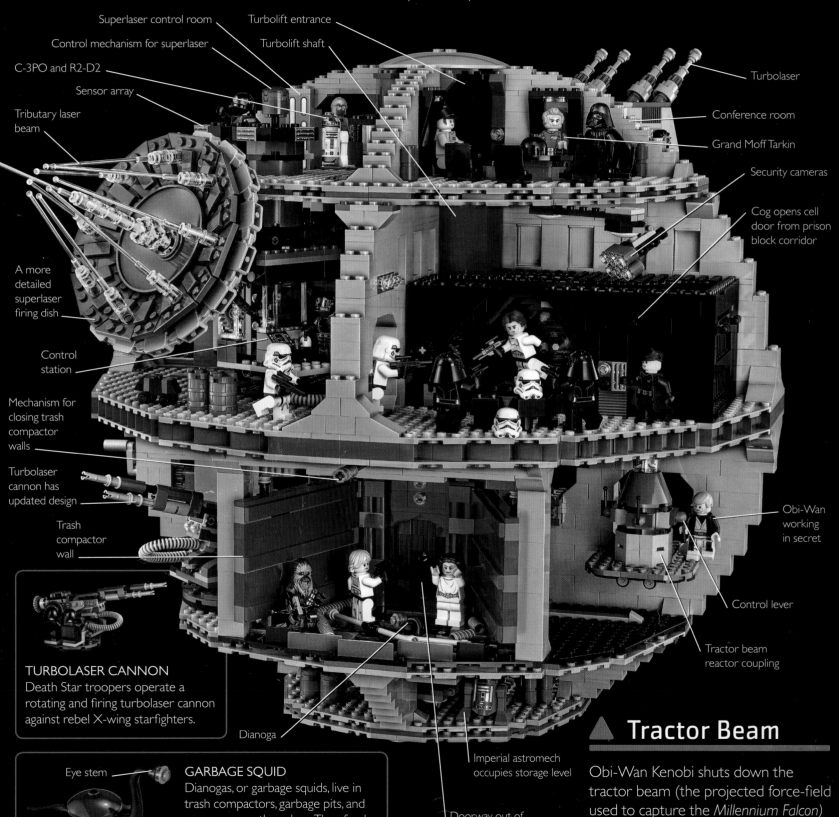

Superlaser control room

Control mechanism for superlaser

C-3PO and R2-D2

Sensor array

Tributary laser beam

Turbolift entrance

Turbolift shaft

Turbolaser

Conference room

Grand Moff Tarkin

Security cameras

Cog opens cell door from prison block corridor

A more detailed superlaser firing dish

Control station

Mechanism for closing trash compactor walls

Turbolaser cannon has updated design

Trash compactor wall

Obi-Wan working in secret

Control lever

Tractor beam reactor coupling

Dianoga

Imperial astromech occupies storage level

Doorway out of trash compactor

TURBOLASER CANNON
Death Star troopers operate a rotating and firing turbolaser cannon against rebel X-wing starfighters.

GARBAGE SQUID
Dianogas, or garbage squids, live in trash compactors, garbage pits, and sewers across the galaxy. They feed on scraps of decaying organic matter.

Eye stem

Tentacle

▲ Tractor Beam

Obi-Wan Kenobi shuts down the tractor beam (the projected force-field used to capture the *Millennium Falcon*) but Darth Vader then confronts him, leading to a lightsaber duel.

Imperial Stormtroopers

The gleaming white ground troops of the Galactic Empire can be found on thousands of planets across the galaxy. Hidden behind imposing masks and blast-proof armor, they present a unified show of strength that few would dare to challenge. Yet, for all their seeming uniformity, there are many different kinds of stormtrooper, especially trained for different duties and environments.

Distinctive bulky helmet brow

Stud shooter

C-PH patrol speeder bike

▶ Patrol Trooper

Wearing lighter armor than standard stormtroopers, patrol troopers act as law enforcement officers on worlds already under Imperial control. They police the streets of planets such as Corellia on sturdy C-PH patrol speeder bikes.

Set name	Imperial Patrol Battle Pack	
Year	2018	Number	75207
Pieces	99	Source	Solo

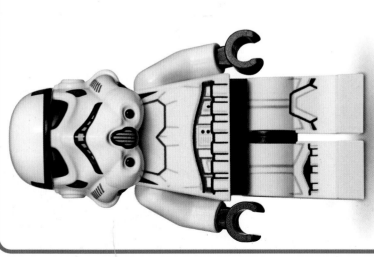

STORMTROOPER

Nameless, faceless stormtroopers are utterly loyal to the Empire. The 2019 minifigure has a new updated helmet mold for the 20th anniversary that replaces a previous mold, in use since 2001.

Fur-lined armor

RANGE TROOPER

These tough troopers serve on the wildest fringes of Imperial space.

Jetpacks allow for flight

JUMPTROOPER

With jetpacks on their backs, these special stormtroopers can actually fly!

SHORETROOPER

Life's a beach for these sand-colored coastal defender stormtroopers.

Helmet has advanced sensors

DEATH TROOPER

The grimly named death troopers are elite warriors clad in all-black armor.

STORMTROOPER SERGEANT

A white pauldron on a storm trooper's shoulder indicates that he or she is a sergeant.

Sandtrooper

With vital supplies of food and water strapped to their backs, sandtroopers are equipped to serve in dry, desert conditions. On the planet Tatooine, they often ride giant green lizards called dewbacks, rather than rely on vehicles that can break down when clogged up with sand.

Set name	Mos Eisley Cantina	
Year	2014	Number 75052
Pieces	616	Source EP IV

Electric prod to control dewback

Sand-stained armor

Survival backpack

Dewback

Steering vanes

74-Z speeder bike

Lightweight armor

Snowtrooper

Trained and outfitted for survival in the coldest environments, snowtroopers wear less armor than other stormtroopers, but a lot more insulation. Battery packs on their backs serve as portable heating systems, while their legs are kept warm by distinctive belt capes.

E-Web heavy repeating blaster cannon

Heated mask

Kama belt cape

Set name	Snowspeeder	
Year	2014	Number 75049
Pieces	279	Source EP V

Scout Trooper

Highly skilled at piloting super-fast speeder bikes, scout troopers are mostly used as advance guards. They can gather information about an area at speed, before racing back to report their findings. Their narrow vehicles and survival training make them especially well suited to deployment in dense forest environments.

Set name	Ewok Village	
Year	2013	Number 10236
Pieces	1,990	Source EP VI

Imperial Army

At the end of the Clone Wars, the Galactic Republic becomes an Empire and its military resources now serve the new regime. Clone troopers become stormtroopers, their ranks made up of clones and, now, human recruits. Stormtroopers have a huge arsenal of powerful ground vehicles to choose from, including giant armored walkers for smashing through enemy armies.

▼ Imperial Conveyex Transport

A long line of armored cargo cars that can travel on both the top and underside of the track is an imposing sight—even for daring smugglers! Range troopers walk up the sides of these fast-moving trains in their magnetic boots, or using the studs on the sides of the LEGO version.

Set name	Imperial Conveyex Transport	
Year 2018	Number 75217	
Pieces 622	Source Solo	

Movable gun turret

Cargo cabin with coaxium hyperfuel containers inside

Door to driver's compartment

Engine section with wrap-around track

▶ AT-AT Walker

AT-AT DRIVER

Equipped with insulated jumpsuits and life-support packs, AT-AT drivers guide the huge walkers.

GENERAL VEERS

General Veers masterminds the devastating assault on the rebel base on Hoth from the cockpit of the lead AT-AT.

During the Battle of Hoth, the Empire deploys All Terrain Armored Transports (AT-ATs) against the rebels, knowing the mere sight of these walking tanks is enough to scare off most soldiers. An AT-AT's side opens to reveal a staging platform for the two snowtrooper minifigures and General Veers, who stand ready to attack the rebel artillery. An AT-AT driver steers the walker from a cockpit in its head.

Set name	AT-AT	
Year 2014	Number 75054	
Pieces 1,138	Source EPV & VI	

▼ Troop Transport

These sturdy, reliable Imperial Troop Transports—or ITTs—constantly move troops between important locations. The Empire also uses them to forcibly relocate locals once their land is seized.

Set name	Imperial Troop Transport	
Year 2015	Number 75078	
Pieces 141	Source Rebels	

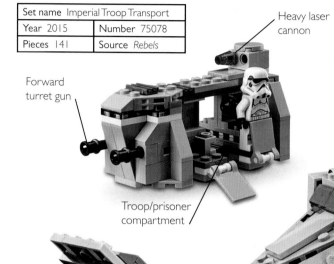

Heavy laser cannon

Forward turret gun

Troop/prisoner compartment

Command cockpit

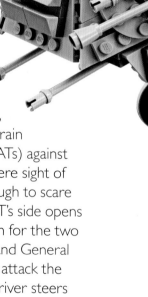

Class II heavy laser cannon

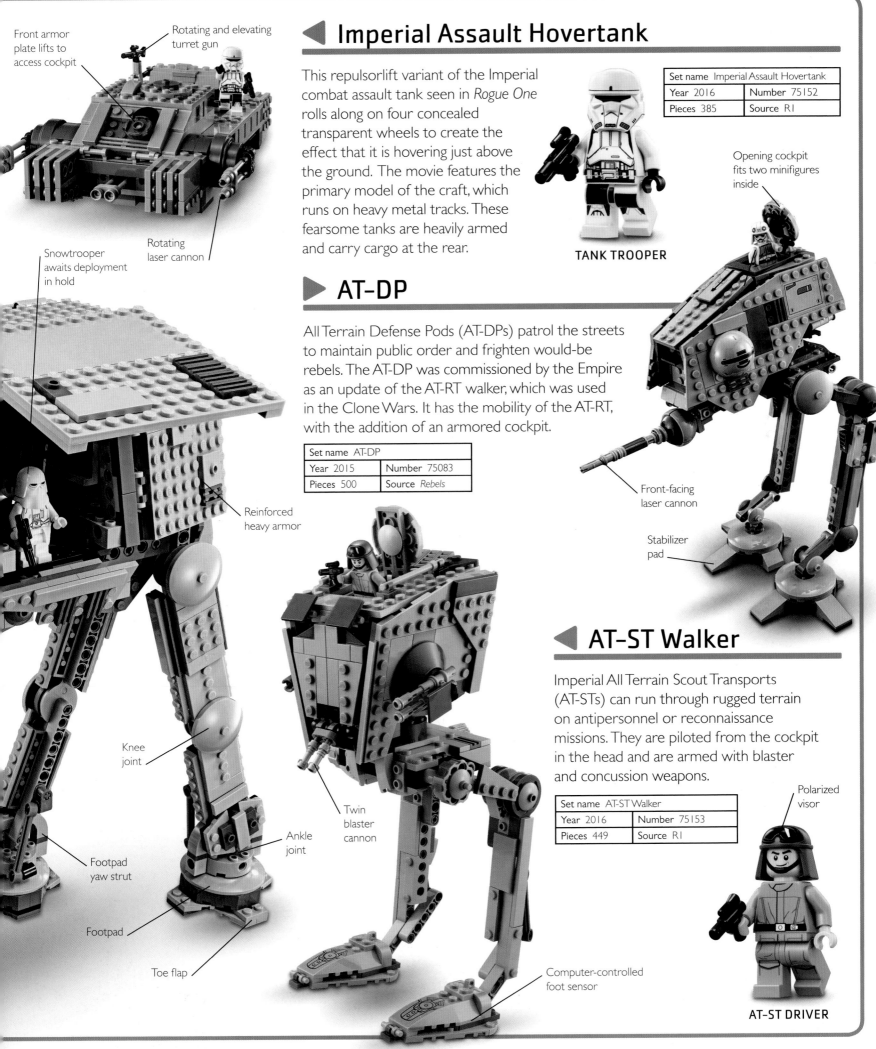

Front armor plate lifts to access cockpit

Rotating and elevating turret gun

Rotating laser cannon

Imperial Assault Hovertank

This repulsorlift variant of the Imperial combat assault tank seen in *Rogue One* rolls along on four concealed transparent wheels to create the effect that it is hovering just above the ground. The movie features the primary model of the craft, which runs on heavy metal tracks. These fearsome tanks are heavily armed and carry cargo at the rear.

Set name	Imperial Assault Hovertank	
Year	2016	Number 75152
Pieces	385	Source R1

TANK TROOPER

Opening cockpit fits two minifigures inside

AT-DP

All Terrain Defense Pods (AT-DPs) patrol the streets to maintain public order and frighten would-be rebels. The AT-DP was commissioned by the Empire as an update of the AT-RT walker, which was used in the Clone Wars. It has the mobility of the AT-RT, with the addition of an armored cockpit.

Set name	AT-DP	
Year	2015	Number 75083
Pieces	500	Source *Rebels*

Snowtrooper awaits deployment in hold

Reinforced heavy armor

Front-facing laser cannon

Stabilizer pad

AT-ST Walker

Imperial All Terrain Scout Transports (AT-STs) can run through rugged terrain on antipersonnel or reconnaissance missions. They are piloted from the cockpit in the head and are armed with blaster and concussion weapons.

Set name	AT-ST Walker	
Year	2016	Number 75153
Pieces	449	Source R1

Polarized visor

Knee joint

Twin blaster cannon

Ankle joint

Footpad yaw strut

Footpad

Toe flap

Computer-controlled foot sensor

AT-ST DRIVER

TIE Variants

When Palpatine establishes his tyrannical Empire, the Republic's massive navy is appropriated and put to brutal use. Jedi-piloted interceptor starfighters, with their solar-panel wings, are reborn as aggressive TIE fighters. Indeed, the Imperial fleet is expanded with a variety of new, ever-deadlier models. The TIE fighter becomes a staple in the Imperial fleet.

R3-J2

This is the only LEGO astromech with a completely transparent dome.

TIE FIGHTER PILOT

Imperial fighter pilots are a specially trained, elite flying corps.

▼ TIE Defender

A prototype starfighter developed in secret by the Empire, the TIE defender is agile and heavily armored to stand up to Rebel fighters. The LEGO set has a unique rotating cockpit and is armed with six flick-fire missiles.

Set name	TIE Defender	
Year 2010	Number	8087
Pieces 304	Source	Rebels

Flick-fire missile

Solar panels

Gyroscopic cockpit lets pilot remain upright

Targeting sensors

▼ TIE Fighter

TIE fighters are armed with cannon and have no deflector shields or hyperdrive, making them light and agile in battle. These craft are mass-produced by the Empire and they swarm an enemy to take them out. This 2018 set includes a highly detailed design with an opening cockpit and two spring-loaded shooters. Four minifigures are included in the set: a TIE fighter pilot, an Imperial mudtrooper, Han Solo, and Tobias Beckett.

Set name	Imperial TIE Fighter	
Year 2018	Number	75211
Pieces 519	Source	Solo

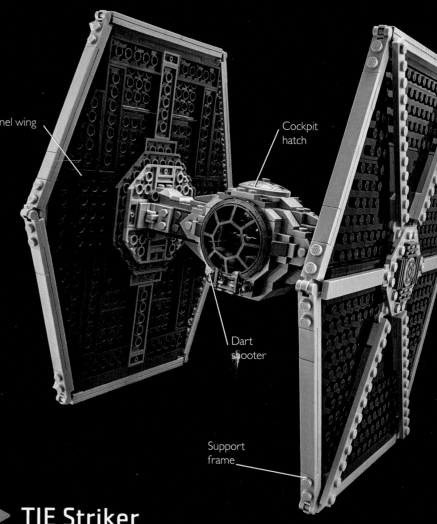

Solar-panel wing

Cockpit hatch

Dart shooter

Support frame

▶ TIE Striker

The TIE striker is deployed to defend the base on Scarif. Levers on the back of this set switch the wings from attack mode to cruising mode. Two spring-loaded darts are mounted below the pilot's canopy.

Set name	TIE Striker	
Year 2016	Number	75154
Pieces 543	Source	R1

Wings are in attack mode

TIE Interceptor

The TIE interceptor is one of the fastest, most maneuverable, and best-armed starfighters in the Imperial fleet. Its upgraded ion engines deliver immense power for dogfights, and each wing-tip boasts a blaster cannon whose linked fire can rip through enemy fighters.

Set name	TIE Interceptor	
Year	2006	Number 6206
Pieces	212	Source EP VI

Wing-tip blaster cannon

Cut-away wing profile

Advanced targeting sensors

TIE minifigure pilot in cockpit

Angled solar wing

TIE Advanced Prototype

The Grand Inquisitor flies a new TIE fighter prototype when Darth Vader assigns him to a new mission. It's a smaller ship than the advanced fighter Darth Vader uses.

Set name	TIE Advanced Prototype	
Year	2015	Number 75082
Pieces	355	Source *Rebels*

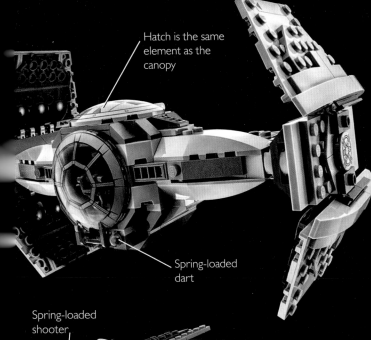

Hatch is the same element as the canopy

Spring-loaded dart

Spring-loaded shooter

IDEN VERSIO

INFERNO SQUAD
Led by the formidable Commander Iden Versio, Inferno Squad are an elite special forces unit. They are sent on the toughest missions by the Empire. Iden has unique printing to denote her military rank.

TIE Bomber

Set name	TIE Bomber	
Year	2003	Number 4479
Pieces	229	Source EP V

Single-pilot TIE bombers make precise "surgical strikes" that would be impractical for the Empire's capital ships. The ship's armaments include laser weapons and proton bombs that can be deployed against shielded targets, blasting open their hiding places.

Solar-panel wings

Cockpit viewscreen

Spring-loaded guided concussion missile port

Imperial Transports

The Empire uses its distinctive tri-wing shuttles for ferrying troops, cargo, and VIPs. In most cases, the vessels have a fixed-position stabilizer wing on top and adjustable stabilizers on the sides. These side wings fold upward when a shuttle lands—not only to take up less space on the ground but also to provide a defensive shield for the central section.

IMPERIAL SHUTTLE PILOT
These pilots are handpicked for their loyalty as many fly to the Empire's most secret bases.

▶ Tydirium

More elegant-looking than most Imperial ships, *Lambda*-class T-4a shuttles are often used to transport dignitaries up to and including the Emperor himself. The *Tydirium* is a T-4a shuttle that was stolen by the Rebel Alliance and used to mount a sneak attack on the second Death Star's shield generator on the forest moon of Endor.

Set name	Imperial Shuttle *Tydirium*	
Year 2015	Number 75094	
Pieces 937	Source EP VI	

LEIA IN CAMOUFLAGE
Leia is well equipped for battle in the forests on the moon of Endor in her camouflage cape.

LANDING MODE

White LEGO Technic beams provide stability

Side panel opens to reveal passenger area

Wings are raised for landing

Cockpit viewscreen

Missile shooter hidden under wing

Double laser cannon can be tilted

Wings constructed out of plates, tiles, and LEGO Technic® beams

Folding wing

AT-Hauler

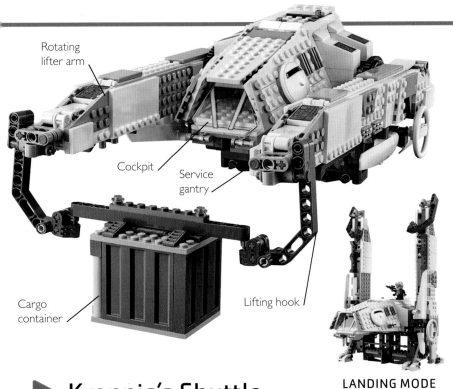

Rotating lifter arm

Cockpit

Service gantry

Cargo container

Lifting hook

The Y-45 Armored Transport (or AT) Hauler is not a shuttle, but is based on the same fold-up format as its less cumbersome cousins. Instead of wings, it has sturdy arms for shifting cargo, which rotate upward when not in use. In LEGO form, it is designed to carry the cargo wagon from the set Imperial Conveyex Transport (set 75217).

Set name	Imperial AT-Hauler	
Year	2018	Number 75219
Pieces	829	Source *Solo*

LANDING MODE

Krennic's Shuttle

As the Empire's Director of Advanced Weapons Research, Orson Krennic has his pick of the best, most cutting-edge ships. When he saw the concept designs for a new stealth ship called the *Delta*-class T-3c shuttle, he insisted that one should be built for his personal use. The ship is heavily armed and all but invisible to enemy sensors.

Set name	Krennic's Imperial Shuttle	
Year	2016	Number 75156
Pieces	863	Source R1

LANDING MODE

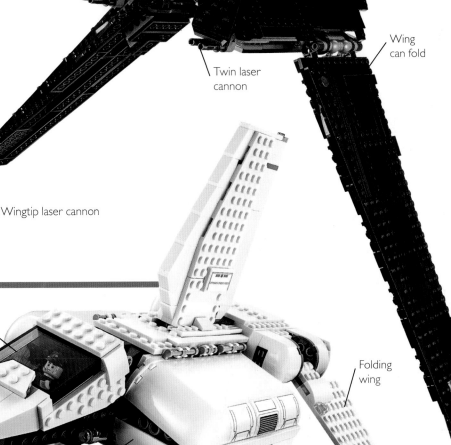

Cockpit

Wing can fold

Twin laser cannon

Wingtip laser cannon

Landing Craft

The *Sentinel*-class landing craft is the bulkier brother of the *Lambda*-class T-4a shuttle. It is mainly used to deploy stormtroopers in battle, but can also be used to carry cargo. The 2018 LEGO version has a fold-out ramp that can extend from either side of the craft.

Set name	Imperial Landing Craft	
Year	2018	Number 75221
Pieces	636	Source EP IV

Space for a sandtrooper on each side

Cockpit

Folding wing

Opening compartment

Retractable ramp

Star Destroyer

Dagger-shaped Star Destroyers are the most feared symbol of Imperial might, armed with fearsome firepower and powerful scanner and tractor-beam arrays. The Republic develops *Victory*-class Star Destroyers as capital ships in the final years of the Clone Wars, and the Emperor expands the fleet with new *Imperial*-class Star Destroyers, employed to crush and subdue worlds.

COMMAND BRIDGE
The bridge is situated at the center of the command tower, in view of any ship under attack. Grand Moff Tarkin and an Imperial officer stand at the flight consoles and tracking systems.

MEDITATION CHAMBER
On long space voyages, Darth Vader sits in his meditation chamber, or hyperbaric pod. In the high-pressure air mix within the chamber, Vader can remove his helmet (using a lifting mechanism) to reveal his horribly scarred face and head.

Defense turret

ESCAPE POD
The ship contains a life-support escape pod for emergency evacuations. Escape pods contain food and oxygen, as well as flares, a porta-shelter, and survival suits for passengers.

MSE-6 droid

Grand Moff Tarkin

R2-D5

Armored hull

Flight deck

Escape pod

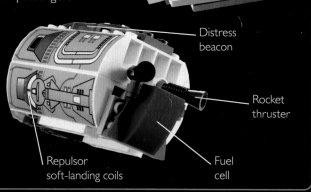

Distress beacon

Rocket thruster

Repulsor soft-landing coils

Fuel cell

▶ Forward Systems

A Star Destroyer's nose contains powerful pursuit tractor beams. The model contains a mechanism that, when pulled, ejects the escape pod through a hatch in the ship's underside.

Escape pod release mechanism

Entrance to escape pod hangar bay

actor beam
rgeting array

Command bridge

Ship instrument
and shield
projector sphere

Rear of command
bridge opens
for access

Ion cannon
(flick missile)

Firing mechanism
for flick missiles

Rotating heavy
turbolaser
battery

Spring-loaded
missile launcher

Wheel hub
caps used for
engine clusters

Set name	Imperial Star Destroyer	
Year 2014		Number 75055
Pieces 1,359		Source EP IV–VI

2014 STAR DESTROYER

The imposing warship was redesigned and updated in 2014. The interior features a movie-accurate bridge with stickers depicting the controls and its exterior features brand-new spring-loaded bricks that can fire missiles at approaching enemy vehicles.

Hologram
projector

Death Star
telemetry screen

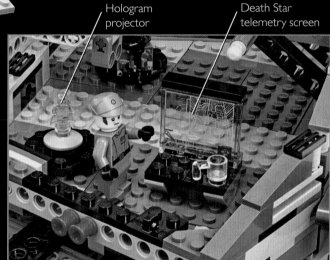

COMM STATION

The communication station is where Imperial officers receive orders from the Empire and occasionally from the foreboding Emperor himself!

Mechanism slides along crane
arm to lift off Vader's helmet

Backup engine

Main engine
thrust nozzle

Meditation
chamber

Lightsaber
storage

Stand for Vader's
helmet when
removed

HOLOGRAM

However far the Star Destroyer travels, Darth Vader can still kneel before his master and receive orders via hologram

Imperial roval

DATA FILE

Set name: Imperial Star Destroyer
Year: 2006   **Set Number:** 6211
Pieces: 1,367   **Source:** EP IV–VI
Dimensions:
length 29 in (74.4 cm)
width 15 in (38.4 cm)
height 3³/₄ in (9.3 cm)
Minifigures: 9—Darth Vader, Grand Moff Tarkin, Imperial officer, 2 stormtroopers, 2 Imperial guards, R2-D5, MSE-6 droid

Early Rebel Craft

From the earliest days of the Empire, pockets of resistance gave people hope that democracy might one day return to the galaxy. Slowly, these rebel groups gained in strength and number, and started to work together to undermine the Empire. These different peoples traveled in a whole host of crafts and vehicles.

Dorsal laser cannon turret

▶ The *Ghost*

The heavily modified VCX-100 light freighter called the *Ghost* is home to the rebel group known as the Spectres. The *Ghost* gets its name from its advanced stealth technology, which allows it to vanish from enemy sensors. At the rear of the ship is a docking station for the Spectres' shuttlecraft, the *Phantom*.

Cockpit

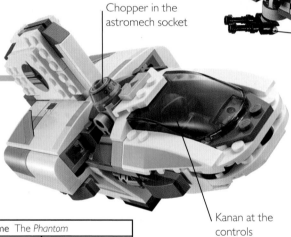

Set name	The *Ghost*	
Year	2014	Number 75053
Pieces	929	Source *Rebels*

Chopper in the astromech socket

Forward laser cannon turret

▶ The *Phantom*

The Spectres have owned two different shuttlecraft called the *Phantom*. Both have been recreated in LEGO form—in 2014 (set 75048) and 2017—and both are designed to connect with the back of the *Ghost*.

Kanan at the controls

Set name	The *Phantom*	
Year	2017	Number 75170
Pieces	269	Source *Rebels*

▼ Wookiee Gunship

Most Wookiees are made to work as slaves for the Empire, but some have escaped Imperial clutches and now fight for their species' freedom. Former slaves such as Wullffwarro stand ready to assist other rebels in their *Auzituck*-class anti-slaver gunships.

Set name	Wookiee Gunship	
Year	2015	Number 75084
Pieces	570	Source *Rebels*

KANAN JARRUS   **EZRA BRIDGER**   **HERA SYNDULLA**   **ZEB ORRELIOS**

THE SPECTRES
The rebel cell known as the Spectres is made up of the Jedi Kanan Jarrus; his apprentice Ezra Bridger; the captain of the *Ghost*, Hera Syndulla; the Lasat warrior Zeb Orrelios; the graffiti artist Sabine Wren; and their droid, C1-10P.

SABINE WREN   **C1-10P (CHOPPER)**

Twin laser cannon

Cockpit

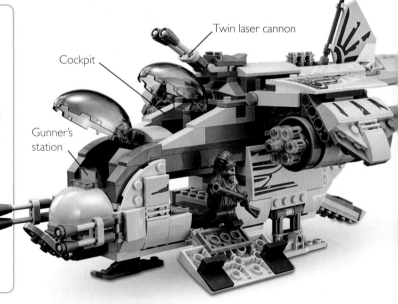

Gunner's station

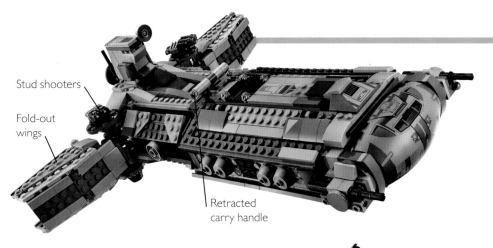

Stud shooters

Fold-out wings

Retracted carry handle

◀ Phoenix Home

The Phoenix cell is one of the largest early rebel groups, led by Commander Jun Sato and Anakin Skywalker's former Jedi Padawan, Ahsoka Tano. Their HQ is the *Pelta*-class frigate known as *Phoenix Home*.

Set name	Rebel Combat Frigate	
Year 2016	Number 75158	
Pieces 936	Source *Rebels*	

AHSOKA TANO

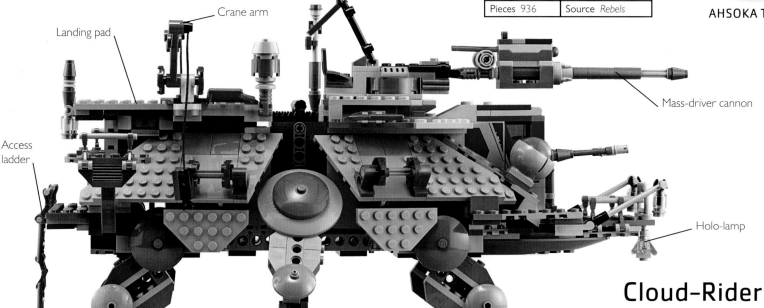

Crane arm

Landing pad

Access ladder

Mass-driver cannon

Holo-lamp

▼ Cloud-Rider Swoop Bikes

The Cloud-Riders are a band of rebels and pirates who make raids against the Imperial sympathizers on fast and dangerous swoop bikes. Their leader, Enfys Nest, pilots a Skyblade-330 swoop, while her sidekick Weazel rides a larger 221 model with a sidecar.

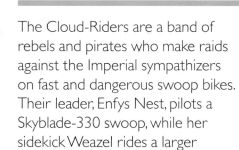

ENFYS NEST

Set name	Cloud-Rider Swoop Bikes	
Year 2018	Number 75215	
Pieces 355	Source *Solo*	

▲ Captain Rex's AT-TE

After the Clone Wars, three retired clone soldiers made their home in a battered old AT-TE on the planet Seelos. Captain Rex and his friends, Commander Wolffe and Commander Gregor, wanted no part in the Rebellion, but found themselves drawn into the fight against the Empire when they met the Spectres. Rex then became a member of the Phoenix rebel cell.

Set name	Captain Rex's AT-TE	
Year 2016	Number 75157	
Pieces 972	Source *Rebels*	

CAPTAIN REX   **COMMANDER WOLFFE**

Weazel

Steering vanes

Rebel Alliance

Freedom fighters who have banded together as the Rebel Alliance are dedicated to the Empire's downfall. Some rebels are deserters from the Imperial forces, but many are untrained volunteers. With skilful leaders and a rag-tag assortment of ships and weapons, the rebels prove a serious threat to Emperor Palpatine's iron rule.

PRINCESS LEIA ORGANA

PRINCESS LEIA
A bold leader of the Rebellion, Princess Leia is kidnapped by the Empire and taken to the Death Star. Luke Skywalker and Leia try to outwit the battle station's crew in the LEGO set Death Star Escape (75229).

▼ Y-Wing Fighter

BTL-A4 Y-wings are old but tough workhorses of the rebel fleet, famously employed in the attacks on both Death Stars. They have hyperdrives, ion fission engines, and massive firepower. This trusty fighter was used during the Battle of Scarif to retrieve the plans for the Death Star. LEGO Technic gears open the bottom of the ship to deploy bombs.

Set name	Y-Wing Starfighter	
Year 2017	Number	75172
Pieces 691	Source	R1

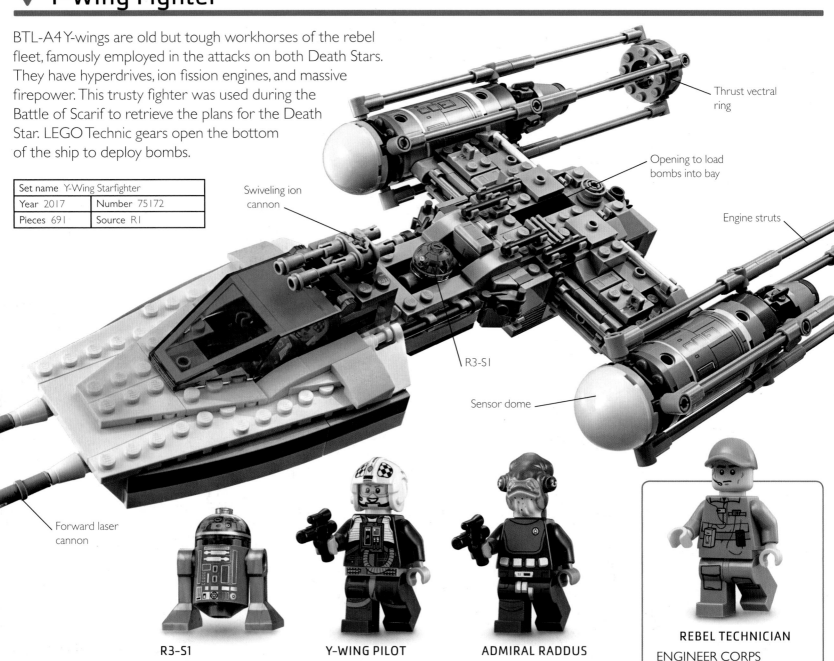

Thrust vectral ring

Opening to load bombs into bay

Engine struts

Swiveling ion cannon

R3-S1

Sensor dome

Forward laser cannon

R3-S1
This astromech droid is unusually vain. The silver design on her torso is a standard astromech droid print pattern.

Y-WING PILOT
This rebel pilot's torso has detailed printing depicting a Guidenhauser ejection harness and a life-support unit.

ADMIRAL RADDUS
Raddus is in charge of the rebel fleet. He perishes, along with his flagship *Profundity*, at the Battle of Scarif.

REBEL TECHNICIAN ENGINEER CORPS
Rebel engineers and technicians maintain and repair spaceships and vehicles, among other tasks.

▼ Tantive IV

As a senator for Alderaan, Princess Leia Organa travels in a diplomatic starship, the *Tantive IV*. The ship also carries out covert missions for the Rebel Alliance—until Darth Vader pursues the ship and captures it.

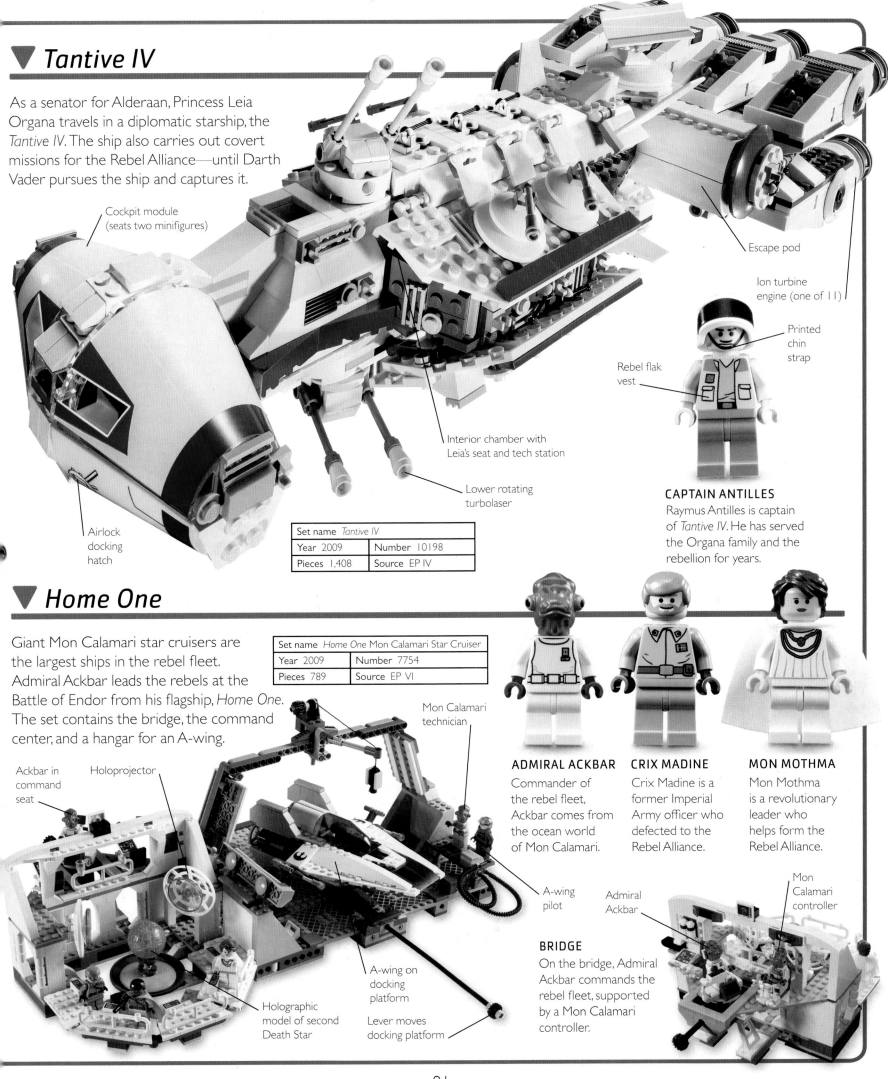

Cockpit module (seats two minifigures)

Escape pod

Ion turbine engine (one of 11)

Printed chin strap

Rebel flak vest

Interior chamber with Leia's seat and tech station

Lower rotating turbolaser

Airlock docking hatch

Set name	*Tantive IV*	
Year	2009	Number 10198
Pieces	1,408	Source EP IV

CAPTAIN ANTILLES
Raymus Antilles is captain of *Tantive IV*. He has served the Organa family and the rebellion for years.

▼ Home One

Giant Mon Calamari star cruisers are the largest ships in the rebel fleet. Admiral Ackbar leads the rebels at the Battle of Endor from his flagship, *Home One*. The set contains the bridge, the command center, and a hangar for an A-wing.

Set name	*Home One* Mon Calamari Star Cruiser	
Year	2009	Number 7754
Pieces	789	Source EP VI

Ackbar in command seat

Holoprojector

Mon Calamari technician

A-wing pilot

Holographic model of second Death Star

A-wing on docking platform

Lever moves docking platform

ADMIRAL ACKBAR
Commander of the rebel fleet, Ackbar comes from the ocean world of Mon Calamari.

CRIX MADINE
Crix Madine is a former Imperial Army officer who defected to the Rebel Alliance.

MON MOTHMA
Mon Mothma is a revolutionary leader who helps form the Rebel Alliance.

Admiral Ackbar

Mon Calamari controller

BRIDGE
On the bridge, Admiral Ackbar commands the rebel fleet, supported by a Mon Calamari controller.

81

Rogue Heroes

When Jyn Erso finds out about a new Imperial superweapon, she realizes that the fate of the galaxy lies with whoever knows its secrets. She commits herself to the rebel cause and convinces a rag-tag band of heroes to join her on a mission to steal the Death Star plans. Calling their ship *Rogue One,* Jyn, Captain Cassian Andor, the droid K-2SO, and the rest of the team set course for the Imperial archive on the planet Scarif.

ALWAYS PREPARED
Jyn Erso's practical, protective clothes reflect the harsh environments in which she has often found herself. Her warm poncho comes in useful on the rain-soaked world of Eadu.

JYN ERSO

◀ U-Wing

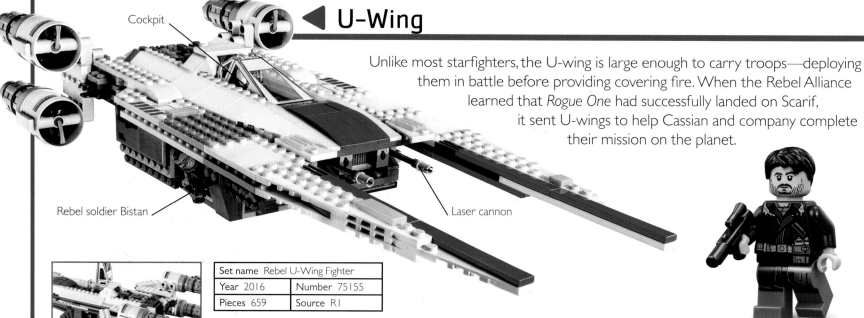

Cockpit

Rebel soldier Bistan

Laser cannon

Unlike most starfighters, the U-wing is large enough to carry troops—deploying them in battle before providing covering fire. When the Rebel Alliance learned that *Rogue One* had successfully landed on Scarif, it sent U-wings to help Cassian and company complete their mission on the planet.

Set name	Rebel U-Wing Fighter	
Year	2016	Number 75155
Pieces	659	Source R1

Prong-like wings fold backward for combat mode

COMBAT MODE

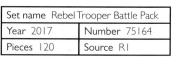

CASSIAN ANDOR

▼ Rogue Reinforcements

After the core team of Cassian, K-2SO, Bodhi, Chirrut, and Baze assembles around Jyn, a number of other rebels also offer their services. In the Rebel Trooper Battle Pack, four unnamed troopers join the fight with stud shooters, a speeder bike, and a laser cannon.

Set name	Rebel Trooper Battle Pack	
Year	2017	Number 75164
Pieces	120	Source R1

Laser cannon

Defensive trench

Stud shooter

EMPIRE STATE OF MIND
A reprogrammed rebel droid, K-2SO was loyal to the Empire—until Cassian Andor got inside his head! He's much happier as a rebel, though he hates to let it show. He is found in just one LEGO set: Krennic's Imperial Shuttle (set 75156).

K-2SO

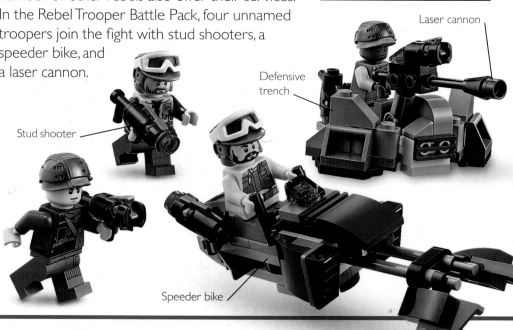

Speeder bike

ROGUES' GALLERY

Joining Jyn, Cassian, and K-2SO on the *Rogue One* mission are the blind warrior monk Chirrut Îmwe and his best friend Baze Malbus; the former Imperial pilot Bodhi Rook; and the Drabatan commando, Pao. Pao's full name is Paodok'Draba'Takat Sap'De'Rekti Nik'Linke'Ti' Ki'Vef'Nik'NeSevef'Li'Kek!

CHIRRUT ÎMWE   **BAZE MALBUS**   **BODHI ROOK**   **PAO**

▼ Battle of Scarif

On sandy Scarif, the rogue rebels fight their way to the top-secret archive where the Death Star plans are kept. This set features locking doors, exploding floor panels, and two shoretroopers to keep Jyn and Cassian from their goal.

Set name	Battle on Scarif	
Year	2017	Number 75171
Pieces	419	Source R1

"Exploding" floor panel

Cassian Andor

Death Star Plans

Jyn in Imperial Ground Crew disguise

Shoretrooper

Echo Base

On the ice planet Hoth, the Rebel Alliance establishes its secret Echo Base, protected by an immense energy shield. When the Empire discovers the location of the base, it deploys AT-ATs and AT-STs to destroy the shield generator. The combined strength of rebel artillery emplacements and snowspeeder squadrons cannot prevent one of the Alliance's worst battlefield defeats.

PROTOCOL DROIDS

K-3PO is a white protocol droid who was given the rank of lieutenant in Hoth Rebel Base (set 7666). Exclusive to Hoth Echo Base (set 7879), R-3PO has special programming designed to ferret out Imperial spies.

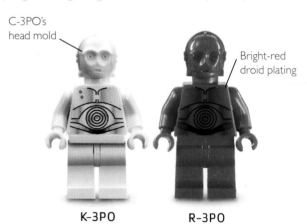

C-3PO's head mold

Bright-red droid plating

K-3PO   R-3PO

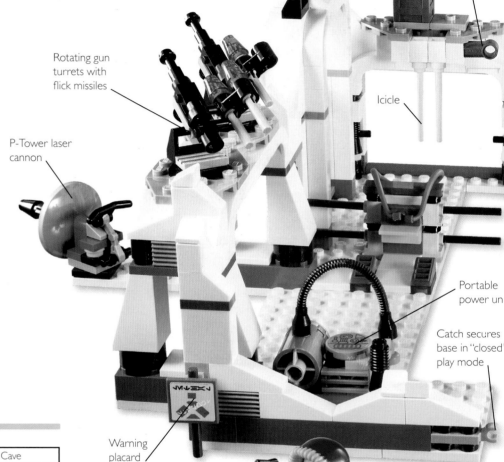

Slide out pin to activate icicle trap

Rotating gun turrets with flick missiles

Icicle

P-Tower laser cannon

Portable power un

Catch secures base in "closed" play mode

Warning placard

Han Solo

Saddle for minifigures

▼ Wampa Cave

After a wampa captures Luke, the rebel hero must use the Force to escape the beast. Minifigures can attach to the wampa's hand, but the ice monster also has an oversized turkey leg in case his prey should elude him.

Set name	Hoth Wampa Cave	
Year	2010	Number 8089
Pieces	297	Source EP V

Head, torso, and tail is a single mold

Horn

Remnants of former meal

"Force" launcher for Luke's lightsaber

Sharp claws on hands and feet for gripping ice

WAMPA

TAUNTAUN

Rebel troops on Hoth make patrols on domesticated snow lizards called tauntauns. Tauntauns can withstand freezing winds, but are not the sweetest-smelling animals!

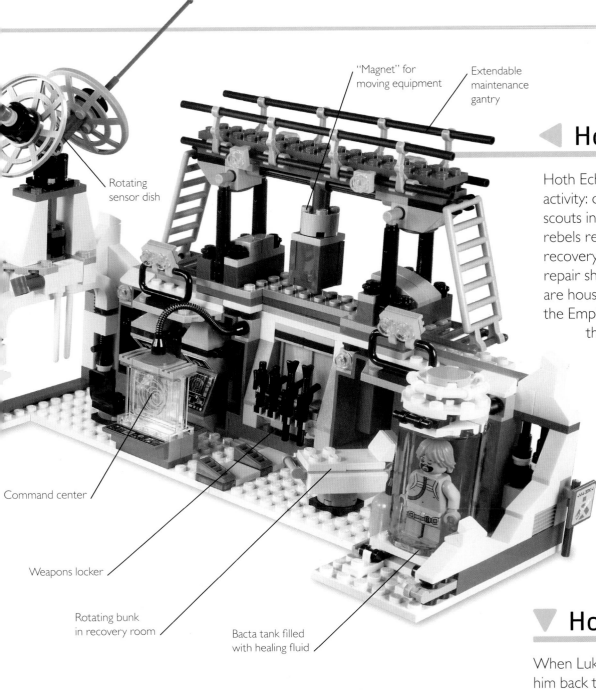

Rotating
sensor dish

"Magnet" for
moving equipment

Extendable
maintenance
gantry

Hoth Base

Hoth Echo Base (set 7879) hums with activity: droids keep watch for Imperial scouts in the command center, wounded rebels recuperate in the bacta tank and recovery room, technicians maintain and repair ships in the gantries, and tauntauns are housed in a secure paddock. When the Empire attacks, the rebels defend their home with gun turrets, hand-held blasters from the weapons locker, and a pair of strategically located icicle traps.

Set name	Hoth Echo Base	
Year 2011	Number 7879	
Pieces 773	Source EP V	

Command center

Weapons locker

Rotating bunk
in recovery room

Bacta tank filled
with healing fluid

Hoth Medical Chamber

When Luke is wounded by a wampa, Han takes him back to Echo Base for recovery. Leia and the rebels' medical droids 2-1B and FX-7 watch over him as he heals in a bacta tank. This set is packed with equipment including a sink, an operating chair, and a bacta tank.

Tank opens at
the back so the
minifigure can
be removed

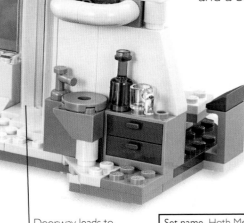

Doorway leads to
operating table

Set name	Hoth Medical Chamber	
Year 2018	Number 75203	
Pieces 255	Source EP V	

Grenades on torso

Goggles attach to helmet

Rebels on Hoth

After the rebels established Echo Base in a secret location on Hoth, it was only a matter of time before Imperial probe droids tracked them down. Very soon the rebels have to use all their technology and firepower to counter an Imperial assault.

HOTH REBEL SOLDIER

The first Hoth soldiers, released in 1999, had yellow faces and brown visors. The latest minifigures have squared-off, movie-accurate ski goggles and detailed printing, which includes grenades on their torsos.

▼ Laser Ice Cutter

Turret rotates

Vehicles often break down in the bitter cold of Hoth, forcing the rebels to patrol with tauntauns and one-man laser ice cutters while adapting their airspeeders to the frigid conditions. Laser ice cutters are combat speeders, with swiveling gun turrets and skirts designed to push through accumulated ice and snow.

Flick-fire missile

Repulsorlift skirt

Snow goggles

HOTH REBEL OFFICER

Set name	Rebel Trooper Battle Pack	
Year	2010	Number 8083
Pieces	79	Source EP V

▼ Snowspeeder

Rebel snowspeeders are civilian T-47 airspeeders adapted for military use with laser cannon bolted to the wings, as well as souped-up engines and armor plating (but no shields). Although similar to previous sets, the 2014 snowspeeder has redesigned wings and engines, with the back portion of the laser cannons being much larger. The harpoon can be triggered to launch a grappling hook, which is attached to a spool of rope.

Hinged flap opens and closes

Clip on grappling hook allows it to be fired

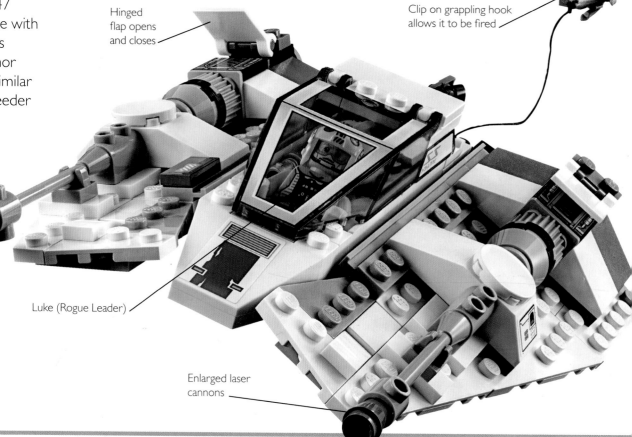

Luke (Rogue Leader)

Enlarged laser cannons

Set name	Snowspeeder	
Year	2014	Number 75049
Pieces	279	Source EP V

HAPPY DAYS

Zev Senesca looks happy—probably because he saves the rebellion by finding Luke and Han after a night on Hoth. His minifigure is one of many in the bright-orange rebel fight suit, but the latest variant of Senesca has a unique gun-metal helmet with silver printing to show scratches.

ZEV SENESCA

Flick-fire missile

Imperial officer

▼ Imperial Battle Station

Hoth's rebels defend their base against Imperial invaders with giant AT-ATs supported by artillery squads. These squads' mobile equipment includes rotating gun turrets and sensor emplacements.

Sensor dish

Set name	Snowtrooper Battle Pack	
Year	2010	Number 8084
Pieces	74	Source EP V

▶ Turret Defense

Large laser cannon in rotating turret

In trenches and behind snow-packed ridges, supported by tall, cylindrical anti-infantry batteries, rebel soldiers are the first line of defense against Imperial walkers.

Set name	Hoth Attack	
Year	2016	Number 75138
Pieces	233	Source EP V

Knob for rotating turret

Power cable runs between tower and control panel

Snowy terrain is hinged so it can be rearranged

IMPERIAL PROBE DROID

Probe droids (or probots) are programmed to seek out the rebels and report back to Imperial officers. A probot detects telltale signs of habitation on Hoth, prompting Vader to initiate a full-scale Imperial assault.

▼ Tower Cannon and Trench

Echo Base is protected by an energy shield and a ring of trenches and artillery emplacements manned by brave rebel troopers. These soldiers defend their base against AT-ATs and supporting units: snowtrooper scouts riding speeder bikes and Imperial artillery squads.

GENERAL RIEEKAN

Rieekan is Echo Base's grim commander. His gray hairpiece can be switched for a cap.

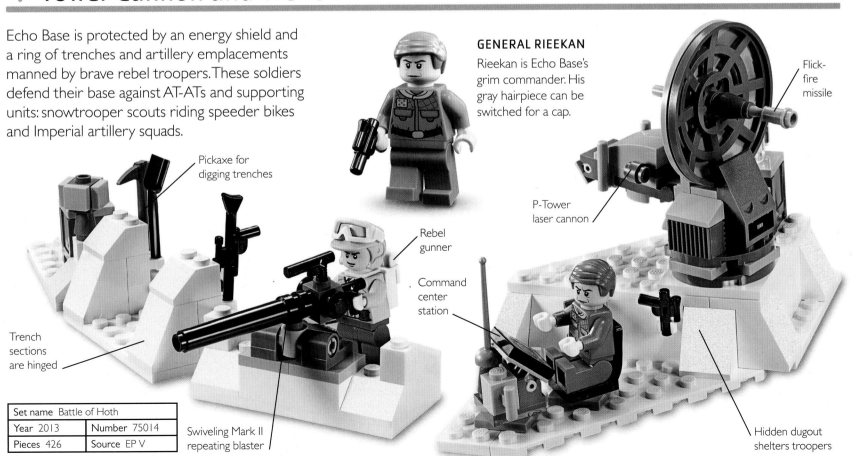

Pickaxe for digging trenches

Flick-fire missile

Rebel gunner

Command center station

P-Tower laser cannon

Trench sections are hinged

Swiveling Mark II repeating blaster

Hidden dugout shelters troopers

Set name	Battle of Hoth	
Year	2013	Number 75014
Pieces	426	Source EP V

Jedi in Hiding

After swearing allegiance to the Sith, Anakin Skywalker helps Darth Sidious hunt down the Jedi and turn the Republic into the Galactic Empire. The few Jedi who survive become refugees, hoping to avoid detection by Darth Vader and his Emperor. Obi-Wan Kenobi gives the infant Luke Skywalker to the Lars family on Tatooine and then dwells in the desert, while Yoda hides on a little-known planet in the Outer Rim.

▼ Yoda's Hut

Yoda survives the Great Jedi Purge at the end of the Clone Wars to live in exile on Dagobah. He lands on the planet in an escape pod, which he makes into a hut. Yoda's lifestyle on the swamp planet is frugal: his dwelling is furnished with a simple bed, table, cooking pot, and barrels.

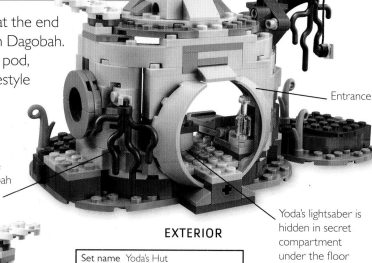

Vine for swinging

Entrance

Native Dagobah foliage

Yoda's lightsaber is hidden in secret compartment under the floor

EXTERIOR

Set name	Yoda's Hut	
Year 2018	Number 75208	
Pieces 229	Source EP V & VI	

Yoda's bed

Luke uses the force to make the box levitate.

Training area with flip mechanism that propels Luke into the air

INTERIOR

YODA (DAGOBAH)

Eight hundred years of life have taught Yoda patience, and changed his appearance. There have been many incarnations of Yoda's minifigure, including three main head types. His torso, featuring a ragged robe and blissl flute, is exclusive to this Yoda's Hut set.

Brackets attach Yoda to Luke

JEDI IN TRAINING
Luke carries Yoda when he's training. Luke's double-sided head has a meditative face on the other side.

Gray hair

Jedi robes

BEN KENOBI (TATOOINE)
In exile on Tatooine, Obi-Wan becomes known as "Ben Kenobi." He keeps a quiet watch over Luke, Anakin's son, waiting for the day he can teach him about the Force.

BEN KENOBI (JEDI MASTER)
Obi-Wan's exile comes to an end when he receives a distress call from Princess Leia. He puts on his Jedi cloak and hood to lead Luke on a rescue mission.

Boba Fett

Son of the bounty hunter Jango Fett, Boba Fett follows in his father's footsteps to become the most feared bounty hunter in the galaxy. Thanks to his talent and an arsenal of exotic weapons, Fett brings in many "impossible" bounties. Working for Darth Vader, Fett captures Han Solo and loads Solo's carbon-frozen body into his ship, *Slave I*.

▶ Boba Fett's *Slave I*

Boba Fett inherits *Slave I* from his father, Jango. He has added modifications of his own, including several upgraded weapons systems. The 2010 set features an opening cargo bay, a cockpit, and wings that automatically rotate into flight mode. It also features spring-loaded cannons, a hidden missile carousel, and swiveling short-range twin blasters on the tail.

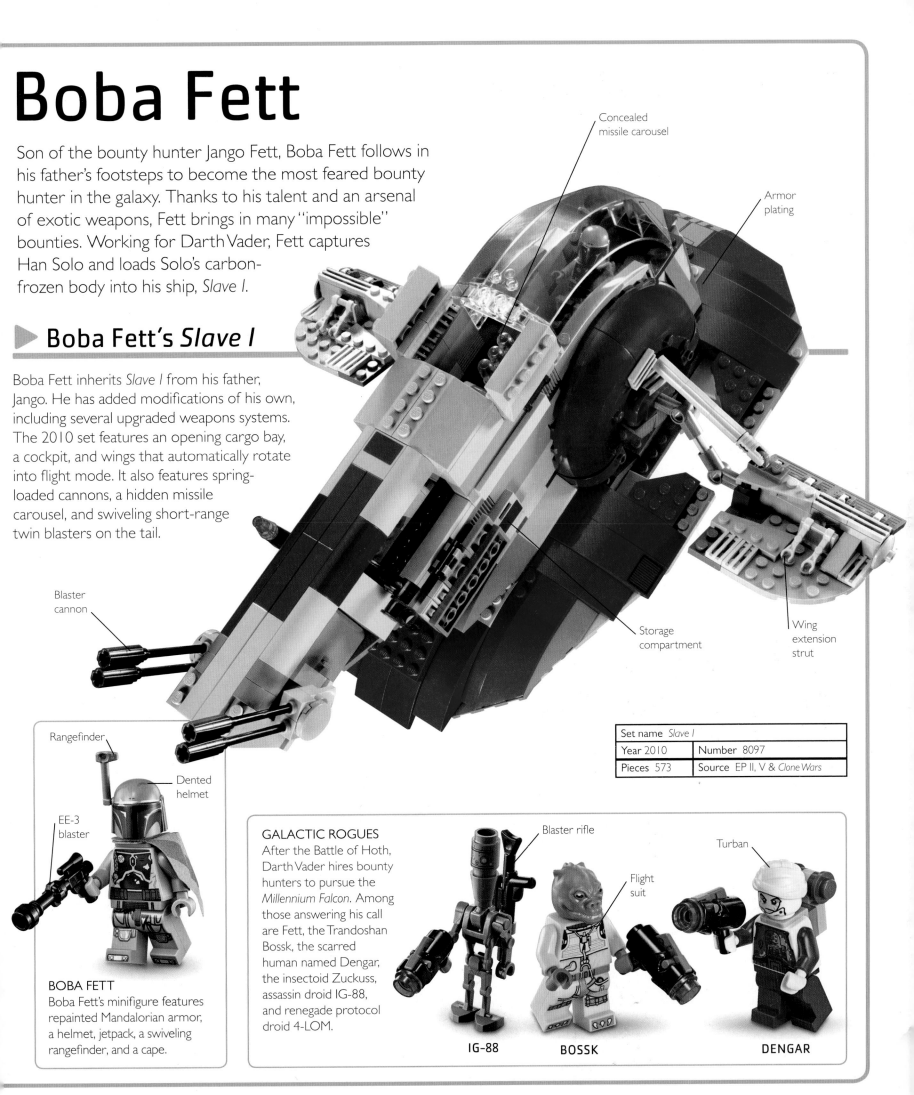

Concealed missile carousel

Armor plating

Blaster cannon

Storage compartment

Wing extension strut

Rangefinder

Dented helmet

EE-3 blaster

BOBA FETT
Boba Fett's minifigure features repainted Mandalorian armor, a helmet, jetpack, a swiveling rangefinder, and a cape.

Set name *Slave I*	
Year 2010	Number 8097
Pieces 573	Source EP II, V & *Clone Wars*

GALACTIC ROGUES
After the Battle of Hoth, Darth Vader hires bounty hunters to pursue the *Millennium Falcon*. Among those answering his call are Fett, the Trandoshan Bossk, the scarred human named Dengar, the insectoid Zuckuss, assassin droid IG-88, and renegade protocol droid 4-LOM.

Blaster rifle

Turban

Flight suit

IG-88

BOSSK

DENGAR

Custom-made shirt

Cloud City

After the Battle of Hoth, Han Solo and Chewbacca escape with Leia and C-3PO to a floating pleasure resort and mining colony called Cloud City, located near a gas planet called Bespin. Its administrator, Lando Calrissian, is Han Solo's longtime friend and sometime rival. The arrival of Solo and the others, however, is preceded by Boba Fett and Darth Vader, who spring a trap and lure Luke Skywalker to a confrontation with Vader himself!

Dashing cape

LANDO CALRISSIAN

The 2018 minifigure for smartly dressed Lando Calrissian features a beautifully textured cape.

Interrogation chamber

Cloud car pilot

▼ Duel with Vader

When Luke arrives at Cloud City to rescue his friends, Vader is waiting for him in the carbon freezing chamber. They ignite their lightsabers and duel through the chamber into a control room overlooking a huge reactor shaft. Luke is sucked through a smashed window and a final clash takes place on a treacherous gantry.

Luke and Vader are engaged in an epic duel

LEGO foil piece used for top of atmosphere sensor

Turning lever encases Solo in carbonite

Han Solo is about to be frozen!

Opulent dining room for entertaining guests

Cloud car has two cockpits

CLOUD CITY CAR

The Cloud City pilots use these fast vehicles to patrol the area surrounding Cloud City. This LEGO version of the craft has space for one pilot in each cockpit. The top and the outer side of each pod open up to let them sit in it.

Stud shooter attached to hull

BRICK FACTS

Released in 2018, the Betrayal at Cloud City set is the first set of the Master Builder Series (MBS). These large playsets are complicated builds with exciting dioramas, many play functions, and a large assortment of minifigures.

SLAVE I
Boba Fett's *Slave I* is a powerful vehicle. The set's wings move depending on whether the ship is in flight or landing mode. The Han Solo in carbonite piece can fit under the ship's hull.

Cloud City guard

◀ Landing Platform

Arriving starships dock on a landing platform outside the main wall of Cloud City. When Han and the others arrive in the *Millennium Falcon*, Lando Calrissian meets them.

C-3PO has discovered a stormtrooper

SITH SURPRISE

Later, Lando escorts Han and his friends to a dining room—but it's a trap. The Dark Lord of the Sith and his stormtroopers are waiting to capture them.

DATA FILE

Set name: Betrayal at Cloud City
Year: 2018
Set Number: 75222
Pieces: 2,812
Source: EP V
Dimensions: length 22 in (56 cm); width 22 in (56 cm); height 6 in (16 cm)
Minifigures: 20—Luke Skywalker, Han Solo (in Hoth outfit and Bespin outfit), Princess Leia Organa (in Hoth outfit and Bespin outfit), Chewbacca, C-3PO, R2-D2, Lando Calrissian, Lobot, 2 Cloud City Guards, 2 Cloud Car Pilots, Ugnaught, Darth Vader, 2 stormtroopers, Boba Fett, and IG-88

This beam can lock the door in an open position

Conical hat piece used for micro Cloud City build

Jabba the Hutt

A gigantic, slug-like Hutt with slimy skin; an unfathomable appetite; and a large, lascivious mouth, Jabba lives to strike shady deals with other members of the galactic underworld. He is protected by thugs and hirelings on whose loyalty he keeps a careful eye. Luke Skywalker and his friends seek to rescue Han Solo from Jabba's clutches, but run the risk of falling prey to the gangster's wiles and becoming his latest victims.

JABBA THE HUTT

Jabba's single mold minifigure portrays him with wrinkles of flesh, cat-like eyes, and a tattoo on his arm.

Shrewd expression

Many chins

Muscular tail

Belly swollen with gorg snacks

ROTTA THE HUTTLET

Jabba's son Rotta can be clipped onto a minifigure's hand through a circle at his base. He comes with AT-TE Walker (set 7675) and The Twilight (set 7680), which recreates his kidnap and rescue at the beginning of *Star Wars: The Clone Wars.*

ROTTA

▶ Jabba's Palace

Jabba's palace once belonged to the mysterious order of B'omarr monks who continue to go about their business on the lower levels. The palace is armed against external attacks with gun emplacements and missiles, and further dangers await those foolish enough to enter. The fortress is riddled with secret compartments, trap doors, and other unwelcome surprises—not to mention the depraved thugs and criminals who call its dank passages home.

Set name	Jabba's Palace	
Year	2012	Number 9516
Pieces	717	Source EP VI

Lookout post

Gamorrean guard

Trap door

Guard tower

Weapons cache

Binoculars

Hookah

Salacious B. Crumb

Flick-fire missile defends palace

Domed temple roof

Jabba the Hutt seated on dais

Chewbacca

Han Solo frozen in carbonite

Lever opens trap door to rancor pit

▲ Rancor Pit

Set name	Rancor Pit		
Year	2013	Number	75005
Pieces	380	Source	EP VI

The first LEGO rancor dwells beneath Jabba's throne room, devouring those who anger the cruel Hutt. The set stacks with Jabba's Palace, with a trap door so a minifigure can fall between sets, while Jabba's minions watch from above through the grate. A portcullis keeps the rancor in its dreary pen. Accessories include a key, pitchfork, and bucket.

Rancor is 3 in (10cm) tall

Moveable arms and jointed fingers

RANCOR

Leia disguised as Boushh

Luke Skywalker

Remains of the rancor's earlier victim

Entrance door

B'omarr monk

Helmet

Thermal detonator

BOUSHH

Electrostaff

Locked exit gate

Unfortunate Gamorrean guard

Rancor

Walls hewn from Tatooine rock

IN DISGUISE
To infiltrate Jabba's lair, Princess Leia disguises herself as Boushh—a Ubese bounty hunter—and pretends she has captured Chewbacca. When Jabba balks at the price for Chewie, Leia threatens to blow up his palace with a thermal detonator—a gutsy move that earns Jabba's respect.

JABBA'S MINIONS
A bevy of aliens and creatures are resident at Jabba's Palace, from guards to jesters.

BIB FORTUNA
The Twi'lek Bib Fortuna is Jabba's chief lieutenant. His updated minifigure has a fierce expression with bared teeth (set 9516).

OOLA
A green-skinned Twi'lek with printed details and a unique head piece, Oola falls through the trap door and is eaten by the hungry rancor.

MALAKILI
The human Malakili cares for Jabba's fearsome rancor. Swiveling his head reveals a tearful alternate face—Malakili is fond of the beast.

B'OMARR MONK
These strange monks house their brains in jars ferried around by spider-like droid bodies. The monks' legs are repurposed samurai swords.

GAMORREAN GUARD
These pig-like guards serve Jabba as dim-witted muscle. This third incarnation has printed legs and a torso rich in detail.

SALACIOUS B. CRUMB
This Kowakian monkey-lizard, made from a single LEGO piece, serves as court jester. He loves to cackle at guests' misfortunes.

Jabba's Sail Barge

Jabba's Sail Barge is a giant repulsorlift pleasure craft that carries the crime lord and his undesirable entourage from his palace to podraces; gladiatorial contests; and other, shadier activities. It also transports Jabba to the Great Pit of Carkoon to watch Luke Skywalker being fed to the hungry beast that inhabits this basin in the desert.

Decorative sails for shade rather than propulsion

Observation deck

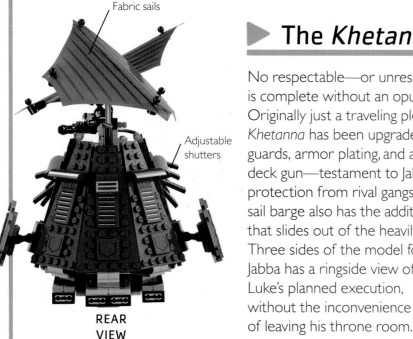

Fabric sails

Adjustable shutters

REAR VIEW

▶ The *Khetanna*

No respectable—or unrespectable—Hutt is complete without an opulent sail barge. Originally just a traveling pleasure craft, the *Khetanna* has been upgraded with prison cells, guards, armor plating, and a custom-mounted deck gun—testament to Jabba's need for protection from rival gangs. Jabba's 2013 LEGO sail barge also has the addition of a large cannon that slides out of the heavily armored hull. Three sides of the model fold down so Jabba has a ringside view of Luke's planned execution, without the inconvenience of leaving his throne room.

Cannon slides out

Craft "floats" on hidden wheels

▼ Sand Skiff

Sand skiffs are repulsorlift platforms used to ferry passengers or prisoners to and from Jabba's palace. Han battles with a skiff guard before Luke is forced to walk the plank over the Sarlacc pit.

Set name	Desert Skiff Escape	
Year	2017	Number 75174
Pieces	277	Source EP VI

Compartment for stowing blasters

Hull railing—the first time this has been included on a LEGO skiff

Exploratory tentacle

Opening mouth with space for minifigure

Teeth prevent victims escaping

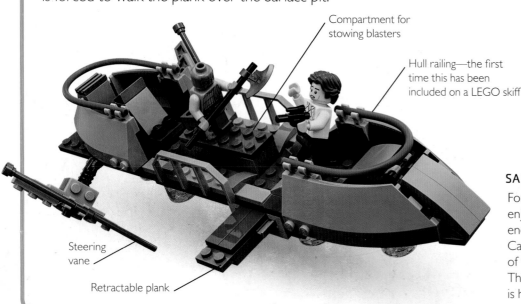

Steering vane

Retractable plank

SARLACC PIT

For years, Jabba has enjoyed feeding his enemies to the Sarlacc at Carkoon. All that can be seen of the Sarlacc is its gaping mouth. The rest of its huge, tentacled body is hidden below the desert sand.

Deck gun

Weequay
skiff guard

Aft deck

Max
Rebo

Red ball
jet organ

Thrust exhaust

Hinged boarding
hatch to
observation
deck

Prison cell

Kitchen for preparing
Jabba's nine daily meals

Neck brace is
attached to a back
plate and chain

Blue head
made from
rubber

Trinocular
vision

Short legs
without
hinges

MAX REBO

Max Rebo is an Ortolan
musician, indentured to
perform for Jabba the Hutt.
His paws play his red ball jet
organ, but also absorb food,
which is his only payment.

REE-YEES

The criminal Gran called Ree-Yees is
on the run, sheltering as part of Jabba
the Hutt's court. This hiding place does
not do him much good, though, when
the sail barge is blown up by Princess
Leia and Luke—with him on board.

DATA FILE

Set name: Jabba's Sail Barge
Year: 2013
Set Number: 75020
Pieces: 850   **Source:** EP VI
Dimensions: length 18 in
(46 cm); width 8$^{1}/_{2}$ in (22 cm);
height 8$^{1}/_{2}$ in (22 cm)
Minifigures: 6—Jabba the Hutt,
Princess Leia, R2-D2 (with serving
tray), Max Rebo, Ree-Yees,
Weequay Skiff Guard

▼ A-Wing

The rebels constructed this lightning-fast ship in secret before the Battle of Endor as an escort craft. A trio of A-wing starfighters play a crucial role in the battle, destroying Darth Vader's gigantic ship, the *Executor*.

Set name	A-Wing Starfighter	
Year 2017	Number 75175	
Pieces 358	Source EP VI, VIII & *Rebels*	

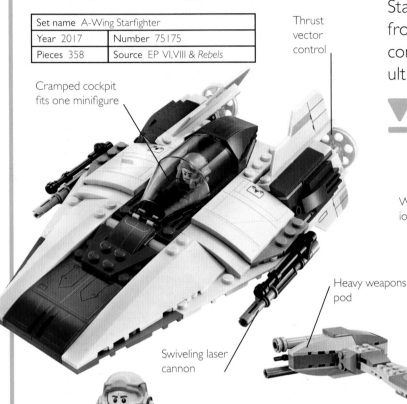

Thrust vector control

Cramped cockpit fits one minifigure

Swiveling laser cannon

A-WING PILOT

Battle of Endor

The Battle of Endor takes place on the surface of Endor's forest moon and in orbit around the planet. The Empire's second Death Star orbits the moon, protected by a defensive shield projected from a generator on the moon's surface. The rebels must concentrate all their resources on a concerted strike that will ultimately bring down the hated Empire.

▼ B-Wing

The B-wing is the most powerful starfighter in the rebel fleet. Its S-foil wings can be deployed for flight and attack modes, and folded for landing. Its vast array of weapons is operated by spring-loaded mechanisms.

Set name	B-Wing	
Year 2014	Number 75050	
Pieces 448	Source EP VI	

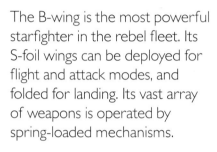

Wingtip ion cannon

Heavy weapons pod

Navigation sensor array

Primary wing

Cooling system intake

Ion cannon

Rotating cockpit

▼ Rebel Control Center

The rebels direct their forces at Endor from a mobile command center on board a massive Mon Calamari star cruiser. A-wings, B-wings, and Y-wings are launched from hangars in the ship as well.

Set name	B-Wing at Rebel Control Center	
Year 2000	Number 7180	
Pieces 338	Source EP VI	

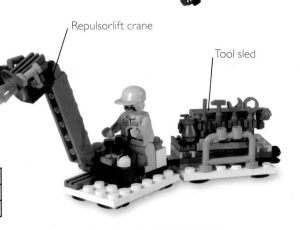

Repulsorlift crane

Tool sled

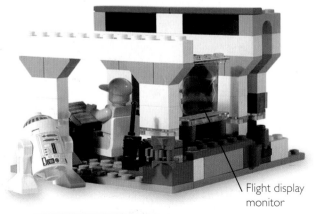

Flight display monitor

Ewok Weapons

Endor's forest moon is inhabited by Ewoks, who help the rebels defeat the Imperial forces guarding the shield generator bunker (including, in this set, a stormtrooper and a scout trooper on a speeder bike). The Ewoks use weapons that are crude—simple wooden catapults and gliders—but these furry creatures are tough and resourceful.

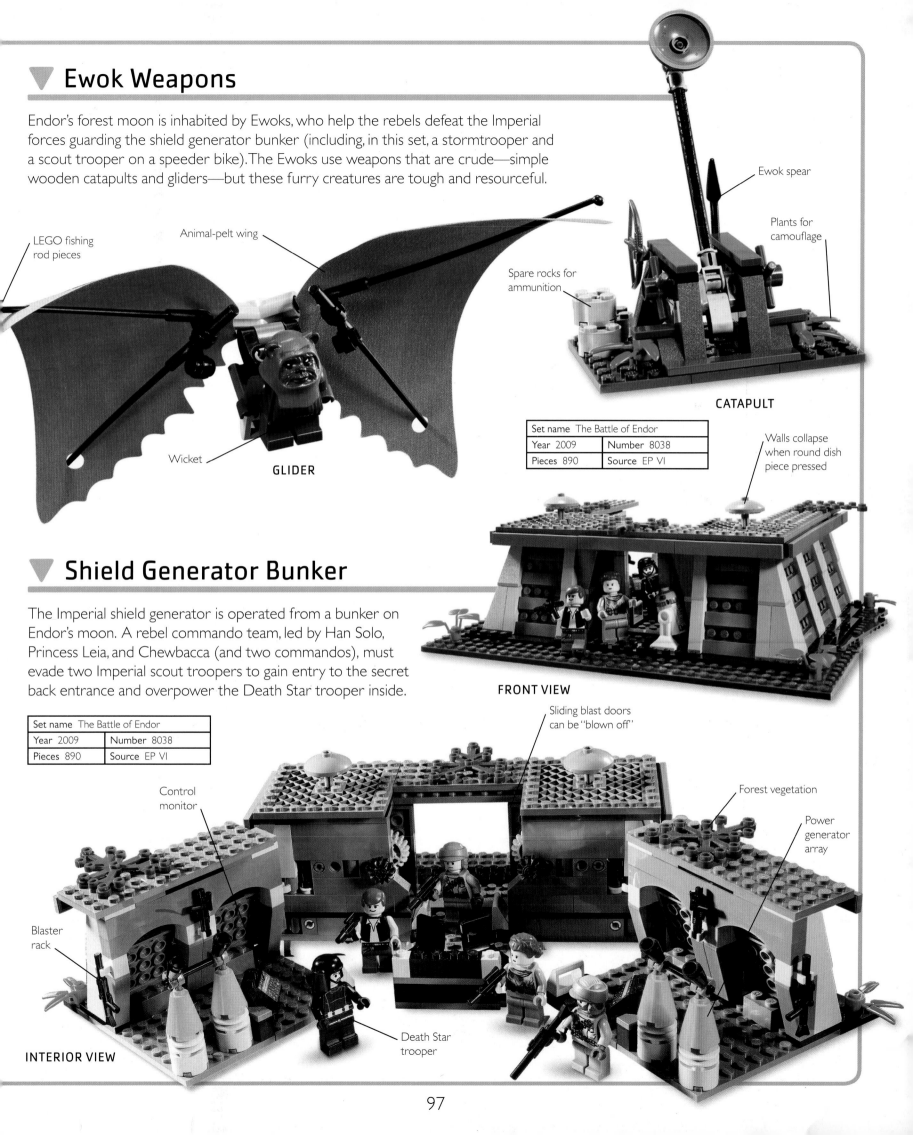

LEGO fishing rod pieces

Animal-pelt wing

Ewok spear

Plants for camouflage

Spare rocks for ammunition

Wicket

GLIDER

CATAPULT

Set name	The Battle of Endor	
Year 2009	Number 8038	
Pieces 890	Source EP VI	

Walls collapse when round dish piece pressed

Shield Generator Bunker

The Imperial shield generator is operated from a bunker on Endor's moon. A rebel commando team, led by Han Solo, Princess Leia, and Chewbacca (and two commandos), must evade two Imperial scout troopers to gain entry to the secret back entrance and overpower the Death Star trooper inside.

FRONT VIEW

Set name	The Battle of Endor	
Year 2009	Number 8038	
Pieces 890	Source EP VI	

Sliding blast doors can be "blown off"

Control monitor

Forest vegetation

Power generator array

Blaster rack

Death Star trooper

INTERIOR VIEW

97

Bright Tree Village

Deep in the primeval woodland of Endor's forest moon is Bright Tree Village, the home of the Ewoks. Although the wooden building materials are primitive, the resourceful Ewoks have created a complex network of tree-top dwellings, protected by hidden fortifications. When the rebels stumble into Ewok territory, they get a mixed reception, but soon win over the furry creatures—who prove to be invaluable allies.

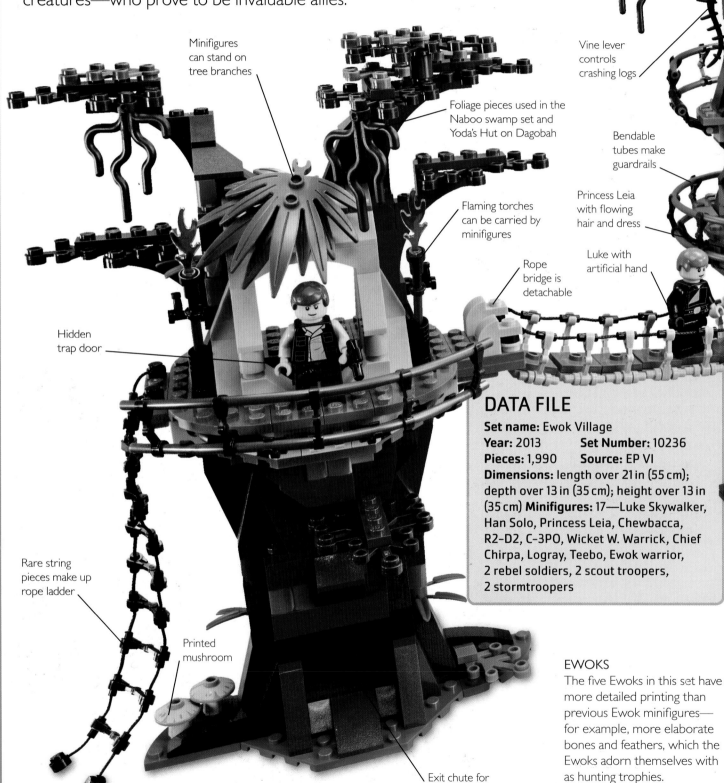

Minifigures can stand on tree branches

Vine lever controls crashing logs

Foliage pieces used in the Naboo swamp set and Yoda's Hut on Dagobah

Bendable tubes make guardrails

Flaming torches can be carried by minifigures

Princess Leia with flowing hair and dress

Rope bridge is detachable

Luke with artificial hand

Hidden trap door

Rare string pieces make up rope ladder

Printed mushroom

Exit chute for hidden trap door

DATA FILE

Set name: Ewok Village
Year: 2013   **Set Number:** 10236
Pieces: 1,990   **Source:** EP VI
Dimensions: length over 21 in (55 cm); depth over 13 in (35 cm); height over 13 in (35 cm) **Minifigures:** 17—Luke Skywalker, Han Solo, Princess Leia, Chewbacca, R2-D2, C-3PO, Wicket W. Warrick, Chief Chirpa, Logray, Teebo, Ewok warrior, 2 rebel soldiers, 2 scout troopers, 2 stormtroopers

EWOKS

The five Ewoks in this set have more detailed printing than previous Ewok minifigures—for example, more elaborate bones and feathers, which the Ewoks adorn themselves with as hunting trophies.

Stitching detail

WICKET W. WARRICK

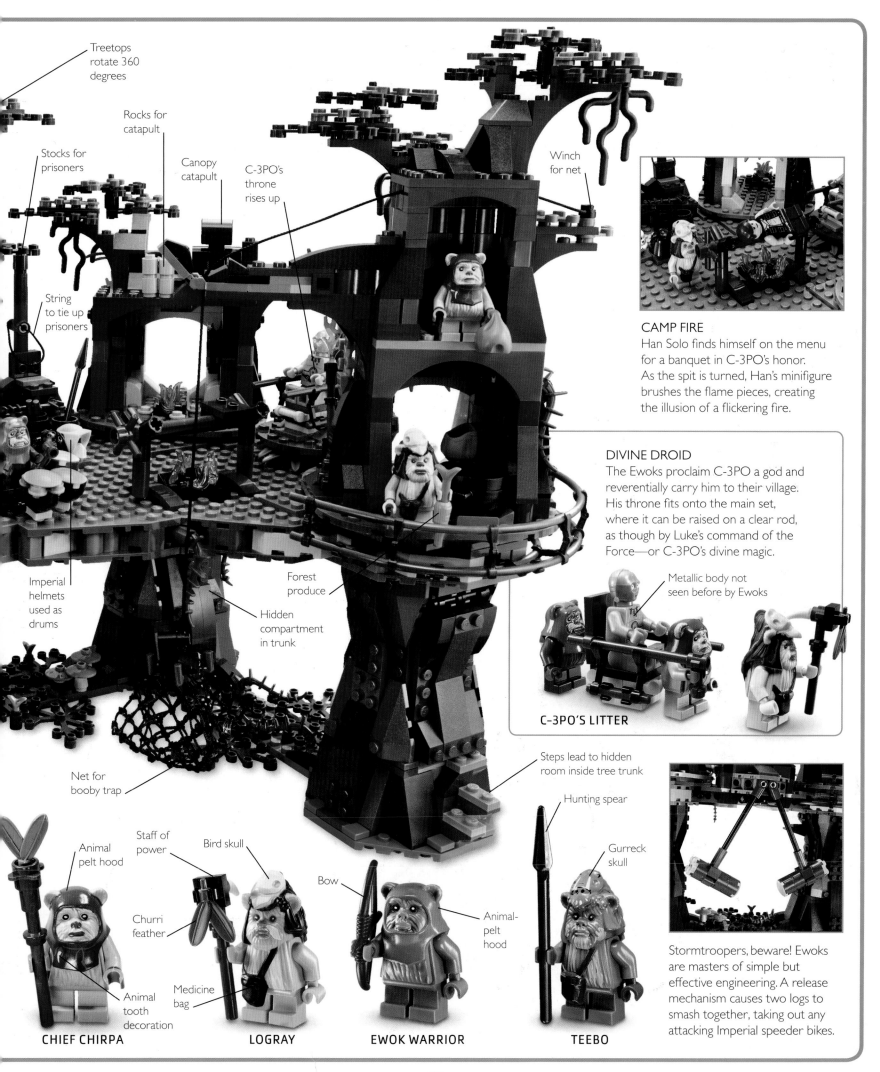

Treetops
rotate 360
degrees

Rocks for
catapult

Stocks for
prisoners

Canopy
catapult

C-3PO's
throne
rises up

Winch
for net

String
to tie up
prisoners

Imperial
helmets
used as
drums

Forest
produce

Hidden
compartment
in trunk

Net for
booby trap

CAMP FIRE

Han Solo finds himself on the menu
for a banquet in C-3PO's honor.
As the spit is turned, Han's minifigure
brushes the flame pieces, creating
the illusion of a flickering fire.

DIVINE DROID

The Ewoks proclaim C-3PO a god and
reverentially carry him to their village.
His throne fits onto the main set,
where it can be raised on a clear rod,
as though by Luke's command of the
Force—or C-3PO's divine magic.

Metallic body not
seen before by Ewoks

C-3PO'S LITTER

Steps lead to hidden
room inside tree trunk

Hunting spear

Gurreck
skull

Animal
pelt hood

Staff of
power

Bird skull

Bow

Animal-
pelt
hood

Churri
feather

Medicine
bag

Animal
tooth
decoration

CHIEF CHIRPA

LOGRAY

EWOK WARRIOR

TEEBO

Stormtroopers, beware! Ewoks
are masters of simple but
effective engineering. A release
mechanism causes two logs to
smash together, taking out any
attacking Imperial speeder bikes.

Chapter 3: The Rise of the First Order

Rey

Abandoned by her parents as a child, Rey has to learn to look after herself. As a lonely scavenger on the desert world of Jakku, she learns how to fly and repair ships and how to defend herself against attack. A chance meeting with the Resistance droid BB-8 soon sees her calling on all those skills to escape the First Order—and discovering new ones as a gifted Force user.

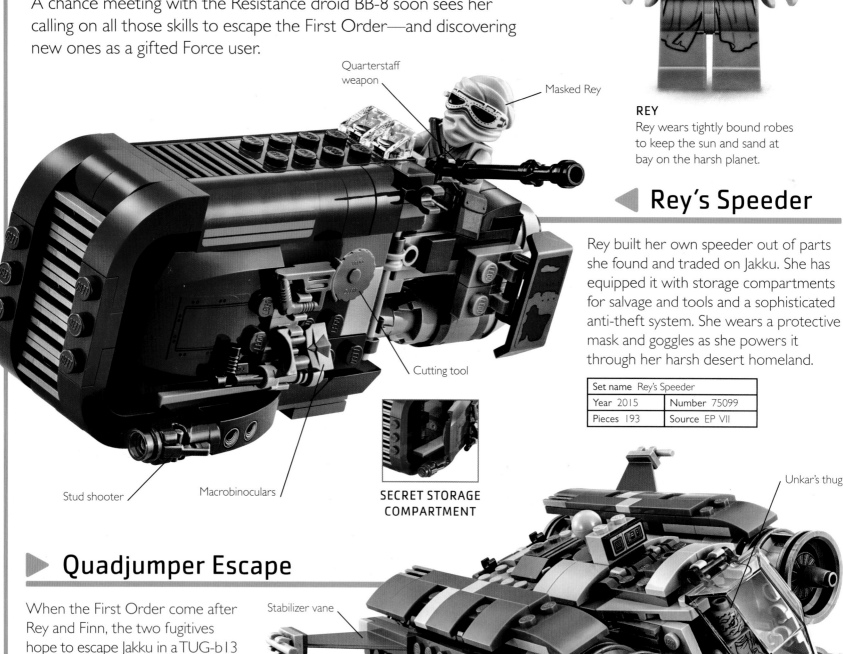

Quarterstaff weapon

Masked Rey

Cutting tool

Stud shooter

Macrobinoculars

SECRET STORAGE COMPARTMENT

REY
Rey wears tightly bound robes to keep the sun and sand at bay on the harsh planet.

◄ Rey's Speeder

Rey built her own speeder out of parts she found and traded on Jakku. She has equipped it with storage compartments for salvage and tools and a sophisticated anti-theft system. She wears a protective mask and goggles as she powers it through her harsh desert homeland.

Set name	Rey's Speeder	
Year	2015	Number 75099
Pieces	193	Source EP VII

Unkar's thug

▶ Quadjumper Escape

When the First Order come after Rey and Finn, the two fugitives hope to escape Jakku in a TUG-b13 quadjumper. But their pursuers blow it up before they can reach it—so they steal the *Millennium Falcon* instead! The LEGO® version is flown by one of Unkar Plutt's thugs.

Stabilizer vane

Explode function sends engines flying

Orientation vane

One of four turbine engines

Set name	Jakku Quadjumper	
Year	2017	Number 75178
Pieces	457	Source EP VII

Niima Outpost

Before she leaves Jakku, Rey makes a living by trading salvage for food at Niima Outpost. Ruthless Unkar Plutt calls the shots at this makeshift marketplace, and Rey has no choice but to accept whatever rations he offers.

Teedo scavenger

Unkar Plutt's concession stand

Luggabeast

BB-8

UNKAR PLUTT
Cruel Plutt uses hired thugs to enforce his stranglehold on barter. His minifigure has a sculpted, detailed head.

Set name	Encounter on Jakku	
Year	2016	Number 75148
Pieces	530	Source EP VII

Jedi Training

When Rey meets Jedi Master Luke Skywalker, she hopes he will leave the planet Ahch-To to fight the First Order. He refuses, but agrees to teach her how to use her Force powers instead.

Set name	Ahch-To Island Training	
Year	2018	Number 75200
Pieces	241	Source EP VIII

Luke's hut has a lift-off roof

Ragged cloth curtain

Rey uses Luke's old lightsaber

Luke's fire pit

Luke's staff

Revolving platform

REY'S NEXT MISSION
After leaving Ahch-To, Rey dons a gray robe to face Snoke in his throne room, and then the First Orders' forces on the planet Crait.

REY
The 2018 minifigure shows Rey in her training outfit and comes with two facial expressions.

LUKE SKYWALKER
Master Luke Skywalker dons a majestic robe with gold detail and a large, textured cape.

PORG
Porgs are sea-dwelling birds native to Ahch-To Island where Luke Skywalker is in exile.

Finn and Friends

When stormtrooper FN-2187 is ordered to destroy a village on the planet Jakku, he sees the true horror of the First Order, and disobeys. He flees in a TIE fighter with help from the Resistance pilot Poe Dameron, who gives him the new name Finn, and sets him on the path to becoming a freedom fighter.

FN-2187
This minifigure of Finn in a weathered First Order stormtrooper uniform comes in a LEGO polybag (set 39695).

THAT'S SO POE
When Finn and Poe crash on Jakku, all Finn can find of his new friend is his jacket, which he puts on in place of his trooper armor.

Guavian security soldier

Chewbacca

◀ Rebels and Rathtars

Finn gets away from Jakku with help from Rey, and the pair soon run into the famous rebels Han Solo and Chewbacca. Han and his co-pilot aren't sure about Finn at first, but they become friendlier after they all survive a rathtar attack inside Han's sprawling freighter, the *Eravana*.

Set name	Rathtar Escape	
Year	2017	Number 75180
Pieces	836	Source EP VII

Han Solo

Rathtar

Kylo Ren

▶ Maz Kanata

Han takes Finn and Rey to Takodana, where they meet the mysterious "pirate queen" Maz Kanata. Finn thinks about leaving his new friends here, but when the First Order attacks, Maz entrusts Finn with Luke Skywalker's lightsaber, and he chooses to fight and get the weapon to Rey.

MAZ KANATA

Exploding wall function

Fallen tree

Finn with lightsaber

Set name	Battle on Takodana	
Year	2016	Number 75139
Pieces	409	Source EP VII

Rose and the Resistance

BACTA FASHION
For DK's LEGO® *Star Wars™: Visual Dictionary: New Edition,* the LEGO Group produced a brand-new exclusive Finn minifigure. This wounded hero has been recovering in a flexypoly bacta suit.

At first, Finn insists that his only loyalty is to Rey, and not to the Resistance. But when he and the Resistance technician Rose Tico set out on a dangerous mission in a tiny transport pod, he starts to realize the importance of taking a side in the battle between good and evil.

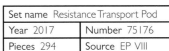

FINN

ROSE TICO

Two-seater transport pod

Stud shooter

Set name	Resistance Transport Pod	
Year 2017	Number 75176	
Pieces 294	Source EP VIII	

AT-ST Pilot

Throughout Finn's adventures, BB-8 is never far from his side. The tiny, ball-shaped droid even saves Finn's life when he and Rose are taken prisoner by Captain Phasma—by piloting an AT-ST walker to save them.

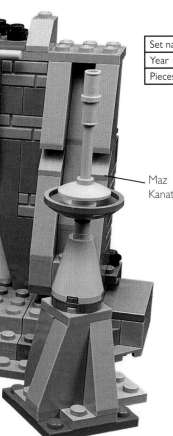

Maz Kanata's castle

Set name	First Order AT-ST	
Year 2018	Number 75201	
Pieces 370	Source EP VIII	

Rose in First Order disguise

Twin blaster cannons

BB-8 sits in the exposed cockpit

Finn in First Order disguise

Captain Phasma

RARE ROGUE
Finn meets the amoral crook DJ on the planet Cantonica, and makes the mistake of trusting him. As befits DJ's shady nature, he is found in just one limited edition LEGO polybag (set 40298).

Millennium Falcon— Flight from Jakku

After many years in the service of Han Solo, plus a stint in a Jakku junkyard, the *Millennium Falcon* is no longer the gleaming white racer it was under Lando Calrissian's command. Now in the hands of Rey, the ship still has it where it counts, however, and forms a vital part of the Resistance fleet.

▶ Rey's Ride

Rey and Finn steal the *Millennium Falcon* from Unkar Plutt's junk as they flee Jakku during a First Order air strike. Its old owner Han Solo picks it up on his new freighter ship's sensors and captures it. He quickly sees that Rey is a skilled pilot and engineer and offers her a job on the *Falcon*, but tragically he never leaves Starkiller Base. Later, Rey and Chewie set out alone in the *Falcon* to find missing Jedi Master Luke Skywalker.

Starboard docking ring

Rey and Fin in cockpit

Press here to fire missiles

Sliding hull section

Spring-loaded missile launcher

DATA FILE

Set name: *Millennium Falcon*
Year: 2015
Set Number: 75105
Pieces: 1,329
Source: EP VII
Dimensions:
length 18½in (47 cm)
width 12½in (32 cm)
height 5½in (14 cm)
Minifigures: 7—Rey, Finn, Han Solo, Chewbacca, Tasu Leech, Kanjiklub Gang Member, BB-8

TASU LEECH   **CROKIND SHAND**

AMBUSH!
When Han Solo's freighter is ambushed by the Kanjiklub gang intent on settling Han's debts, Han is forced to escape on the *Falcon* with Rey and Finn. The Flight from Jakku set comes with two gang member minifigures, Tasu Leech and Crokind Shand.

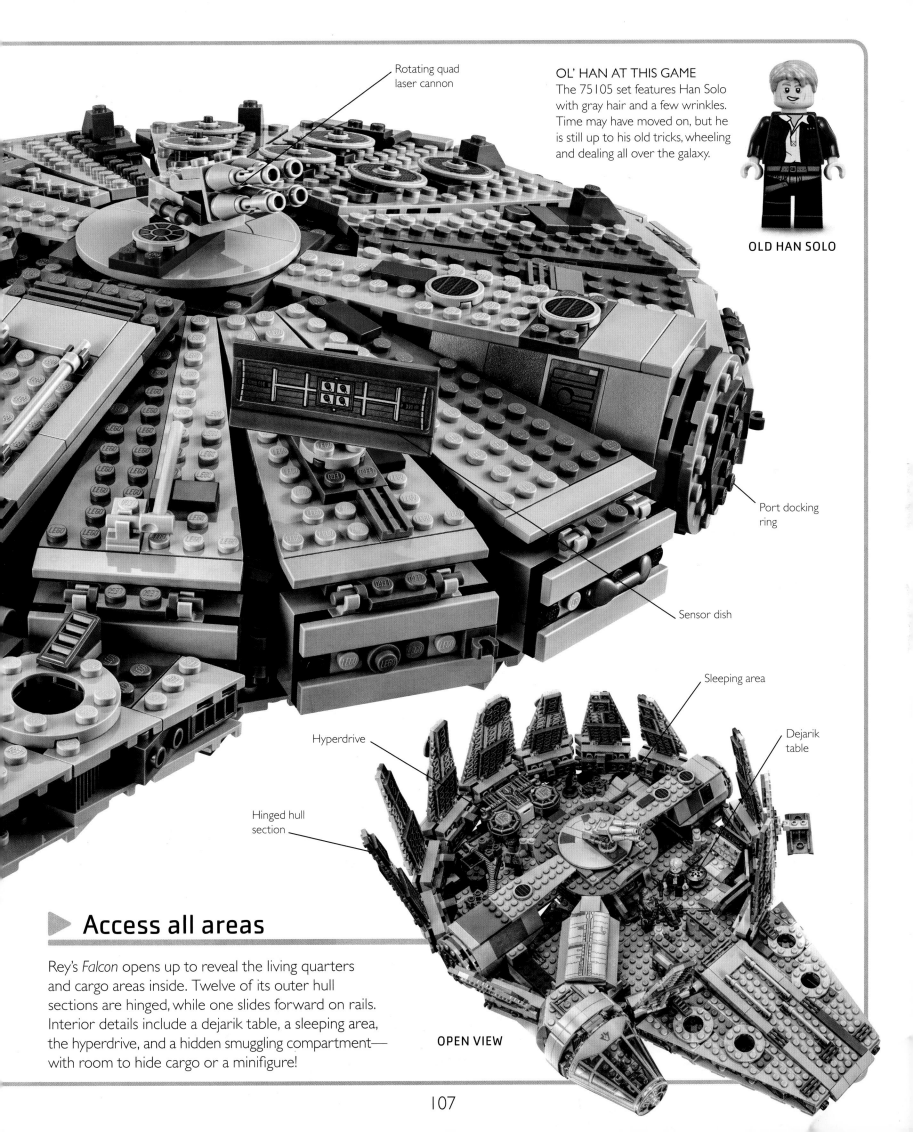

Rotating quad laser cannon

OL' HAN AT THIS GAME
The 75105 set features Han Solo with gray hair and a few wrinkles. Time may have moved on, but he is still up to his old tricks, wheeling and dealing all over the galaxy.

OLD HAN SOLO

Port docking ring

Sensor dish

Sleeping area

Dejarik table

Hyperdrive

Hinged hull section

▶ Access all areas

Rey's *Falcon* opens up to reveal the living quarters and cargo areas inside. Twelve of its outer hull sections are hinged, while one slides forward on rails. Interior details include a dejarik table, a sleeping area, the hyperdrive, and a hidden smuggling compartment—with room to hide cargo or a minifigure!

OPEN VIEW

The Resistance

When the Galactic Empire fell, a New Republic grew up in its place. Its leaders believed in a peaceful future, and most turned their back on military matters. But Leia Organa still saw threats in the galaxy, and so she formed the Resistance to fight the evil First Order.

LIFELONG FRIEND
Protocol droid C-3PO has served General Leia for as long as she can remember. He has been damaged and repaired many times over the years, and sports a red replacement arm during the early days of the Resistance.

C-3PO

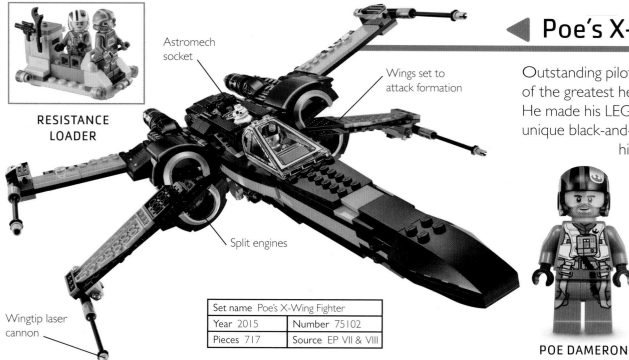

Astromech socket

Wings set to attack formation

RESISTANCE LOADER

Split engines

Wingtip laser cannon

Set name	Poe's X-Wing Fighter	
Year	2015	Number 75102
Pieces	717	Source EP VII & VIII

◀ Poe's X-Wing Fighter

Outstanding pilot Poe Dameron is one of the greatest heroes of the Resistance. He made his LEGO set debut alongside his unique black-and-orange X-wing starfighter, his faithful astromech droid, BB-8, and two brave Resistance colleagues.

POE DAMERON   **BB-8**

▶ Resistance Bomber

The MG-100 StarFortress SF-17 (to give it its full name) is designed to drop proton bombs from its long lower hull, while a pair of gunners defend the ship in rotating ball turrets. Its LEGO incarnation has all these features, plus lift-off sections that reveal the cockpit, flight deck, and targeting station.

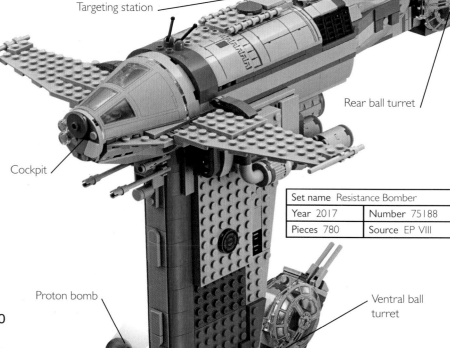

Targeting station

Rear ball turret

Cockpit

Set name	Resistance Bomber	
Year	2017	Number 75188
Pieces	780	Source EP VIII

Proton bomb

Ventral ball turret

RESISTANCE GUNNER PAIGE
Gunner Paige is Rose Tico's sister. Her helmet has a distinctive, colorful print. She comes with two face paintings—including one wearing breathing gear.

VICE ADMIRAL HOLDO
Vice Admiral Holdo's minifigure features a pale-purple hair piece true to the movie character.

Resistance Troop Transporter

The Resistance has good people but poor resources. Its troop transporter is bolted together using bits of B-wing starfighters, cargo ships, and ancient shuttles. Its cramped interior has room for General Leia and Admiral Ackbar, along with a Resistance trooper or two.

Set name	Resistance Troop Transporter	
Year 2016		Number 75140
Pieces 646		Source EP VII

Roof opens up on hinges

INTERIOR VIEW

Heavy laser cannon

Deployment ramp

Repurposed B-wing cockpit

GENERAL LEIA

GENERAL AVAILABILITY
Leia appears in more than 20 sets, but her Resistance General look only appears in a couple of sets.

The Battle of Crait

When the Resistance is all but wiped out by the First Order, its remaining members make a stand on the planet Crait. Making use of the defenses and ski speeders from an old rebel base, they narrowly survive to fight another day.

V-4X-D ski speeder

Rebel command tower

Twin medium laser cannon

Set name	Defense of Crait	
Year 2018		Number 75202
Pieces 746		Source EP VIII

Mono-ski

Open-air cockpit

Rotating laser cannon

Defensive trench

GENERAL EMATT

First Order snowtrooper

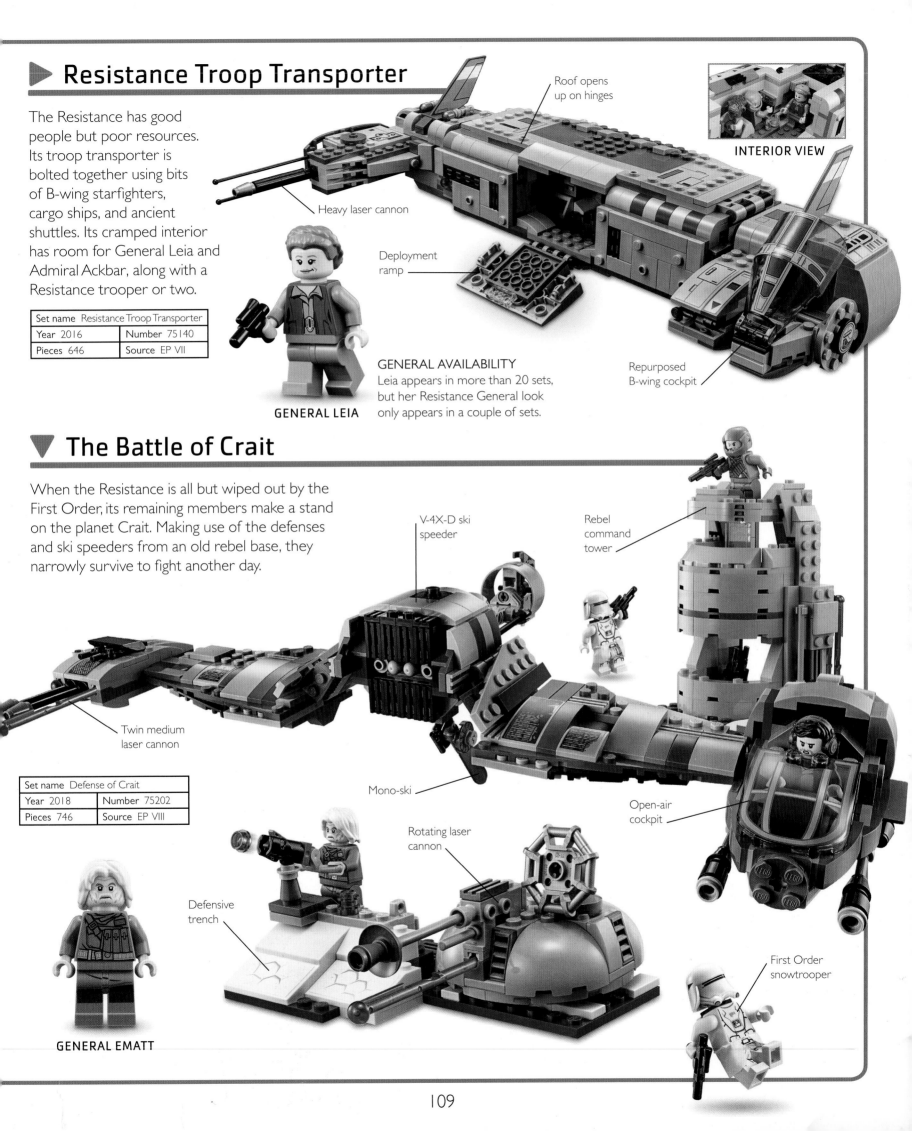

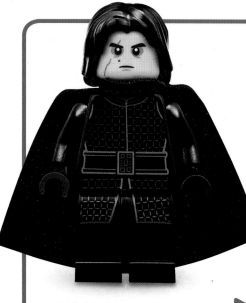

KYLO REN
This Kylo Ren minifigure (set 75179) has a facial scar. Its second face has an angry expression.

Kylo Ren

The Force-sensitive son of Han Solo and Leia Organa, Kylo Ren was lured to the dark side by Supreme Leader Snoke. He longs to be as powerful and confident as his grandfather, Darth Vader, and has risen to become Supreme Leader of the First Order by destroying his former master, Snoke.

▶ Kylo Ren's Command Shuttle

When Kylo Ren's *Upsilon*-class command shuttle comes in to land, its tall, spear-like wings fold down to create a thick defensive wall on both sides of the ship. Black-clad First Order crew members pilot the ship and operate its laser cannons.

Wings fully extended for flight

Twin heavy laser cannon

Command bridge

Cruciform lightsaber

Knights of Ren mask

BEHIND THE MASK
Four minifigure versions of Kylo Ren carry a cruciform lightsaber, but only one wears a Vader-like mask. Its image is also printed on the head piece beneath, so it can still be seen when the mask piece is swapped for a hood.

LANDING MODE

Set name	Kylo Ren's Command Shuttle	
Year 2015	Number 75104	
Pieces 1,005	Source EP VII & VIII	

Access hatch

Heavy laser cannon

Cockpit

Solar energy panels

BB-9E

Wingtip laser cannon

◀ Kylo Ren's TIE Fighter

As an ace pilot, Kylo Ren is the perfect choice to test this prototype TIE craft, known as a TIE silencer. Faster and more powerful than a standard First Order TIE fighter, it is also equipped with stealth technology to baffle an enemy's sensors.

Set name	Kylo Ren's TIE Fighter	
Year 2017	Number 75179	
Pieces 630	Source EP VIII	

Supreme Leader Snoke

Loaded stud shooter

Command bridge

Little is known about the powerful Force user who leads the First Order. A master manipulator, he prefers to operate in the shadows, and relies on others to do his bidding. His greatest wish is to destroy the Jedi once and for all, and he sees his apprentice, Kylo Ren, as the key to that ambition.

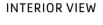

◀ First Order Star Destroyer

Open up this *Resurgent*-class Star Destroyer using its LEGO Technic hinges to reveal the first ever minifigure of Supreme Leader Snoke, along with various First Order functionaries and the devious droid BB-9E.

SNOKE

INTERIOR VIEW

LEGO® Technic hinge

Set name	First Order Star Destroyer	
Year 2017	Number 75190	
Pieces 1,416	Source EP VII & VIII	

Ship opens along center line

Turbolift

Snoke's throne

Operate lever to rotate throne

▲ Snoke's Throne Room

Snoke rules the First Order from a throne room on board the *Mega*-class Star Dreadnought *Supremacy*. Kylo brings Rey to see Snoke here, and a battle ensues between the Force users and the Praetorians.

Set name	Snoke's Throne Room	
Year 2018	Number 75216	
Pieces 492	Source EP VIII	

▼ Praetorian Guard Battle Set

Evoking the Imperial Guard that protected Emperor Palpatine, Snoke is flanked by eight fearsome and mysterious warriors clad in blood-red armor. Called the Praetorian Guard, they train with each other and with droids to hone their skills.

Set name	Elite Praetorian Guard Battle Pack	
Year 2019	Number 75225	
Pieces 109	Source EP VIII	

Bilari electro-chain whip

Twin vibro-arbir blade

Vibro-voulge

Electro-bisento

PRAETORIAN GUARD

First Order Forces

Under the command of General Armitage Hux, the First Order military is an ever-growing threat to peace in the galaxy. Inspired by the might of the old Imperial Navy, its firepower now outstrips the Empire at its apex.

Snowtrooper offic

▶ Snowspeeder

Properly known as the Light Infantry Utility Vehicle or LIUV, the First Order snowspeeder is a rugged repulsorlift craft, well suited to the icy conditions on Starkiller Base. It is designed for patrol duty and supply runs rather than assault missions.

Transparent wheels
for hovering effect

Set name	First Order Sr
Year 2015	N
Pieces 444	Sc

Armor plating
opens for access
to storage bay

MegaCaliber Six
turbolaser cannon

Viewport

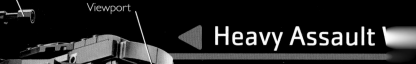

◀ Heavy Assault \

The biggest walker in the Fir
fleet is properly named the ⁄
MegaCaliber Six (AT-M6), af
huge MegaCaliber cannon o
It has tough armor-plating d
a posable head with a cockp

Medium laser
cannon

Set name	First Order Heavy Assault Walker	
Year 2017	Number 75189	
Pieces 1,376	Source EP VIII	

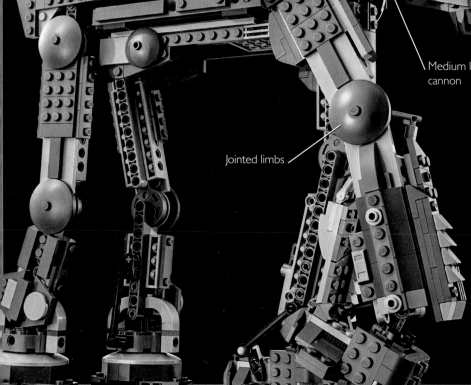

Jointed limbs

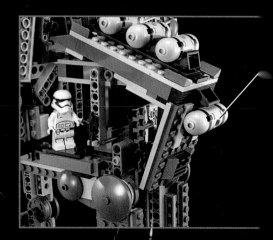

Scout Walker

The All Terrain Heavy Scout, or AT-HS, walker crawls along on eight spider-like legs. Unlike other small walkers—which can topple if just one limb is attacked—it can withstand the destruction of several legs and still keep scuttling on.

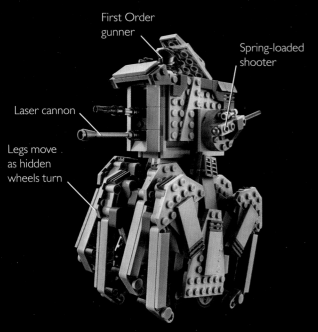

First Order gunner

Spring-loaded shooter

Laser cannon

Legs move as hidden wheels turn

Set name	First Order Heavy Scout Walker	
Year	2017	Number 75177
Pieces	554	Source EP VIII

Special Forces TIE Fighter

While most TIE fighters have only one seat, the Special Forces TIE makes room for two. This allows the pilot to focus solely on flying while a dedicated gunner controls the mission-specific heavy weapons.

Set name	First Order Special Forces TIE Fighter	
Year	2015	Number 75101
Pieces	517	Source EP VII & VIII

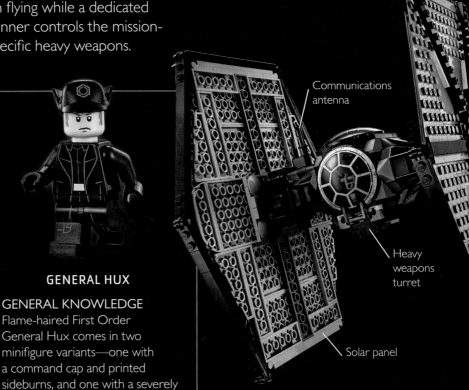

Communications antenna

Heavy weapons turret

Solar panel

GENERAL HUX

GENERAL KNOWLEDGE
Flame-haired First Order General Hux comes in two minifigure variants—one with a command cap and printed sideburns, and one with a severely swept hair piece. Both are resolved to destroy the Resistance!

Transporter

Designed to deliver troops from bigger ships into ground battles, First Order Transporters are little more than heavily armored flying boxes. Even seats are considered a luxury, and stormtroopers have to stand inside as they wait for the deployment ramp to drop.

Set name	First Order Transporter	
Year	2015	Number 75103
Pieces	792	Source EP VII

Emergency escape hatch

Pilot's cabin

Flametrooper

Captain Phasma

Deployment ramp

Dial raises and lowers ramp

First Order Troops

The fighting men and women of the First Order are trained to be emotionless. The majority of the troops are stormtroopers and pilots, who are conditioned for combat from childhood and given ID numbers instead of names. Others are allowed to retain a small amount of their individuality as officers—though their loyalty to the organization must still be absolute.

▶ First Order Army

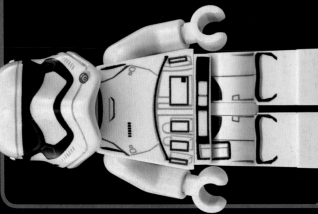

STANDARD ORDER

With updated armor and more streamlined helmets, standard First Order stormtroopers are easy to tell apart from their Imperial predecessors. Though they are not clones, their minifigures all have the same fierce face beneath their headgear.

RIOT TROOPER

Wearing standard First Order stormtrooper armor, riot control units carry betaplast shields and electroshock batons to subdue civilian populations.

SNOWTROOPER

Specially trained to serve in cold conditions, First Order snowtroopers wear insulated belt-capes, glare-resistant helmets, and armor with built-in heating.

HEAVY ASSAULT TROOPER

Armed with oversized blasters, heavy assault troopers can be identified by the extra equipment strapped to their chest and sometimes worn on their back, too.

EXECUTIONER

Bold black markings denote executioner troopers, who serve to strike fear into their fellow stormtroopers—reminding them of the need for total obedience!

FLAMETROOPER

With fuel tanks on their backs and incinerator guns in their grasp, the fearsome flametroopers are outfitted in fireproof armor and glare-resistant helmets.

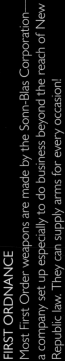

BETAPLAST BALLISTIC RIOT SHIELD

Z6 RIOT CONTROL BATON

FWMB-10 REPEATING BLASTER

D-93W FLAME PROJECTOR GUN

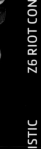

LASER AX

CONFLAGRINE-14 FUEL TANKS

FIRST ORDNANCE

Most First Order weapons are made by the Sonn-Blas Corporation—a company set up especially to do business beyond the reach of New Republic law. They can supply arms for every occasion!

First Order Navy and Special Forces

The pilots and crew of the First Order Navy are essentially the stormtroopers of the skies—though they operate ground vehicles such as walkers, too. They are separate from the Special Forces, an elite branch of the First Order military whose members combine the skills of a pilot and a trooper.

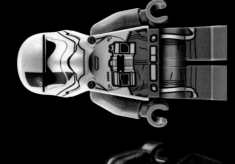

WALKER PILOT

FIRST ORDER FLEET ENGINEER

SHUTTLE PILOT

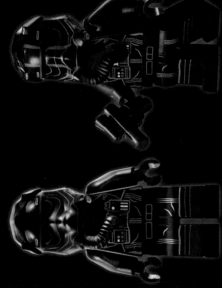

SPECIAL FORCES TIE PILOT

TIE PILOT

BB-9E

First Order warships rely on dark, gleaming BB astromech units to make sure procedures are followed. BB-9E keeps a sharp photoreceptor out for infiltrators, saboteurs, and other threats to Supreme Leader Snoke's flagship. BB-9E has a run-in with his counterpart Resistance droid BB-8 in *Star Wars: Episode VIII The Last Jedi*.

First Order Hierarchy

The First Order military has two distinct classes of officer. The first is made up of the soldiers in dark uniforms and matching command caps who mostly serve on bases and aboard capital ships. The second comprises the senior stormtroopers on the ground, whose rank is denoted by colored shoulder pauldrons.

CHROMIUM CAPTAIN

Clad in unique chromium-plated armor, Captain Phasma is the First Order's most senior stormtrooper. She loathes the Resistance fighter Finn, who once served under her command, and longs to make him pay for his desertion.

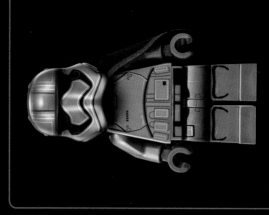

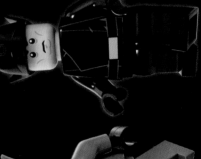

FIRST ORDER GENERAL

FIRST ORDER OFFICER

STORMTROOPER SQUAD LEADER

SNOWTROOPER OFFICER

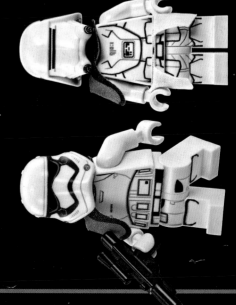

STORMTROOPER OFFICER

LEGO® Legends

In 2014, Lucasfilm reclassified the *Star Wars*™ canon with many stories now considered Legends. These tales come from many different eras of *Star Wars* history and a range of media. The LEGO Group have produced sets based on these Legends.

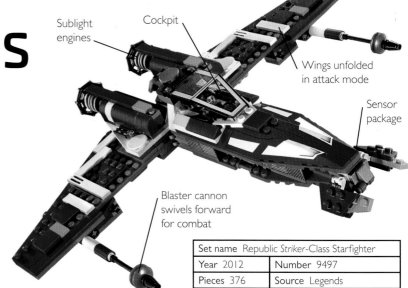

Sublight engines

Cockpit

Wings unfolded in attack mode

Sensor package

Blaster cannon swivels forward for combat

Set name	Republic *Striker*-Class Starfighter	
Year 2012	Number 9497	
Pieces 376	Source Legends	

▲ Republic *Striker*-Class Starfighter

Thousands of years before Luke Skywalker's birth, the Republic battled the fanatical Sith Empire in the *Star Wars: The Old Republic* video game. Jedi Masters such as Satele Shan piloted fast, nimble *Striker*-class fighters, assisted by astromech droids like T7-O1. The *Striker* includes wings and blaster cannons that fold up in landing mode, plus flick missiles and lightsaber storage at the stern.

▼ Sith *Fury*-Class Interceptor

Based on the *Star Wars: The Old Republic* video game, this set depicts the Fury interceptor. This heavily shielded and armed starship's development is personally overseen by the ruthless Sith Lord Darth Malgus. Packed with weapons and filled with Sith troopers, these vicious craft are serious threats to the Republic and the Jedi.

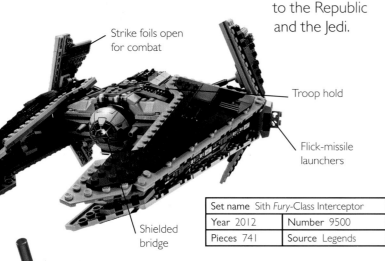

Strike foils open for combat

Troop hold

Flick-missile launchers

Shielded bridge

Set name	Sith *Fury*-Class Interceptor	
Year 2012	Number 9500	
Pieces 741	Source Legends	

VINTAGE VILLAIN
One look at Darth Malgus's burning yellow eyes and unique black cape tell you he's not one to mess with. His shoulder armor and respirator are a single exclusive piece.

DARTH MALGUS

▼ Jedi *Defender*-Class Cruiser

A Jedi mobile command center, the *Defender* has powerful sensors and communications capabilities, and appears in the *Star Wars: The Old Republic* video game. This set has bridge compartments, hidden storage for valuable holocrons, and twin escape pods.

Set name	Jedi *Defender*-Class Cruiser	
Year 2013	Number 75025	
Pieces 927	Source Legends	

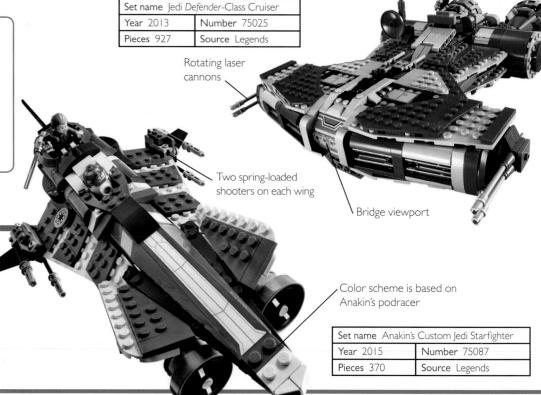

Rotating laser cannons

Two spring-loaded shooters on each wing

Bridge viewport

Color scheme is based on Anakin's podracer

▶ *Azure Angel*

The *Azure Angel* appears in the original *Star Wars: The Clone Wars* animation (2003–2005). It is a Jedi Delta-7 Interceptor that has been heavily customized by Anakin Skywalker to increase its performance. Joined by R4-P22, he must defend his ship from the evil Asajj Ventress.

Set name	Anakin's Custom Jedi Starfighter	
Year 2015	Number 75087	
Pieces 370	Source Legends	

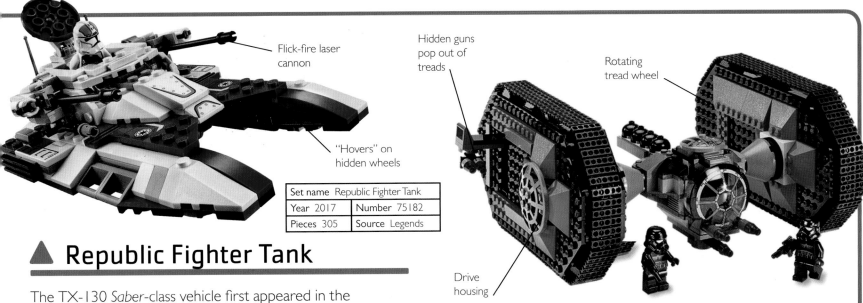

Flick-fire laser cannon

"Hovers" on hidden wheels

Hidden guns pop out of treads

Rotating tread wheel

Drive housing

Set name	Republic Fighter Tank	
Year 2017	Number 75182	
Pieces 305	Source Legends	

▲ Republic Fighter Tank

The TX-130 *Saber*-class vehicle first appeared in the *Star Wars: The Clone Wars* video game. It is a fast-attack tank equipped with laser cannon and concussion missiles. Clone troopers normally pilot this tank, though Jedi have been known to take control.

▼ TIE/D

In the *Star Wars: Dark Empire* comic series, the Empire developed prototype pilotless fighters with programmable droid brains. The droid brain minifigure can be removed from the pod casing.

Set name	TIE Fighter Collection	
Year 2004	Number 10131	
Pieces 682	Source Legends	

DROID BRAIN

Droid brain pod

High-performance solar panels

Blaster cannon

Set name	TIE Crawler	
Year 2007	Number 7664	
Pieces 548	Source Legends	

▲ TIE Crawler

First appearing in the *Star Wars: Dark Empire* comic series, the unusual TIE crawler marries the familiar cockpit of a TIE fighter with tread wheels borrowed from a ground-assault vehicle to make a cheap, effective option for ground combat. The treads rotate, elevating the cockpit to avoid obstacles or shoot the principal flick-fire missiles. The set comes with two shadow stormtroopers, feared servants of the Emperor.

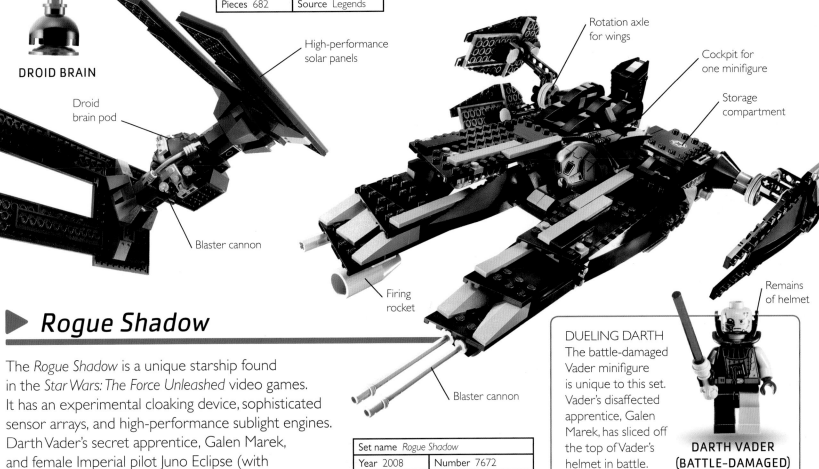

Rotation axle for wings

Cockpit for one minifigure

Storage compartment

Firing rocket

Remains of helmet

Blaster cannon

▶ *Rogue Shadow*

The *Rogue Shadow* is a unique starship found in the *Star Wars: The Force Unleashed* video games. It has an experimental cloaking device, sophisticated sensor arrays, and high-performance sublight engines. Darth Vader's secret apprentice, Galen Marek, and female Imperial pilot Juno Eclipse (with whom Marek falls in love) pilot the ship.

Set name	*Rogue Shadow*	
Year 2008	Number 7672	
Pieces 482	Source Legends	

DUELING DARTH
The battle-damaged Vader minifigure is unique to this set. Vader's disaffected apprentice, Galen Marek, has sliced off the top of Vader's helmet in battle.

DARTH VADER (BATTLE-DAMAGED)

LEGO® Creations

As well as featuring hundreds of sets based on existing settings and spacecraft, the LEGO® *Star Wars*™ theme has occasionally introduced its own inventions to the *Star Wars* universe. Designed for animated TV shows that take place in a brick-built version of the galaxy far, far away, they naturally lend themselves to being LEGO® sets as well!

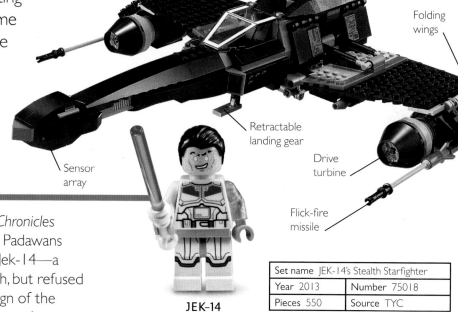

Rotating laser cannon

Astromech socket

Folding wings

Retractable landing gear

Drive turbine

Flick-fire missile

Sensor array

▶ JEK-14's Stealth Starfighter

In 2013, the animated TV series LEGO *Star Wars: The Yoda Chronicles* charted the adventures of Jedi Master Yoda and a group of Padawans during the Clone Wars. The characters they met included Jek-14—a powerful Force-sensitive clone who was created by the Sith, but refused to fight for either the Separatists or the Republic. The design of the starfighter was first visualized in the *Star Wars: Dark Empire* comic.

JEK-14

Set name	JEK-14's Stealth Starfighter	
Year	2013	Number 75018
Pieces	550	Source TYC

◀ Jedi Scout Fighter

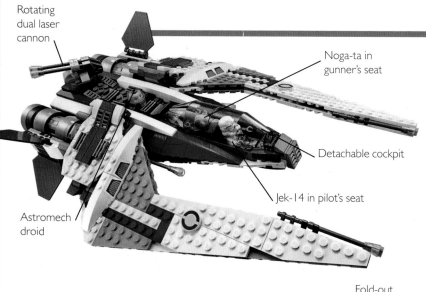

Rotating dual laser cannon

Noga-ta in gunner's seat

Detachable cockpit

Jek-14 in pilot's seat

Astromech droid

Jek-14 returned in new episodes of *The Yoda Chronicles* in 2014. Now a friend of the remaining Jedi in the early days of the Empire, he agreed to help the Ithorian Jedi Knight Noga-ta retrieve vital holocrons from the abandoned Jedi Temple on Coruscant. For this mission, he was equipped with a two-seater Jedi fighter.

Set name	Jedi Scout Fighter	
Year	2014	Number 75051
Pieces	490	Source TYC

▼ *StarScavenger*

Launched in 2016, LEGO *Star Wars: The Freemaker Adventures* is an action-packed animated TV series following the exploits of Force-sensitive Rowan Freemaker and his family of scrap merchants. When we first meet them, all they want is to make a living on board their modular salvage ship, the *StarScavenger*.

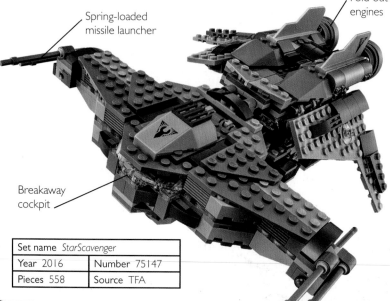

Spring-loaded missile launcher

Fold-out engines

Breakaway cockpit

Set name	*StarScavenger*	
Year	2016	Number 75147
Pieces	558	Source TFA

KORDI FREEMAKER

ZANDER FREEMAKER

ROWAN FREEMAKER

RO-GR

Eclipse Fighter

When Rowan Freemaker starts to flex his untrained Force powers, he attracts some unwanted attention, including from the Sith agent Naare and the bounty hunter Dengar. Naare pretends to be a Jedi and helps the Freemakers at first, but is soon pursuing them in her powerful ship, the *Eclipse Fighter*!

Set name	*Eclipse Fighter*	
Year 2016	Number 75145
Pieces 363	Source TFA

Wings folded back for combat mode

Naare in cockpit

Dengar on speeder bike

Wingtip blaster cannons

Zander at the controls

Kyber crystal power source

Flip-out battering ram

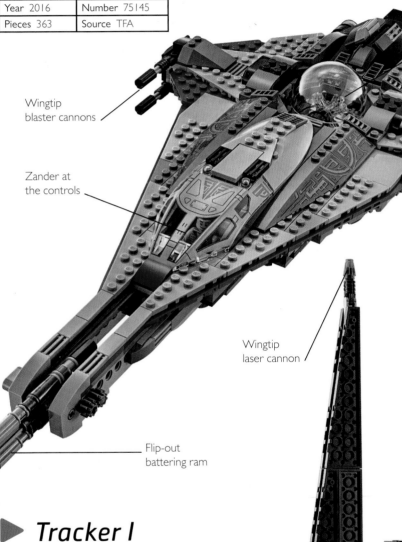

The *Arrowhead*

As Rowan Freemaker's Force powers grow, he experiences a vision of a powerful new ship. With the help of the seasoned Mon Calamari shipbuilder Quarrie, he succeeds in building the *Arrowhead*—a new kind of fighter powered by a giant kyber crystal. The Freemakers hope it could bring down the Empire!

Set name	The *Arrowhead*	
Year 2017	Number 75186
Pieces 775	Source TFA

Wingtip laser cannon

M-OC

INITIALLY FUNNY

Droid M-OC comes with the *Tracker 1* (75185 set). The Emperor created the hunter droid M-OC with his own hands. His name is an in-joke inspired by initials used by many LEGO fan builders—standing for "My Own Creation."

Spring-loaded shooter

Tracker 1

When Emperor Palpatine realizes the threat posed by the Freemakers, he dispatches the Imperial hunter droid M-OC to find and capture Rowan. The multi-talented M-OC pilots the sleek and stealthy *Tracker 1*—a fast-moving ship with a built-in prison cell that even a Force user can't escape from!

Set name	*Tracker 1*	
Year 2017	Number 75185
Pieces 557	Source TFA

Open prison cell

Planet Sets

In 2012 and 2013, the LEGO Group offered a dozen mini-ships, each accompanied by a minifigure, a planet (or other celestial phenomenon) introduced in the first six *Star Wars* movies, and a plaque. The planets can be hung from a wire for display, and several of the minifigures are unique or reworked from their previous LEGO set appearances.

Set name	Naboo Starfighter & Naboo	
Year	2012	Number 9674
Pieces	56	Source EP I

Finial is a flagpole element

Droid is silver stud

NABOO

Flight goggles

NABOO PILOT

▼ Death Star

Built in secret on the Emperor's orders, the first Death Star threatens to extinguish freedom in the galaxy, and destroys the planet Alderaan. The Death Star has a great deal of detail, from the indented superlaser "dish" to the trenches on its surface.

DEATH STAR

Set name	TIE Interceptor & Death Star	
Year	2012	Number 9676
Pieces	65	Source EP IV

Cockpit window shared with TIE bomber

Binoculars used as cannon

TIE PILOT

▲ Naboo

The planet Naboo is a lush world co-inhabited by human settlers known as the Naboo and the aquatic species named Gungans. Naboo's starfighter pilots must defend their home against the droid fighters of the Trade Federation.

Set name	X-Wing Starfighter & Yavin 4	
Year	2012	Number 9677
Pieces	77	Source EP IV

YAVIN 4

S-foils in attack position

Nose also used as roof tile

X-WING PILOT

◀ Bespin

"Radiator grille" is common part

Bespin is a gas giant in the galaxy's Outer Rim notable for the floating habitation known as Cloud City. Lobot's minifigure is reworked from his 2002 incarnation, with a flesh-colored face and a blaster.

BESPIN

LOBOT

Set name	Twin-Pod Cloud Car & Bespin	
Year	2012	Number 9678
Pieces	78	Source EP V

▲ Yavin 4

Yavin 4 is the jungle moon in the Outer Rim that provides a home for the main rebel base. The X-wing pilot shares a helmet with Dak Ralter, whose minifigure first appeared in the Snowspeeder set in 1999 and was updated in 2004 and 2007.

Transparent pink saber blades

Control pod "floats" on clear rod

▶ Tatooine

A forlorn desert world in the Outer Rim, Tatooine is controlled by the Hutts and populated by hard-working moisture farmers, Jawas, and Sand People. Sebulba comes with a wrench for fixing (or perhaps building) his podracer.

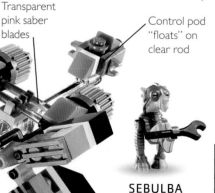

SEBULBA

TATOOINE

Set name	Sebulba's Podracer & Tatooine	
Year	2012	Number 9675
Pieces	80	Source EP I

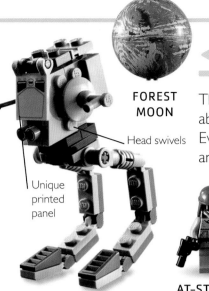

FOREST
MOON

Head swivels

Unique
printed
panel

◀ Forest Moon of Endor

The Empire builds its second Death Star above Endor's forest moon, home to the Ewoks. AT-STs guard a shield generator and bunker constructed among the trees.

AT-ST DRIVER

Set name	AT-ST & Endor	
Year 2012	Number 9679	
Pieces 65	Source EP VI	

KAMINO

R4-P17

Set name	Jedi Starfighter & Kamino	
Year 2013	Number 75006	
Pieces 61	Source EP II	

Republic
symbol
is unique

▲ Kamino

The stormy water world of Kamino is home to a cloning facility that builds the massive clone army. This set includes the first full-body version of astromech R4-P17.

▶ Coruscant

Coruscant is the capital of the Republic (and later the Empire) and is an immensely crowded city-planet. This is one of only two LEGO versions of the Republic assault ship, first used at Geonosis.

Set name	Republic Assault Ship & Coruscant	
Year 2013	Number 75007	
Pieces 74	Source EP II	

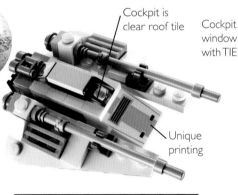

Bridge made
from saber hilt
and stud

CLONE TROOPER

CORUSCANT

Set name	TIE Bomber & Asteroid Field	
Year 2013	Number 75008	
Pieces 60	Source EP V	

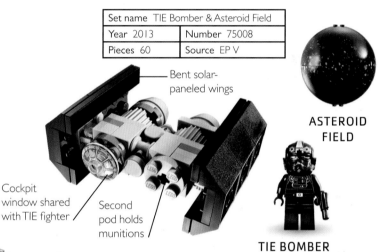

Bent solar-
paneled wings

Cockpit
window shared
with TIE fighter

Second
pod holds
munitions

ASTEROID
FIELD

TIE BOMBER
PILOT

▶ Hoth

The remote ice planet Hoth is the hiding place of the rebels after the destruction of the first Death Star. They defend their base against the Empire with snowspeeders.

HOTH

Cockpit is
clear roof tile

Unique
printing

SNOWSPEEDER
PILOT

Set name	Snowspeeder & Hoth	
Year 2013	Number 75009	
Pieces 69	Source EP V	

▲ Asteroid Field

After the *Millennium Falcon* flees Hoth, TIE bombers search for the freighter amid the tumbling rocks of a nearby asteroid field.

Cockpit is
unique
printed piece

Wings fold

◀ Endor

Above the giant gas planet of Endor, rebels battle in B-wings against the Empire. The B-wing pilot has been updated with a detailed body, legs, and visor.

B-WING PILOT   ENDOR

Set name	B-Wing Starfighter & Endor	
Year 2013	Number 75010	
Pieces 83	Source EP VI	

Antenna
used as gun
turret

ALDERAAN

Set name	Tantive IV & Alderaan	
Year 2013	Number 75011	
Pieces 102	Source EP IV	

Element
known as
a "palisade
brick"

▲ Alderaan

Long a center for culture and learning, the Core World of Alderaan is Princess Leia's home world and the base of operations for her blockade runner, known as the *Tantive IV*.

REBEL TROOPER

Microfighters

The galaxy got a little smaller in 2014 with the launch of LEGO® *Star Wars*™ Microfighters. Designed with key details exaggerated for a fun, stylized look, each set depicts a classic vehicle as if it were a single-seater craft, with room for a minifigure on top. Built for battle, every Microfighters set comes with flick-fire missiles or stud shooters and is made from around 100 bricks.

BRICK FACTS

Before there were Microfighters, there were four other LEGO *Star Wars* sets in a similar scale released in 2012 and 2013. Boba Fett's Mini *Slave I*, Darth Maul's Mini Sith Infiltrator, Luke Skywalker's Mini Landspeeder, and Jek-14's Mini Stealth Starfighter were all special event-exclusive sets.

JEK-14'S MINI STEALTH STARFIGHTER

Sith Infiltrator

Two trans-red slope pieces for the cockpit

Radiator fins can open and close

In 2012, the first iteration of the Sith Infiltrator at this scale was an exclusive release for San Diego Comic-Con. The 2019 Microfighter version is smaller, but has the addition of two stud shooters under its hull.

Set name	Sith Infiltrator
Year 2019	Number 75224
Pieces 92	Source EP I

Naboo Starfighter

Flick-fire missile

Young Anakin and R2 bravely take part in the Battle of Naboo in this Microfighter-scale N-1 Starfighter. This ship's sleek design is created with a combination of angled and curved pieces.

Set name	Naboo Starfighter
Year 2019	Number 75223
Pieces 62	Source EP I

Clone Turbo Tank

The first LEGO Clone Turbo Tank (set 7261) from 2005 had more than 800 pieces. The 2014 Microfighters version has just 96, but still boasts 10 turning wheels, two flick-fire missiles and an exclusive clone trooper minifigure.

Flick-fire missile

Wheels are 2x2 round bricks

Set name	Clone Turbo Tank
Year 2014	Number 75028
Pieces 96	Source EP III

AAT

Rotating cannon turret

Pilot battle droid

The blue body of the minifigure in this set marks him out as a pilot battle droid. At the controls of a Trade Federation Armored Assault Tank, he is surrounded by flick-fire missiles and a rotating, tilting laser cannon.

Set name	AAT
Year 2014	Number 75029
Pieces 95	Source EP I

ARC-170 Starfighter

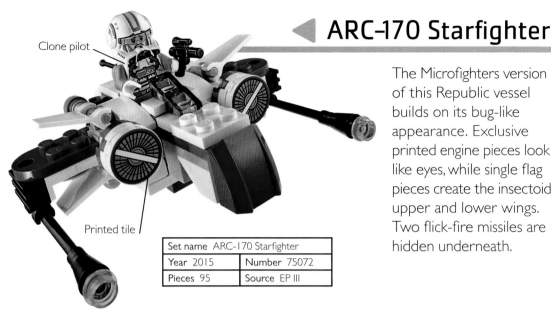

Clone pilot

Printed tile

The Microfighters version of this Republic vessel builds on its bug-like appearance. Exclusive printed engine pieces look like eyes, while single flag pieces create the insectoid upper and lower wings. Two flick-fire missiles are hidden underneath.

Set name	ARC-170 Starfighter	
Year	2015	Number 75072
Pieces	95	Source EP III

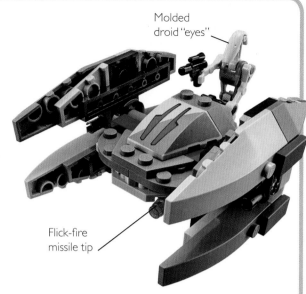

Molded droid "eyes"

Flick-fire missile tip

Vulture Droid

Standard Separatist vulture droids don't need an operator, but the Microfighters version comes with a pilot droid pal. Its wings fold down to form four legs, so they can even go on walks together!

Set name	Vulture Droid	
Year	2015	Number 75073
Pieces	77	Source EP III

The *Ghost*

In 2014, Microfighters-style versions of the *Ghost* piloted by Chopper and Kanan Jarrus were exclusively available at San Diego Comic-Con and Toronto FAN EXPO respectively. Two years later, Hera Syndulla took the controls of an even more compact edition.

Set name	The *Ghost*	
Year	2016	Number 75127
Pieces	104	Source *Rebels*

Captain Hera Syndulla

Stud shooter

U-Wing

Just like the 659-piece version released the previous year, the Microfighters U-wing has two forward-facing S-foils that sweep backward in combat mode. It comes with an exclusive rebel pilot minifigure and a pair of stud shooters.

Set name	U-Wing	
Year	2017	Number 75160
Pieces	109	Source R1

Unnamed rebel pilot

Stud shooter

S-Foil

Exclusive torso print

Stud shooter

Krennic's Imperial Shuttle

Director Krennic himself is exclusive to the much larger version of Krennic's Imperial Shuttle (set 75156), so the Microfighters version is flown by an equally exclusive Imperial Shuttle Pilot. The craft's wings fold upward for landing.

Wing in flight mode

Set name	Krennic's Imperial Shuttle	
Year	2017	Number 75163
Pieces	78	Source R1

Escape Pod vs. Dewback

ESCAPE POD

In the second wave of Microfighter dual packs, this set recreates the Empire's hunt for the Death Star plans. Can C-3PO and R2 evade the sandtrooper on a brick-built Dewback?

Set name	Escape Pod vs. Dewback	
Year	2019	Number 75228
Pieces	177	Source EP IV

LEGO roller skate piece

Head is connected by a ball joint to body

DEWBACK

Smiling face

Y-Wing

Based on the Y-wings in *Rogue One: A Star Wars Story*, this Microfighters set comes with a blue-clad rebel pilot from Blue Squadron. Like most minifigures in the range, his head can be turned to show happy or scared expressions.

Set name	Y-Wing	
Year	2017	Number 75162
Pieces	90	Source R1

Rebel Alliance symbol

AT-DP

The smallest set in the Microfighters range captures the distinctive look of an Imperial walker in fewer than 80 pieces. Each leg is jointed in three places, giving it just as much maneuverability as the 500-piece AT-DP (set 75083)!

Set name	AT-DP	
Year	2016	Number 75130
Pieces	76	Source *Rebels*

Laser cannons made from LEGO® Technic pieces

Snowspeeder

Rebel snowspeeders have appeared in more than a dozen sets, but this one still boasts an exclusive pilot's helmet! Two flick-fire missiles are hidden beneath its remarkably accurate angular hull, which fits together using click-hinge pieces.

Set name	Snowspeeder	
Year	2015	Number 75074
Pieces	97	Source EP V

Imperial combat driver

Posable click-hinge connection

Resistance X-Wing Fighter

Though the minifigure in this set is not named, his facial hair and helmet decals suggest he is Temmin "Snap" Wexley— a member of Poe Dameron's celebrated Black Squadron. The ship's four wingtip laser cannons are, in fact, flick-fire missiles.

Set name	Resistance X-Wing Fighter	
Year	2016	Number 75125
Pieces	87	Source EP VII

Adjustable wings

Sensor dish

Exclusive printed piece

▲ Millennium Falcon

In 2014, one of the first Microfighters sets was the *Millennium Falcon* flown by Han Solo. This Episode VIII update swaps flick-fire missiles for stud shooters; the round sensor dish for a rectangular one; and Han for his former co-pilot, Chewbacca.

Set name	*Millennium Falcon*	
Year	2018	Number 75193
Pieces	92	Source EP VIII

▶ First Order TIE Fighter

With its bold red flash, this ship resembles a First Order Special Forces TIE fighter, though its pilot does not wear a Special Forces helmet. It is the fourth TIE ship in the Microfighters range, after the TIE Interceptor (set 75031), TIE Advanced Prototype (set 75128) and TIE Striker (set 75161).

Set name	First Order TIE Fighter	
Year	2018	Number 75194
Pieces	91	Source EP VIII

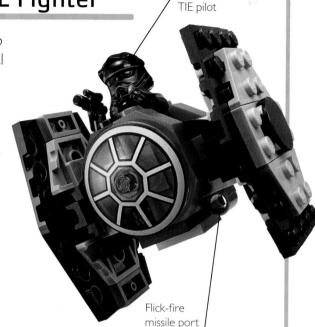

First Order TIE pilot

Flick-fire missile port

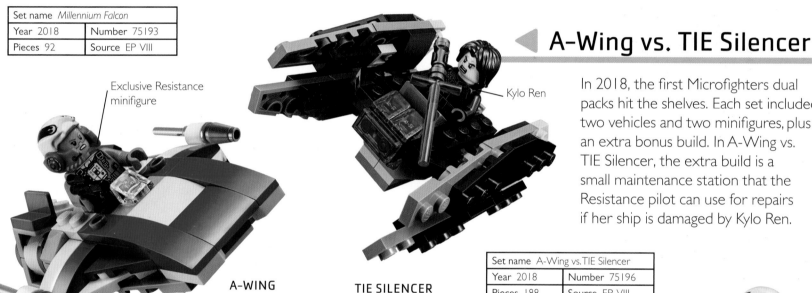

Kylo Ren

Exclusive Resistance minifigure

A-WING

TIE SILENCER

Flick-fire missile

◀ A-Wing vs. TIE Silencer

In 2018, the first Microfighters dual packs hit the shelves. Each set included two vehicles and two minifigures, plus an extra bonus build. In A-Wing vs. TIE Silencer, the extra build is a small maintenance station that the Resistance pilot can use for repairs if her ship is damaged by Kylo Ren.

Set name	A-Wing vs. TIE Silencer	
Year	2018	Number 75196
Pieces	188	Source EP VIII

▶ Ski Speeder vs. First Order Walker

The huge First Order Heavy Assault Walker is brought down to size in this set recreating the Battle of Crait. Both vehicles come with stud shooters and another is included as part of a defensive trench build that captures the distinctive red-and-white surface of Crait in just a handful of pieces.

Set name	Ski Speeder vs. First Order Walker	
Year	2018	Number 75195
Pieces	216	Source EP VIII

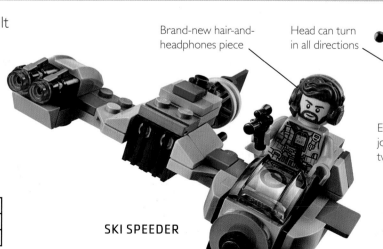

Brand-new hair-and-headphones piece

Head can turn in all directions

Each leg is jointed in two places

SKI SPEEDER

FIRST ORDER WALKER

Mini Sets

In 2002, the LEGO Group created the first mini sets. They are smaller than the normal sets, with fewer pieces. Though less detailed, mini sets are incredibly accurate. The LEGO Group has issued sets based on many vehicles from across the *Star Wars* saga.

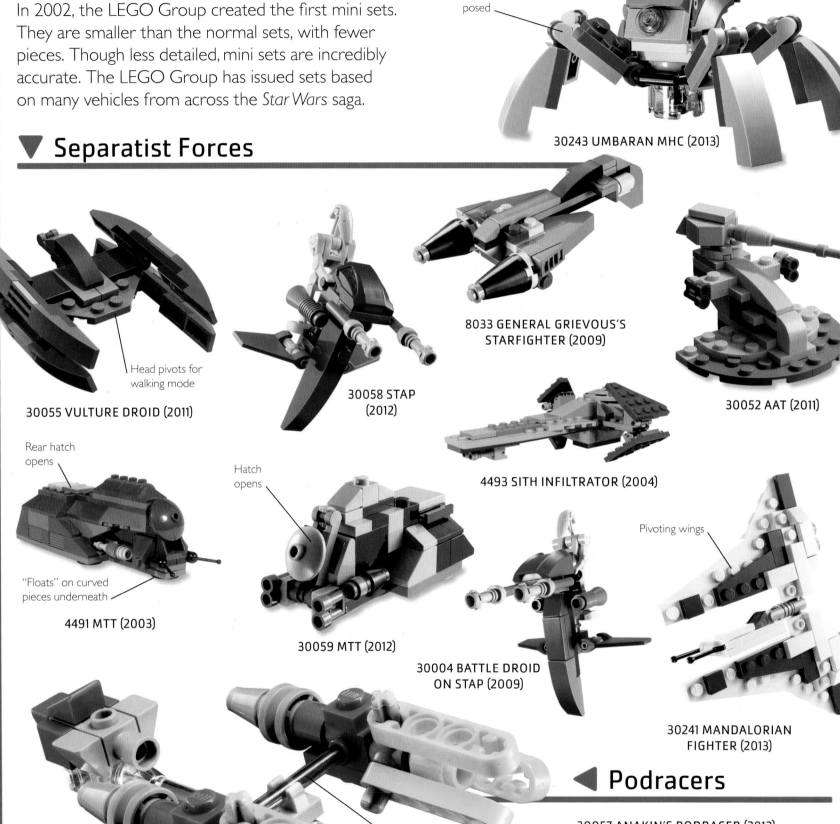

Legs can be posed

30243 UMBARAN MHC (2013)

▼ Separatist Forces

Head pivots for walking mode

30055 VULTURE DROID (2011)

30058 STAP (2012)

8033 GENERAL GRIEVOUS'S STARFIGHTER (2009)

30052 AAT (2011)

Rear hatch opens

"Floats" on curved pieces underneath

4491 MTT (2003)

Hatch opens

30059 MTT (2012)

4493 SITH INFILTRATOR (2004)

Pivoting wings

30004 BATTLE DROID ON STAP (2009)

30241 MANDALORIAN FIGHTER (2013)

◀ Podracers

Pink lightsaber blade used as energy binder arc

LEGO Technic parts used as engine nacelles

30057 ANAKIN'S PODRACER (2012)
The second LEGO incarnation of Anakin's Podracer uses just 38 pieces to make a convincing replica of the future Jedi's custom-built racing machine. Clear pieces allow the control pod to look like it's floating behind the massive engines.

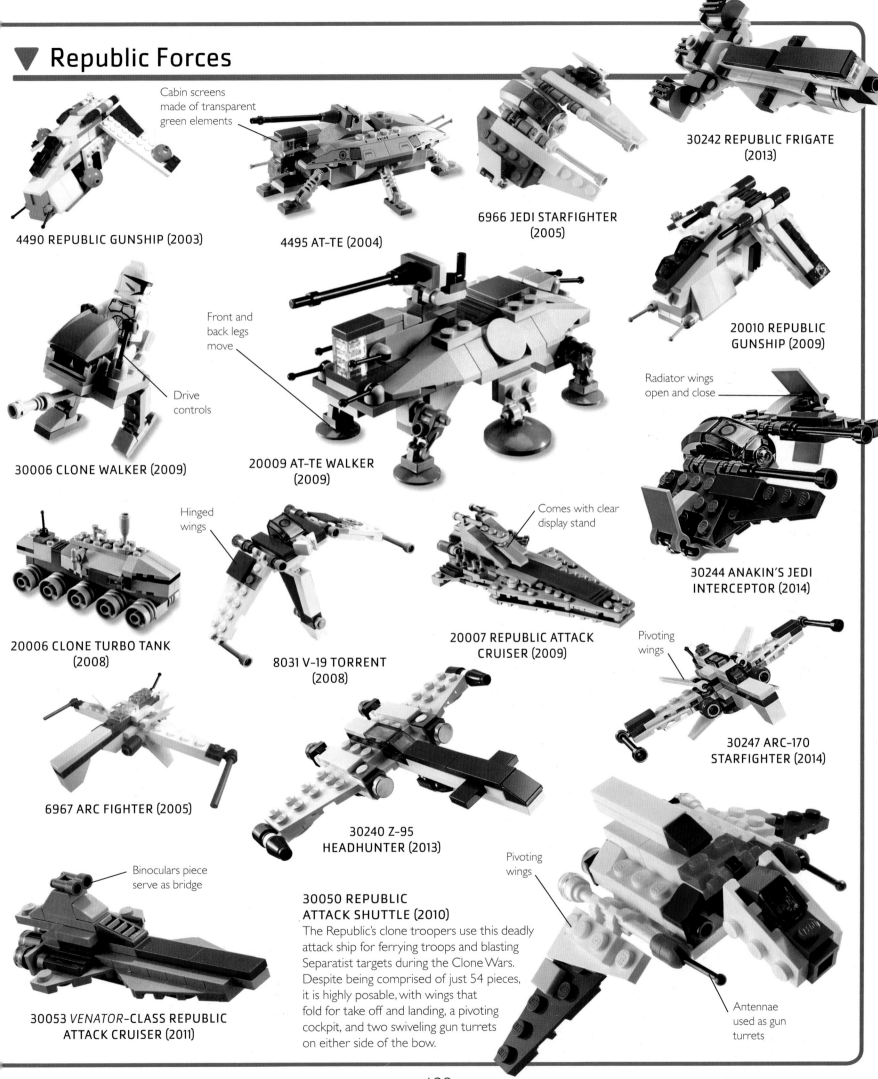

Cabin screens made of transparent green elements

4490 REPUBLIC GUNSHIP (2003)

4495 AT-TE (2004)

6966 JEDI STARFIGHTER (2005)

30242 REPUBLIC FRIGATE (2013)

Drive controls

30006 CLONE WALKER (2009)

Front and back legs move

20009 AT-TE WALKER (2009)

20010 REPUBLIC GUNSHIP (2009)

Radiator wings open and close

30244 ANAKIN'S JEDI INTERCEPTOR (2014)

Hinged wings

Comes with clear display stand

20006 CLONE TURBO TANK (2008)

8031 V-19 TORRENT (2008)

20007 REPUBLIC ATTACK CRUISER (2009)

Pivoting wings

30247 ARC-170 STARFIGHTER (2014)

6967 ARC FIGHTER (2005)

30240 Z-95 HEADHUNTER (2013)

Pivoting wings

Binoculars piece serve as bridge

30053 *VENATOR*-CLASS REPUBLIC ATTACK CRUISER (2011)

30050 REPUBLIC ATTACK SHUTTLE (2010)

The Republic's clone troopers use this deadly attack ship for ferrying troops and blasting Separatist targets during the Clone Wars. Despite being comprised of just 54 pieces, it is highly posable, with wings that fold for take off and landing, a pivoting cockpit, and two swiveling gun turrets on either side of the bow.

Antennae used as gun turrets

▼ Bounty Hunter Craft

Minifigure
pistol used
as cannon

**20021 BOUNTY HUNTER
ASSAULT GUNSHIP (2011)**

Rotating wings

Swiveling
cannon

20019 *SLAVE I* (2011)

▼ Imperial Vehicles

**30381 IMPERIAL
TIE FIGHTER (2018)**

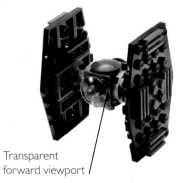

Transparent
forward viewport

8028 TIE FIGHTER (2008)

Laser cannon
made from
lightsaber blade

6965 TIE INTERCEPTOR (2004)

The TIE Interceptor is an exclusive for
certain retailers, including Japanese candy
company Kabaya (who sold it with
bubblegum!). X-Wing (set 6963) and
Slave I (6964) are also Kabaya exclusives.

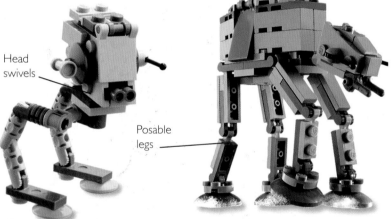

Head
swivels

Posable
legs

**30056 STAR
DESTROYER (2012)**

30054 AT-ST (2011)

20018 AT-AT WALKER (2010)

**30275 TIE ADVANCED
PROTOTYPE (2015)**

30005 IMPERIAL SPEEDER BIKE (2009)

The Imperial Speeder Bike, STAP, and
Clone Walker are all firsts: mini sets
that are minifigure-sized!

Ax becomes
a thruster!

**30274 AT-DP
(2015)**

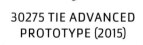

**30246 IMPERIAL
SHUTTLE (2014)**

Rebel Craft

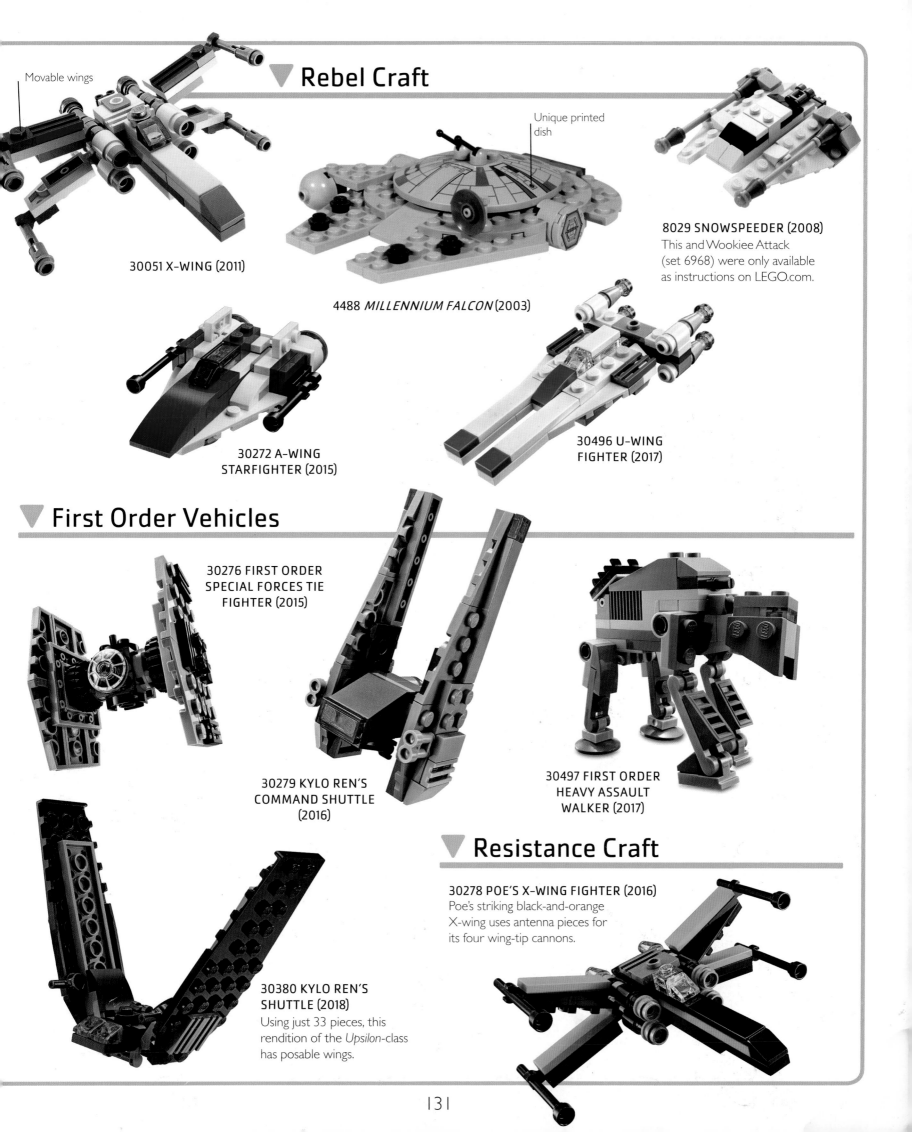

Movable wings

30051 X-WING (2011)

Unique printed dish

4488 *MILLENNIUM FALCON* (2003)

8029 SNOWSPEEDER (2008)
This and Wookiee Attack (set 6968) were only available as instructions on LEGO.com.

30272 A-WING STARFIGHTER (2015)

30496 U-WING FIGHTER (2017)

First Order Vehicles

30276 FIRST ORDER SPECIAL FORCES TIE FIGHTER (2015)

30279 KYLO REN'S COMMAND SHUTTLE (2016)

30497 FIRST ORDER HEAVY ASSAULT WALKER (2017)

30380 KYLO REN'S SHUTTLE (2018)
Using just 33 pieces, this rendition of the *Upsilon*-class has posable wings.

Resistance Craft

30278 POE'S X-WING FIGHTER (2016)
Poe's striking black-and-orange X-wing uses antenna pieces for its four wing-tip cannons.

LEGO® Technic

LEGO® Technic is an advanced building range that utilizes gears and interconnecting rods to create complex models with moving parts. In 2000, the LEGO Group released the first LEGO Technic *Star Wars* models, with a pit droid, battle droid, and destroyer droid (or droideka). Since then, new LEGO Technic sets have appeared for each Prequel Trilogy movie as well as the Classic Trilogy movies.

▼ Pit Droid

Utilizing elastic bands, the pit droid folds up into its compressed form (for storage). A tap on the nose makes the model stand up again.

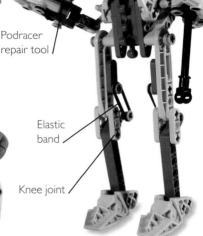

Podracer repair tool

Elastic band

Knee joint

COMPRESSED FORM

Head plate

Folded limb

Monocular receptor

Set name	Pit Droid	
Year 2000		Number 8000
Pieces 217		Source EP I

▼ Battle Droid

The battle droid measures over 13 in (33 cm) tall when standing and can fold up for transportation. When a dial on the back is turned, its arm reaches to the side of its backpack to grab a blaster. The model also comes with spare parts to convert it into a security droid or a battle droid.

Battle droid blaster

Set name	Battle Droid	
Year 2000		Number 8001
Pieces 328		Source EP I–III

▶ Destroyer Droid

The destroyer droid can fold up into a ball, then, when rolling, it will stop after a few turns and unfold into attack position, with its blasters raised—just like it does in the movie. The model utilizes elastic bands in its construction.

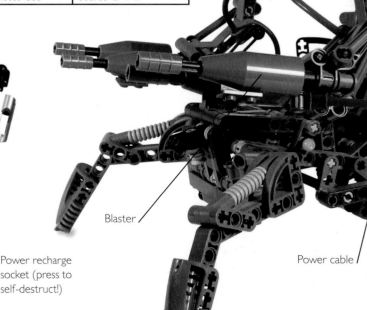

Sensor antenna

Blaster

Power cable

Foot claw

Set name	Destroyer Droid	
Year 2000		Number 8002
Pieces 553		Source EP I–III

▶ C-3PO

Vocoder plate

C-3PO stands 13 in (33 cm) tall when upright. Just like the scene in *The Empire Strikes Back* when a stormtrooper blasts C-3PO, the model's head and arms blow off (when the "belly button" socket is pressed).

Power recharge socket (press to self-destruct!)

Set name	C-3PO	
Year 2001		Number 8007
Pieces 339		Source EP I–VI

Stormtrooper

The 13-in- (33-cm-) tall stormtrooper carries a firing BlasTech E-11 rifle blaster. A wheel in the back allows the arms to move, so the model can aim the blaster—it could even hit C-3PO's socket to blow him up!

Set name	Stormtrooper	
Year	2001	Number 8008
Pieces	361	Source EP IV–VI

Knee joint

R2-D2

R2-D2 has a rotating dome and, when the front is pressed, his third leg extends for stability (the other two drive treads also roll). A lever mechanism at the back of the model operates one of R2-D2's utility/repair arms.

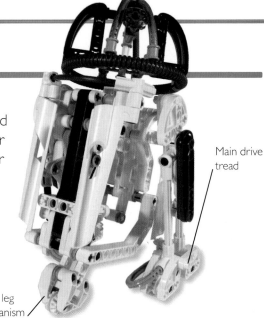

Main drive tread

Set name	R2-D2	
Year	2002	Number 8009
Pieces	242	Source EP I–VI

Third leg mechanism

Darth Vader

The LEGO Technic model of Darth Vader is armed with his lightsaber, which the figure's hands can grasp and hold. The lightsaber can be raised and lowered using a lever in the back of the model. The cape is made from real cloth.

Set name	Darth Vader	
Year	2002	Number 8010
Pieces	400	Source EP III–VI

Sith red eyes

Real fabric cape

Jango Fett

All Jango Fett's limbs and digits (and antenna) are moveable, and a missile can be launched from the jetpack when the model is leaned forward.

Set name	Jango Fett	
Year	2002	Number 8011
Pieces	429	Source EP II

Blaster

Super Battle Droid

The super battle droid's wrist blasters can be raised and lowered using a lever on the back of the model. The model uses BIONICLE® parts for extra posability.

Set name	Super Battle Droid	
Year	2002	Number 8012
Pieces	381	Source EP II & III

Eye stalks

All limbs are posable

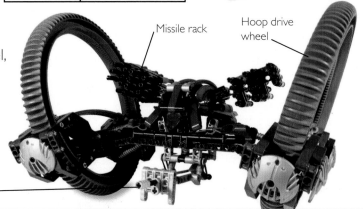

Wrist blaster

BRICK FACTS

In 2008, a LEGO Technic model of General Grievous was issued as an Ultimate Collector's Set (set 10186). Unusually, it consisted of a mix of regular LEGO bricks alongside LEGO Technic pieces.

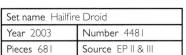

Hailfire Droid

This sturdy model of the hailfire droid rolls on its giant hoop wheels. The central blaster gun snaps into place and flick-fires missiles. The model, which is not packaged as a LEGO Technic set, is in proportion to LEGO *Star Wars* minifigures.

Set name	Hailfire Droid	
Year	2003	Number 4481
Pieces	681	Source EP II & III

Missile rack

Hoop drive wheel

Flick-firing blaster gun

Flexible lightsaber blade piece

Printed battle-damage detail

Buildable Figures

Designed to stand up to rough-and-ready action play, large-scale LEGO *Star Wars* buildable figures hit the shelves in 2015. Built using ball-and-socket connections rather than traditional LEGO bricks, each figure is infinitely posable for play and display, and many have mechanical arm movements and firing weapons for full-on battle functionality.

◄ Obi-Wan Kenobi

With a stylized beard and modified clone armor, this buildable figure is based on General Kenobi's appearance in *Star Wars: The Clone Wars*. He stands ready for battle with General Grievous (set 75112), whose four-armed figure was released at the same time.

Set name Obi-Wan Kenobi	
Year 2015	Number 75109
Pieces 83	Source CW

Exclusive fabric cape

Antenna is a minifigure fencing sword

Thin arms are buildable figure lightsaber hilt pieces

► Darth Vader

Standing more than 11 in (28 cm) tall, the Dark Lord of the Sith towers above most other buildable figures—and is seven times taller than his minifigure equivalent! This updated Vader figure from 2018 has a creepy white face beneath his mask.

INTERIOR VIEW

Set name Darth Vader	
Year 2018	Number 75534
Piece 168	Source EP VI

Unique helmet piece

▲ K-2SO

One of six buildable figures released to tie-in with *Rogue One: A Star Wars Story*, the distinctive rebel droid K-2SO features an adjustable arm-swinging battle function, operated by a wheel built into his back.

Set name K-2SO	
Year 2016	Number 75120
Pieces 169	Source R1

Limbs can angle in any direction

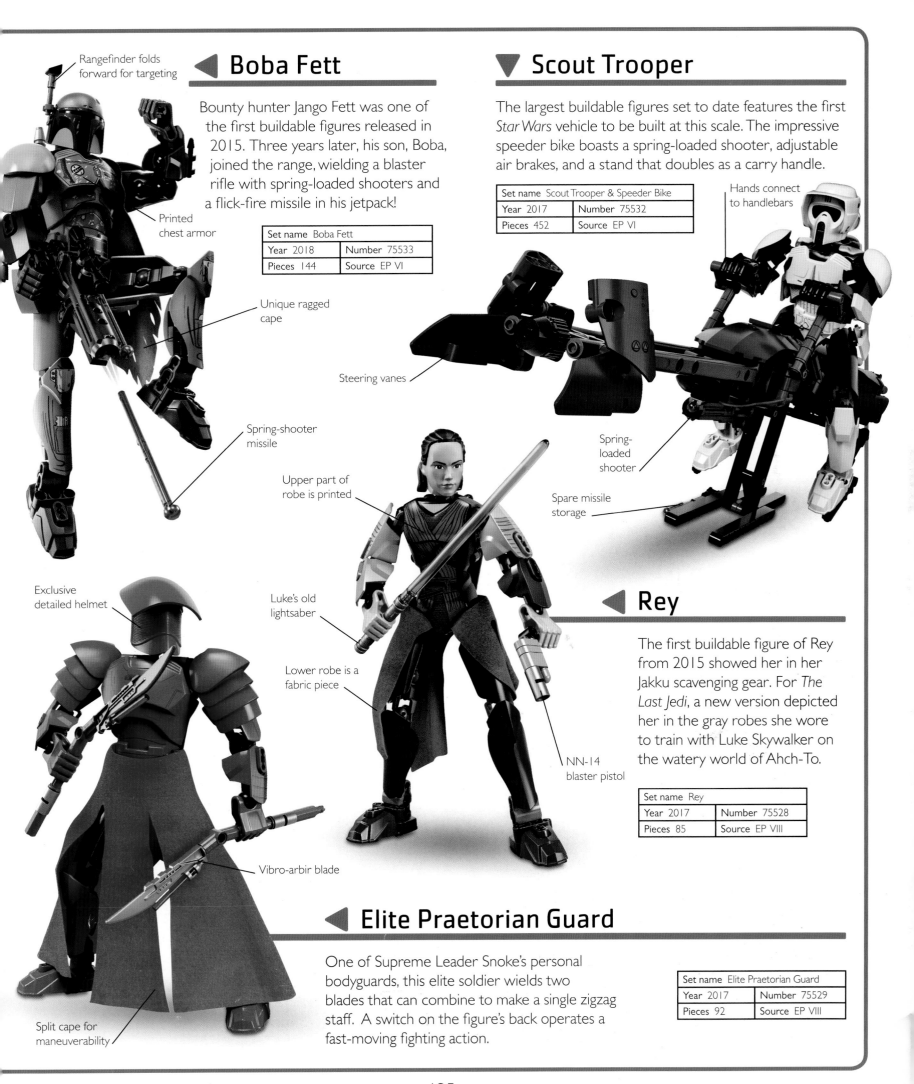

◀ Boba Fett

Bounty hunter Jango Fett was one of the first buildable figures released in 2015. Three years later, his son, Boba, joined the range, wielding a blaster rifle with spring-loaded shooters and a flick-fire missile in his jetpack!

Rangefinder folds forward for targeting

Printed chest armor

Unique ragged cape

Spring-shooter missile

Set name	Boba Fett	
Year 2018		Number 75533
Pieces 144		Source EP VI

▼ Scout Trooper

The largest buildable figures set to date features the first *Star Wars* vehicle to be built at this scale. The impressive speeder bike boasts a spring-loaded shooter, adjustable air brakes, and a stand that doubles as a carry handle.

Set name	Scout Trooper & Speeder Bike	
Year 2017		Number 75532
Pieces 452		Source EP VI

Hands connect to handlebars

Steering vanes

Spring-loaded shooter

Spare missile storage

Upper part of robe is printed

Luke's old lightsaber

Lower robe is a fabric piece

NN-14 blaster pistol

◀ Rey

The first buildable figure of Rey from 2015 showed her in her Jakku scavenging gear. For *The Last Jedi*, a new version depicted her in the gray robes she wore to train with Luke Skywalker on the watery world of Ahch-To.

Set name	Rey	
Year 2017		Number 75528
Pieces 85		Source EP VIII

Exclusive detailed helmet

Split cape for maneuverability

Vibro-arbir blade

◀ Elite Praetorian Guard

One of Supreme Leader Snoke's personal bodyguards, this elite soldier wields two blades that can combine to make a single zigzag staff. A switch on the figure's back operates a fast-moving fighting action.

Set name	Elite Praetorian Guard	
Year 2017		Number 75529
Pieces 92		Source EP VIII

Ultimate Collector Series

The LEGO Group has issued a small number of highly detailed *Star Wars* models called Ultimate Collector Series (or UCS). Intended for older builders and primarily for display, each set includes a collector's card and, in many cases, a display stand. Most are not scaled for minifigures, though some, such as *Millennium Falcon*, are minifigure-scaled.

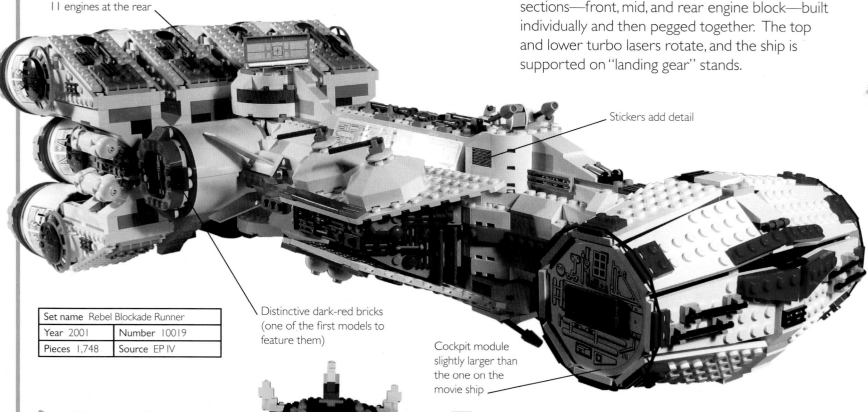

11 engines at the rear

Distinctive dark-red bricks (one of the first models to feature them)

Set name	Rebel Blockade Runner	
Year 2001	Number 10019	
Pieces 1,748	Source EP IV	

▼ *Tantive IV*

Princess Leia Organa's consular starship, *Tantive IV* (otherwise known as the *Blockade Runner*), is one of the largest LEGO Ultimate Collector sets, at over 2 ft (60 cm) long and almost 1 ft (30 cm) wide. The highly detailed model is made up of separate sections—front, mid, and rear engine block—built individually and then pegged together. The top and lower turbo lasers rotate, and the ship is supported on "landing gear" stands.

Stickers add detail

Cockpit module slightly larger than the one on the movie ship

▶ Darth Maul

The 18-in- (45-cm-) tall bust of Sith apprentice Darth Maul has to be constructed from the bottom up and utilizes building techniques employed on expert models at LEGOLAND® Parks. This remarkably detailed model weighs almost 9 lb (4 kg).

Bust can be supported on a special stand

Menacing eyes

Set name	Darth Maul	
Year 2001	Number 10018	
Pieces 1,868	Source EP I	

▼ Naboo Starfighter

The iconic yellow Naboo starfighter has fewer bricks than other UCSs, but among them are unique chrome and curved elements, which give the finished model a sleek look. The 11½-in- (29-cm-) long model features twin laser cannons, a proton torpedo launch tube, and R2-D2, as well as a display stand and plaque.

R2-D2 (dome only)

Sticker elements

Chrome element

Sleek finial

Set name	Naboo Starfighter	
Year 2002	Number 10026	
Pieces 187	Source EP I	

Imperial Star Destroyer

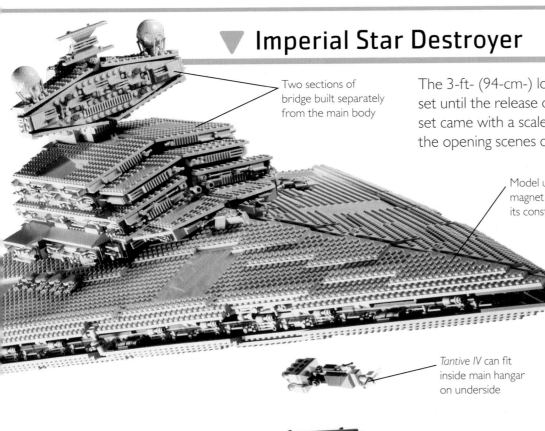

Two sections of bridge built separately from the main body

The 3-ft- (94-cm-) long Star Destroyer was the largest UCS set until the release of Death Star II (set 10143). The former set came with a scaled model of the *Tantive IV* to recreate the opening scenes of *Star Wars: Episode IV A New Hope*.

Model uses a magnet system in its construction

Tantive IV can fit inside main hangar on underside

Set name Imperial Star Destroyer	
Year 2002	Number 10030
Pieces 3,104	Source EP IV–VI

Yoda

This sculptural bust of Jedi Grand Master Yoda is an impressive 14 in (35.5 cm) tall. Like the Darth Maul bust, Yoda is built in layers from the bottom upward: the instructions show a bird's-eye view from above rather than a three-dimensional view. When complete, the head can be rotated to different positions.

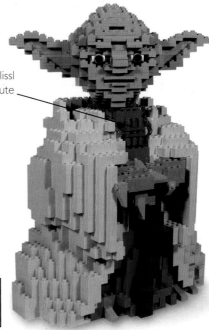

Blissl flute

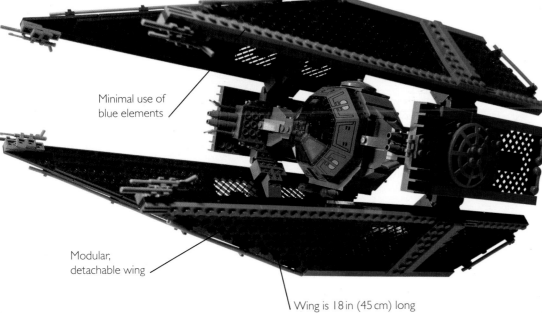

Minimal use of blue elements

Modular, detachable wing

Wing is 18 in (45 cm) long

Set name Yoda	
Year 2002	Number 7194
Pieces 1,075	Source EP I, II, III, V, VI

TIE Interceptor

The TIE interceptor is captured accurately, with its long dagger-like wings (which can be folded to lie flat) and a hinged cockpit with a detailed interior featuring a pilot seat, controls, a HUD (heads-up display or transparent data screen), and several monitor screens. The model sits on an adjustable stand, which allows it to be displayed in a variety of positions.

Set name TIE Interceptor	
Year 2000	Number 7181
Pieces 703	Source EP VI

BRICK FACTS

The year 2000 saw the release of a UCS X-Wing Fighter (set 7191) with 1,304 pieces, a gearbox to operate the S-foils, moving controls in the cockpit, and an R2-D2 minifigure. The model is nearly 2 ft (60 cm) long, with a wingspan of 18 in (45.5 cm).

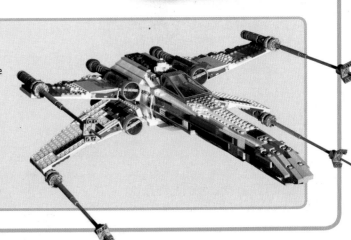

Imperial AT-ST

The Imperial AT-ST, or chicken walker, stands over 16½in (42 cm) tall and is constructed from LEGO bricks and LEGO Technic elements. The cockpit interior features no details, although the model has rotating weapons, an opening pilot hatch and moving window panels.

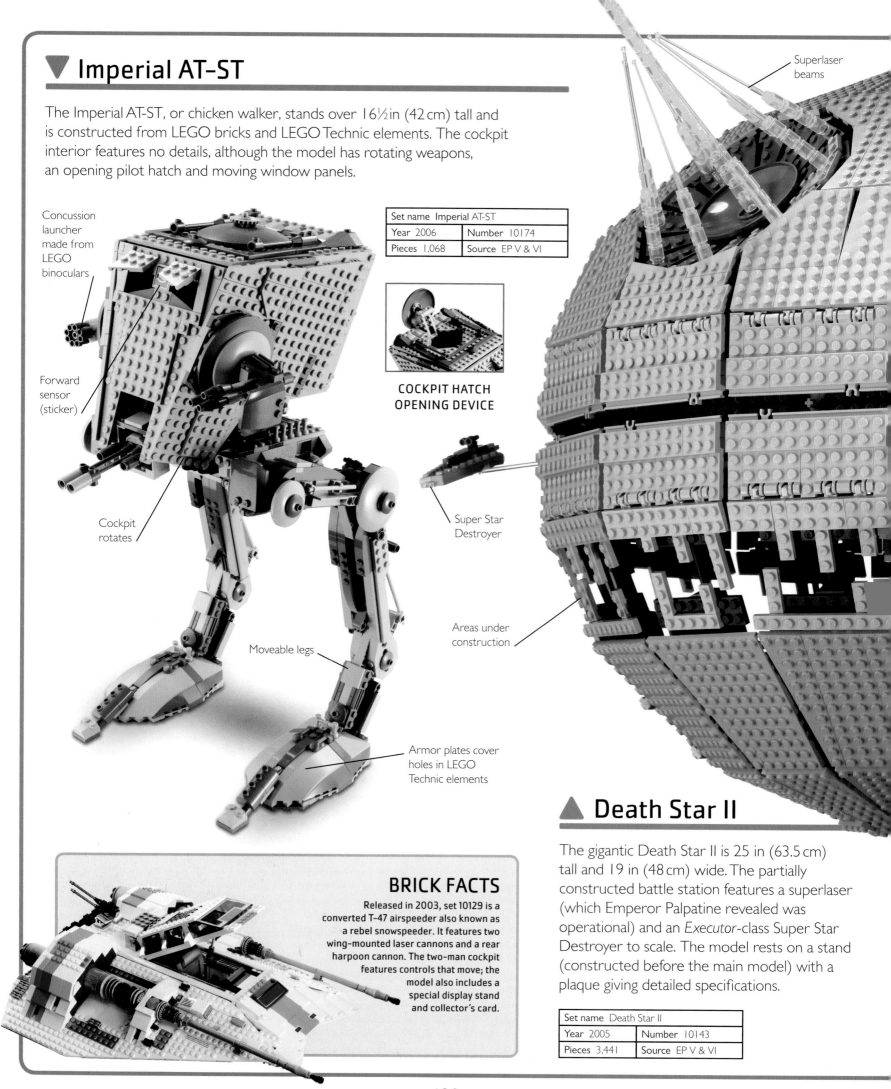

Concussion launcher made from LEGO binoculars

Forward sensor (sticker)

Cockpit rotates

Moveable legs

Armor plates cover holes in LEGO Technic elements

COCKPIT HATCH OPENING DEVICE

Super Star Destroyer

Areas under construction

Superlaser beams

Set name	Imperial AT-ST		
Year	2006	Number	10174
Pieces	1,068	Source	EP V & VI

BRICK FACTS

Released in 2003, set 10129 is a converted T-47 airspeeder also known as a rebel snowspeeder. It features two wing-mounted laser cannons and a rear harpoon cannon. The two-man cockpit features controls that move; the model also includes a special display stand and collector's card.

Death Star II

The gigantic Death Star II is 25 in (63.5 cm) tall and 19 in (48 cm) wide. The partially constructed battle station features a superlaser (which Emperor Palpatine revealed was operational) and an *Executor*-class Super Star Destroyer to scale. The model rests on a stand (constructed before the main model) with a plaque giving detailed specifications.

Set name	Death Star II		
Year	2005	Number	10143
Pieces	3,441	Source	EP V & VI

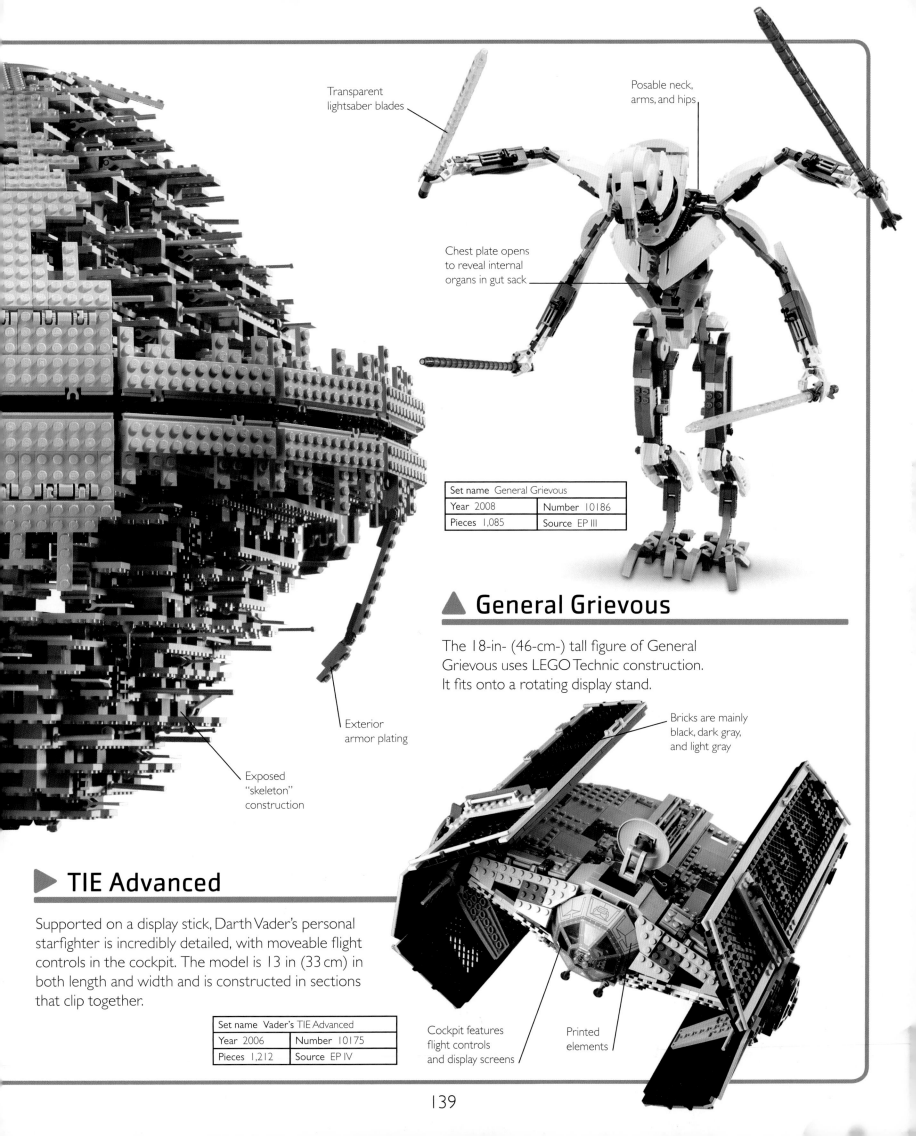

Transparent
lightsaber blades

Posable neck,
arms, and hips

Chest plate opens
to reveal internal
organs in gut sack

Set name General Grievous

Year 2008	Number 10186
Pieces 1,085	Source EP III

▲ General Grievous

The 18-in- (46-cm-) tall figure of General
Grievous uses LEGO Technic construction.
It fits onto a rotating display stand.

Exterior
armor plating

Exposed
"skeleton"
construction

Bricks are mainly
black, dark gray,
and light gray

▶ TIE Advanced

Supported on a display stick, Darth Vader's personal
starfighter is incredibly detailed, with moveable flight
controls in the cockpit. The model is 13 in (33 cm) in
both length and width and is constructed in sections
that clip together.

Set name Vader's TIE Advanced	
Year 2006	Number 10175
Pieces 1,212	Source EP IV

Cockpit features
flight controls
and display screens

Printed
elements

Imperial Shuttle

The *Lambda*-class shuttle that carries Luke Skywalker from Endor to the Death Star measures 22½in (57 cm) wide with the wings unfolded and 28in (71 cm) tall on its display stand. Keys at the rear raise and lower the wings, and the craft has landing gear that attaches to the bottom of the hull.

Navigation light

Reactor heat sink

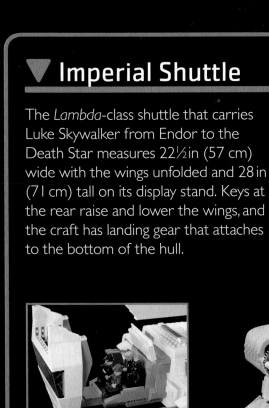

OPEN COCKPIT

Wings fold up for landing

Rotating dual cannons

Cockpit holds four minifigures

Set name	Imperial Shuttle	
Year	2010	Number 10212
Pieces	2,503	Source EP VI

Obi-Wan's Jedi Starfighter

Obi-Wan Kenobi pursues bounty hunters across the galaxy in his Delta-7 *Aethersprite*-class light interceptor, which is 18½in (47 cm) long and 8½in (22 cm) wide when built. The Jedi starfighter has twin laser cannons and a fully detailed cockpit interior. The domed head of astromech droid R4-P17 attaches to the wing and rotates. The fighter also comes with a display stand and plaque.

Set name	Obi-Wan's Jedi Starfighter	
Year	2010	Number 10215
Pieces	676	Source EP II

Opening cockpit

Laser cannons

Communications transceiver

R4-P17

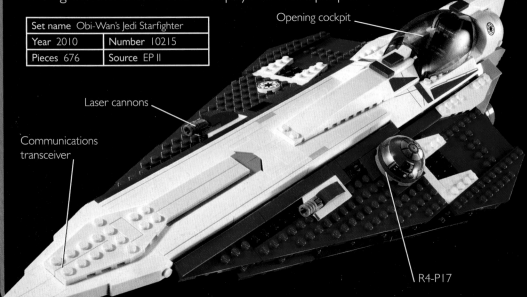

Super Star Destroyer

The first-ever Super Star Destroyer produced by the LEGO Group is also the largest UCS, measuring 50in (124.5 cm) from bow to stern and weighing nearly 8lb (3.6 kg). A section of the fuselage lifts up to reveal a command center where Darth Vader meets with bounty hunters searching for the *Millennium Falcon* (and takes orders from a unique, hand-held hologram of the Emperor). A scaled version of the Imperial Star Destroyer connects to the hull with a clear rod.

Armored hull plates

Display stand

BOTTOM VIEW

Heavy laser cannon

Squadron markings

B-Wing Starfighter

A powerful starfighter used by the rebels at the Battle of Endor, this B-wing measures 26in (66 cm) wide and 15in (38 cm) high. Its cockpit rotates and remains level in flight mode and its wings fold for take off and landing. Its designer decided on the scale by searching for parts for the cockpit, settling on motorcycle wheels and treads originally used in a LEGO bulldozer set from the 1970s.

Ion cannon

Set name	B-Wing Starfighter	
Year	2012	Number 10227
Pieces	1,487	Source VI

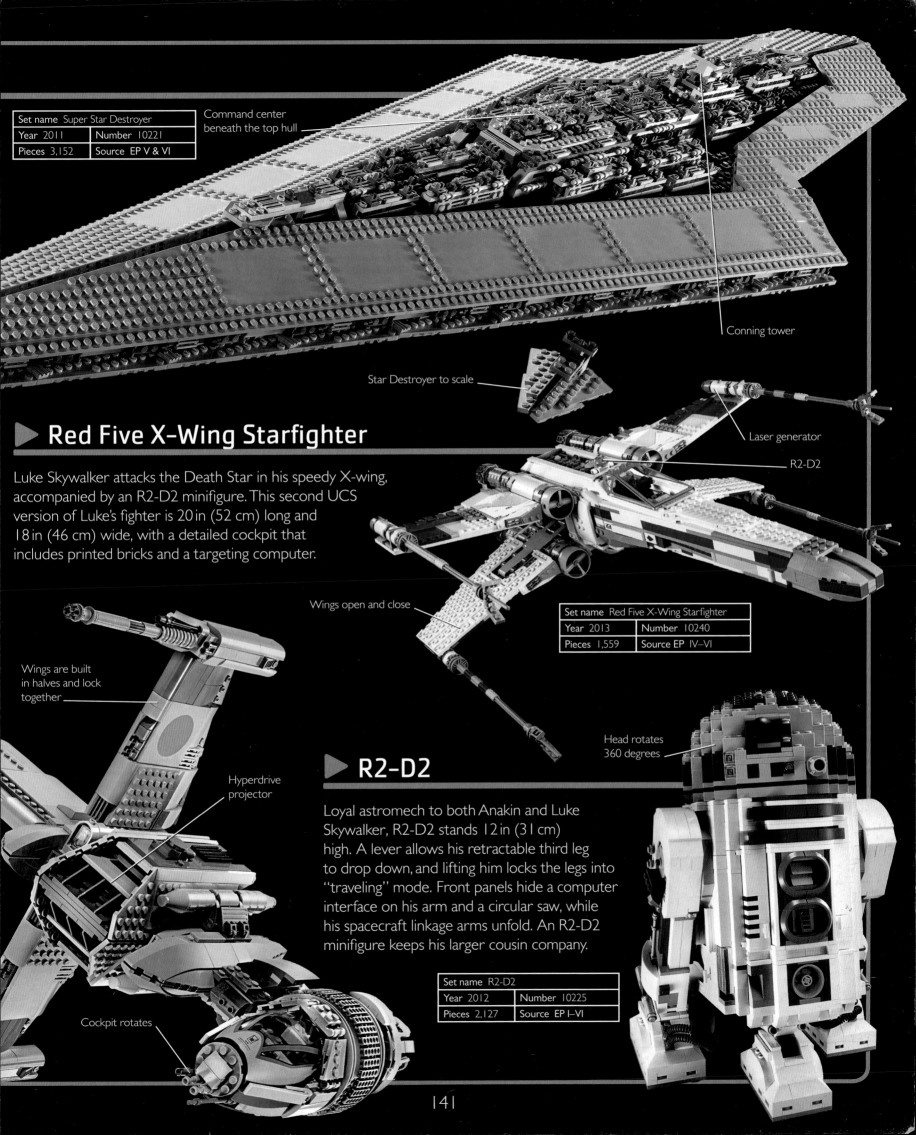

Set name	Super Star Destroyer	
Year 2011	Number 10221	
Pieces 3,152	Source EP V & VI	

Command center
beneath the top hull

Conning tower

Star Destroyer to scale

Laser generator

R2-D2

Red Five X-Wing Starfighter

Luke Skywalker attacks the Death Star in his speedy X-wing, accompanied by an R2-D2 minifigure. This second UCS version of Luke's fighter is 20 in (52 cm) long and 18 in (46 cm) wide, with a detailed cockpit that includes printed bricks and a targeting computer.

Wings open and close

Set name	Red Five X-Wing Starfighter	
Year 2013	Number 10240	
Pieces 1,559	Source EP IV–VI	

Wings are built
in halves and lock
together

Hyperdrive
projector

Head rotates
360 degrees

R2-D2

Loyal astromech to both Anakin and Luke Skywalker, R2-D2 stands 12 in (31 cm) high. A lever allows his retractable third leg to drop down, and lifting him locks the legs into "traveling" mode. Front panels hide a computer interface on his arm and a circular saw, while his spacecraft linkage arms unfold. An R2-D2 minifigure keeps his larger cousin company.

Set name	R2-D2	
Year 2012	Number 10225	
Pieces 2,127	Source EP I–VI	

Cockpit rotates

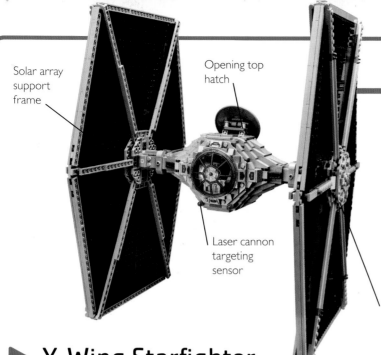

Solar array support frame

Opening top hatch

Laser cannon targeting sensor

◀ TIE Fighter

Standing 18½ in (47 cm) tall, the UCS TIE Fighter rotates on its display stand so it can be admired from all angles without picking it up. It is also guarded by an exclusive TIE pilot minifigure.

Set name TIE Fighter	
Year 2015	Number 75095
Pieces 1,685	Source EP IV

EXCLUSIVE TIE PILOT

Solar energy collector

▶ Y-Wing Starfighter

With 494 more pieces than the first UCS Y-wing, Dutch Vander's ship is based on the vessel seen in *Rogue One: A Star Wars Story*, complete with astromech navigator R2-BHD.

Set name Y-Wing Starfighter	
Year 2018	Number 75181
Pieces 1,967	Source R1

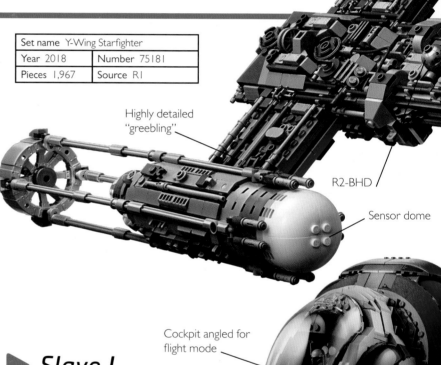

Highly detailed "greebling"

R2-BHD

Sensor dome

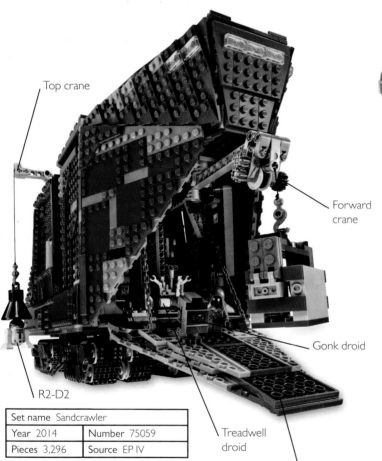

Top crane

Forward crane

Gonk droid

R2-D2

Treadwell droid

Entry ramp

Set name Sandcrawler	
Year 2014	Number 75059
Pieces 3,296	Source EP IV

▲ Sandcrawler

Measuring 19 in (48 cm) long, the UCS version of the Jawas' rolling home comes with two working cranes, opening top and side panels, working steering, a chain-operated entry ramp, and an array of characterful droids!

Cockpit angled for flight mode

▶ *Slave I*

The UCS *Slave I* is the fifth minifigure-scale version of the famous bounty-hunting ship, and is by far the largest. It boasts a rotating cockpit, adjustable wings, hidden weapon compartments, and an opening cargo hold with space to store Han Solo frozen in carbonite.

Set name *Slave I*	
Year 2015	Number 75060
Pieces 1,996	Source EP V

Rotating twin blaster cannon

Weapons hatch

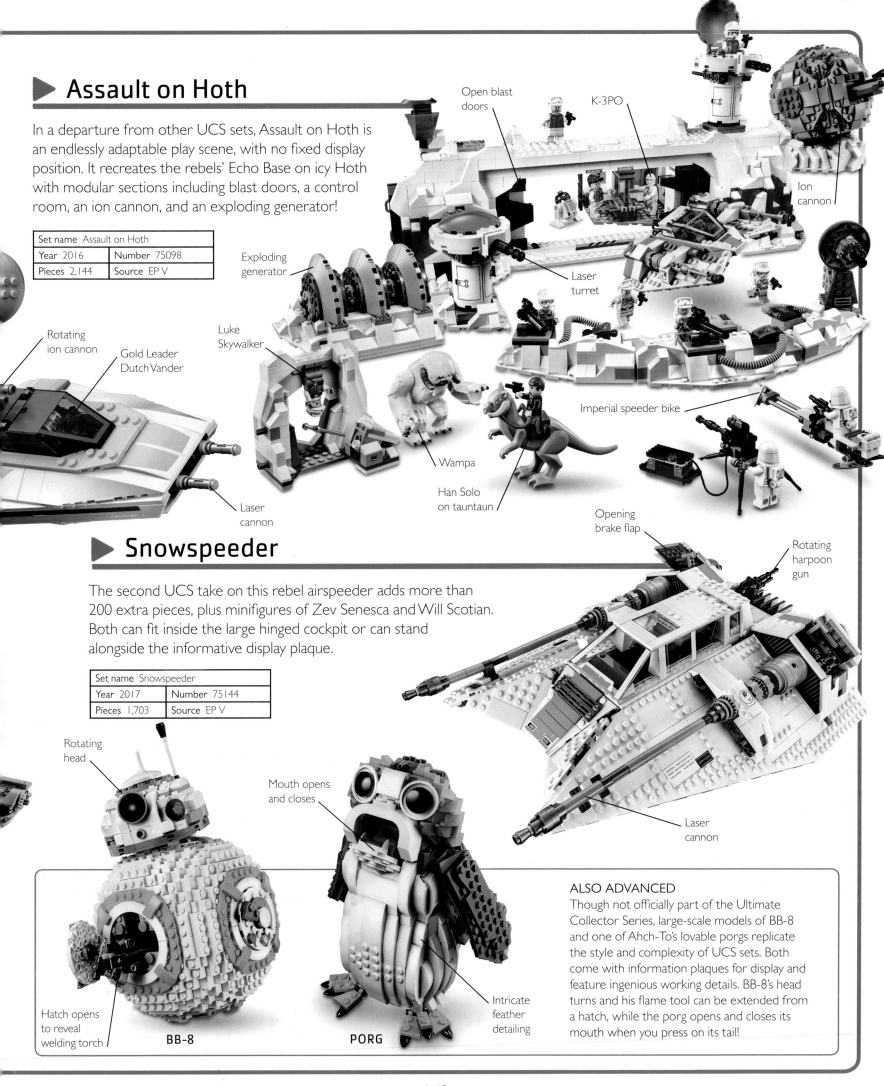

Assault on Hoth

In a departure from other UCS sets, Assault on Hoth is an endlessly adaptable play scene, with no fixed display position. It recreates the rebels' Echo Base on icy Hoth with modular sections including blast doors, a control room, an ion cannon, and an exploding generator!

Set name	Assault on Hoth	
Year	2016	Number 75098
Pieces	2,144	Source EP V

Open blast doors

K-3PO

Ion cannon

Rotating ion cannon

Gold Leader Dutch Vander

Exploding generator

Luke Skywalker

Laser turret

Wampa

Han Solo on tauntaun

Imperial speeder bike

Laser cannon

Snowspeeder

The second UCS take on this rebel airspeeder adds more than 200 extra pieces, plus minifigures of Zev Senesca and Will Scotian. Both can fit inside the large hinged cockpit or can stand alongside the informative display plaque.

Set name	Snowspeeder	
Year	2017	Number 75144
Pieces	1,703	Source EP V

Opening brake flap

Rotating harpoon gun

Laser cannon

Rotating head

Mouth opens and closes

Hatch opens to reveal welding torch

BB-8

Intricate feather detailing

PORG

ALSO ADVANCED

Though not officially part of the Ultimate Collector Series, large-scale models of BB-8 and one of Ahch-To's lovable porgs replicate the style and complexity of UCS sets. Both come with information plaques for display and feature ingenious working details. BB-8's head turns and his flame tool can be extended from a hatch, while the porg opens and closes its mouth when you press on its tail!

Seasonal Sets

Since 2011, the LEGO Group has released an annual seasonal set offering minifigures and parts for making micro sets of *Star Wars* vehicles. Children (or adults) open a window for each day of Advent for the countdown to Christmas, revealing a toy. Each seasonal set has surprises, such as a Christmas tree or a unique minifigure or two, dressed in garb appropriate for the holiday season.

BRICK FACTS
Attendees of the 2011 San Diego Comic-Con could take home that year's advent calendar in special packaging telling them to open it by December 1. Only 1,000 were made.

▼ 2011 Advent Calendar

The countdown to Christmas 2011 began for LEGO fans with a miniature Republic cruiser and ended with Yoda resplendent in a Santa costume. Other highlights included a Republic gunship with movable wings, tools and weapons racks, and a Christmas tree from a galaxy far, far away. The calendar art shows Yoda and a rebel pilot watching the Battle of Endor unfold around them.

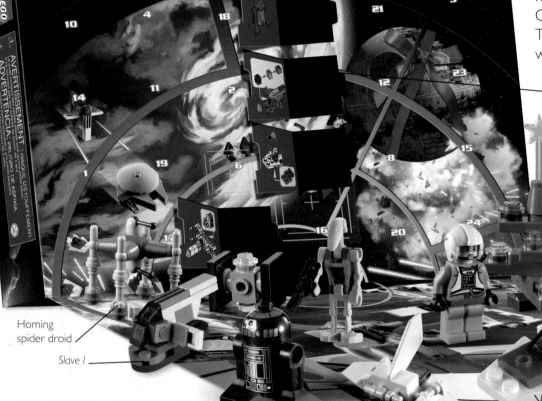

Calendar window, complete with building instructions

Intergalactic Christmas tree

TIE Fighter pilot

Clone pilot

Homing spider droid

Slave I

R2-Q5

A-wing

Chewbacca with bowcaster

Set name	2011 Advent Calendar	
Year	2011	Number 7958
Pieces	266	Source EP I–VI

FESTIVE FIGURES
Throughout the years, LEGO fans have delighted in seeing their favorite minifigures donned in Christmas gear, not least Chewbacca looking merry covered in snow and C-3PO dressed as Santa with a sack of goodies.

YODA
Feeling festive, you are. Yoda carries a heavy sack of presents to deliver to the younglings.

DARTH MAUL
Even Sith celebrate Christmas! Darth Maul donned a Santa suit complete with a fur-lined hood for the season.

DARTH VADER
Nothing feels more festive then when Vader says "I am your Father ... Christmas." Don't be naughty!

C-3PO
Fluent in over seven million forms of communication, C-3PO is the perfect droid to deliver gifts.

CHEWBACCA
Chewie loves snow and is covered in it! His bowcaster shoots snowballs and he is carrying a mini Christmas tree.

Snowspeeder

TIE fighter

AAT

Lambda-class shuttle

Rebel defenses

General Rieekan

Republic equipment stand

2014 Advent Calendar

Including three festive—and exclusive—minifigures, fans were in for a treat in December 2014. The season began with an AAT and ended with one of the exclusives—Darth Vader dressed up as Father Christmas. The other two minifigures are a clone trooper with a Santa hat, who is behind door number four, and a festive astromech, which is the build on day 22. The box art reimagines the Battle of Hoth as a snowball fight!

Set name	2014 Advent Calendar	
Year 2014		Number 75056
Pieces 274		Source EP I–VI, CW

2017 Advent Calendar

The theme for this LEGO *Star Wars* seasonal set is *Star Wars*: Episode VII *The Force Awakens*, and the box art has a decorated Jakku and Starkiller Base with festive fun. For this year, micro sets include a Luggabeast, Krennic's shuttle, Rey's speeder, and the *Ghost*. BB-8 has donned a festive hat and is on his favorite blue snowboard for the holiday.

Krennic's shuttle

Blaster cannon

AAL

AT-DP

Luggabeast

First Order snow blower

BB-8 on a snowboard

Set name	2017 Advent Calendar	
Year 2017		Number 75184
Pieces 309		Source EP I–VII, R1, *Rebels*

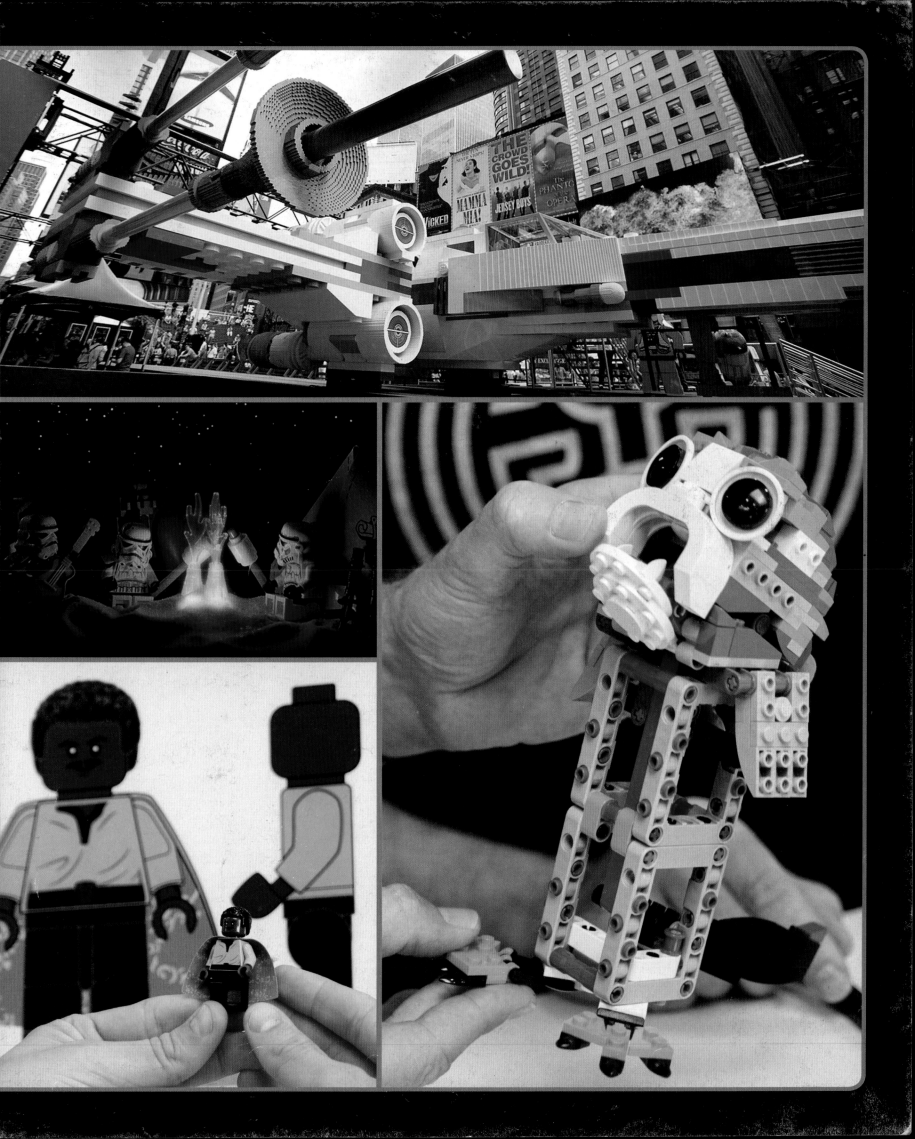

Meet the Team

Since 1999, the LEGO Group has been bringing the *Star Wars*™ galaxy to life in an ever-expanding and imaginative world of LEGO® bricks!

Every brick has been chosen carefully by the LEGO® *Star Wars*™ design team who use their creativity and the latest technology to produce incredible builds.

Let's take a look behind the scenes to discover some of the secrets behind the success of 20 awesome years of LEGO *Star Wars*. LEGO Creative Director Jens Kronvold Frederiksen and Design Master Kurt Kristiansen reveal the ideas, steps, processes, and teamwork behind your favorite LEGO *Star Wars* sets.

"Sets based on locations need to be iconic scenes from the movies, with key characters and memorable moments."

Jens Kronvold Frederiksen

The LEGO *Star Wars* design team. Standing from left to right: Jens Kronvold Frederiksen (Creative Director), César Carvalhosa Soares (Designer), Madison Andrew O'Neil (Graphic Designer), Henrik Andersen (Senior Designer), Kurt Kristiansen (Design Master), Niels Mølgård Frederiksen (Designer), Aaron Douglas Anderson (Designer). **Sitting on the bench from left to right:** Michael Lee Stockwell (Design Manager), Martin Fink (Graphic Designer), Hans Burkhard Schlömer (Designer), Christian Minick Vonsild (Senior Designer), Jan Neergaard Olesen (Designer).

▼ Starting Out

A LEGO *Star Wars* set starts life with a discussion between LEGO designers and Lucasfilm to decide what the location, vehicle, or minifigure will be. For models taken from new movies, the conversation starts many months ahead of the movie's release so the models can be ready in time. For models based on the original trilogy, the LEGO *Star Wars* team listens to suggestions from fans. Sometimes, a set or minifigure is updated with improvements or new features every three to four years.

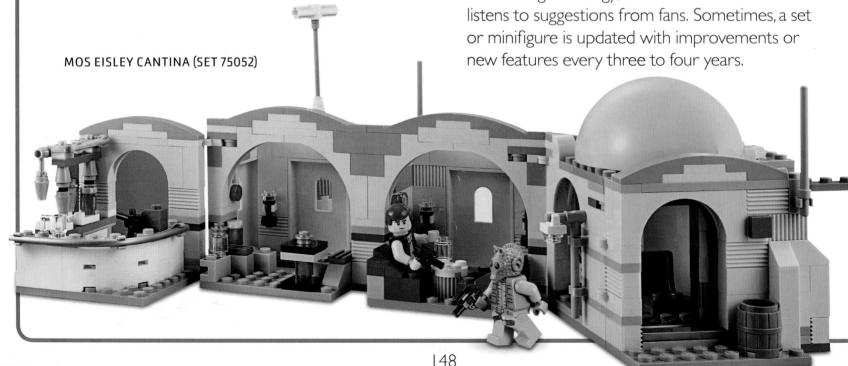

MOS EISLEY CANTINA (SET 75052)

▼ Sketching and Drafting

Often, the designers make sketches of the models before they start building with bricks. Or they may draft the simple model on a computer.

The designers then experiment with the bricks to develop special effects and features, such as the layering of bricks to create the effect of feathers on the Porg.

"Some of us like to start with a drawing to get it right in our own head and see how it will work."

Kurt Kristiansen

This Porg set started out as a simple sketch on a sticky note.

Large eyes and open jaw reflect the Porg's alarmed character

Bricks are layered to look like feathers

PORG (SET 75230)

Jens and Kurt discuss the Porg model.

▼ Feedback from Fans

The LEGO *Star Wars* team asks children to test the models at various stages of the design process. This helps the team to decide which products to develop and what features to include. They get direct feedback by seeing how the children play with the models. If one is left standing in the corner, they won't move forward with it.

The dewback from the Microfighters series is a great example of a model that's popular with children. It's simple and brick-built with movable parts. It looks friendly and kids love it.

Checking the dewback's movable head against the 3D draft.

**ESCAPE POD VS DEWBACK
(SET 75228)**

"It is really important to us to get direct feedback from kids on the models."

Kurt Kristiansen

▼ Using New Technology

Some models are more of a technical challenge than others. Enfys Nest's elaborate helmet, for example, was created with two different types of plastic: one hard for the head part and one softer for the spikes. LEGO technology is developing all the time.

Distinctive spikes on helmet

**ENFYS NEST
(SET 75215)**

A line-up of minifigure head and helmet molds.

▼ True to the Movies

To make the models as accurate as possible, the LEGO *Star Wars* designers look closely at movie stills and on-set photos supplied by Lucasfilm.

Sometimes models, such as the Cloud-Rider Swoop Bikes from the *Solo* movie, are made at the same time as the movies. The LEGO *Star Wars* team and Lucasfilm have to keep closely in touch to make sure the details of the LEGO models match the vehicles in the films. Sometimes, the LEGO designers have an exciting chance to invent the insides of vehicles that are only seen from the outside in the movies.

When creating the LEGO *Star Wars* minifigures, the designers keep in mind the appearance and characteristics of the actors playing the roles. They try to make the minifigures as lifelike as possible, even down to details such as the textures and patterns of Lando Calrissian's cape.

Each LEGO *Star Wars* minifigure captures the personality of the on-screen character.

CLOUD-RIDER SWOOP BIKES (SET 75215)

LANDO CALRISSIAN (SET 75222)

FINN IN BACTA SUIT

The exclusive minifigure included with DK's LEGO® *Star Wars*™ *Visual Dictionary: New Edition* is Finn in his bacta suit from *Star Wars: The Last Jedi.* According to Jens and Kurt, "Finn in his bacta suit was fun to make because it was based on a humorous moment in the movie."

Checking the accuracy of the model against the movie-set vehicle.

▼ 20 Years of LEGO *Star Wars*

Over the past 20 years there have been around 500 LEGO *Star Wars* sets created. What have been the personal highlights for the LEGO *Star Wars* designers? For Kurt, it was designing all the different rooms and creatures for Jabba's Palace and also the challenge of creating the BB-8 model. The first *Millennium Falcon* UCS was a highlight for Jens, as were the Death Star sets, which he thinks are a great family challenge because kids and parents can build them together.

DEATH STAR
(SET 75159)

BB-8 (SET 75187)

JABBA'S PALACE (SET 9516)
AND RANCOR PIT (SET 75005)

"A real highlight for me is to see a set you have designed sitting on a shelf in the store and to hear kids asking for it for Christmas!"

Kurt Kristiansen

MILLENNIUM FALCON
(SET 10179)

Celebrating the Anniversary

The LEGO *Star Wars* team chose popular, iconic sets to refresh for the 20th anniversary. Fan favorites, such as the Battle Packs with stormtroopers, were given an update for 2019. The 20th-anniversary minifigures feature five iconic *Star Wars* characters. Over the years they have had new elements, but they are based on the original 1999 minifigure print cards.

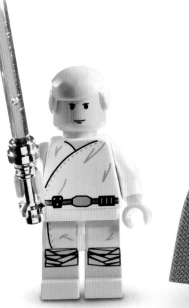

LUKE SKYWALKER
(1999)

LUKE SKYWALKER
(2018)

"To celebrate the 20th anniversary of LEGO® *Star Wars*™, we wanted to refresh classic models and ones that we knew fans would love."

Jens Kronvold Frederiksen

The Future ...

As to the future, the LEGO *Star Wars* team always keep fan requests at the front of their minds when they think about what's coming next. The team are actively involved in the LEGO *Star Wars* fan community and are able to understand first-hand what the fans want.

With so many exciting LEGO *Star Wars* sets available, it may appear that the team have covered everything! However, there are many more models from the ever-expanding *Star Wars* universe still waiting to be created. The designers also look for opportunities to sneak new minifigures into updated sets. One thing's for sure, there's a lot more to come from the LEGO *Star Wars* design team—watch this space!

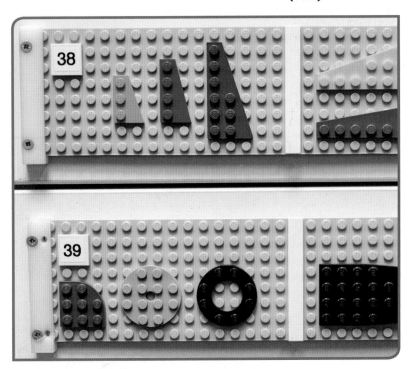

Drawers containing LEGO *Star Wars* bricks; what exciting future builds will the bricks be made into?

Promotional Pieces

All around the world, LEGO *Star Wars* fans get together in small venues and giant convention centers to learn the latest LEGO news, share their creations, and encourage fellow builders. The LEGO Group often attends these events to showcase new sets and interact with its enthusiastic builders and collectors. Loyal fans are often rewarded with exclusive LEGO *Star Wars* sets or minifigures—the space race to locate collectible promotional items is on!

To celebrate 30 years of the LEGO minifigure, 10,000 metallic gold C-3PO minifigures were randomly inserted into LEGO *Star Wars* sets in 2007. Even rarer are the five C-3PO minifigures made of solid 14kt gold! In 2010 Boba Fett joined the highest ranks of exclusivity when two solid bronze variants were released as part of a "May the Fourth" promotion. That year also saw 10,000 white Bobas given away at toy fairs and *Star Wars* Days.

▼ Life-Size X-Wing in Times Square

To celebrate the May 2013 launch of the new animated TV series *The Yoda Chronicles*, the LEGO Group unveiled a life-size X-wing (scaled for humans rather than minifigures) in Times Square, New York. The build is an exact replica of the X-Wing Starfighter (set 9493), magnified 42 times, and consisting of 5,335,200 LEGO bricks. It took a team of 32 builders 17,336 hours (about 4 months) to construct. The event also included a LEGO R2-D2 and X-wing pilot model ready for photo opportunities and a LEGO Yoda bearing a t-shirt with the slogan "NY I Love."

The X-wing builders had to make sure that their model, weighing 45,980 lb (20,856 kg), would be safe above the New York subway system!

The super-sized starfighter measures 11 ft (3.35 m) in height, 43 ft (13.1 m) in length, and has a wingspan of 44 ft (13.44 m).

The model was carefully built to withstand transportation—from its original base in the LEGO Model Shop in Kladno, Czech Republic, to New York and finally on to LEGOLAND® California.

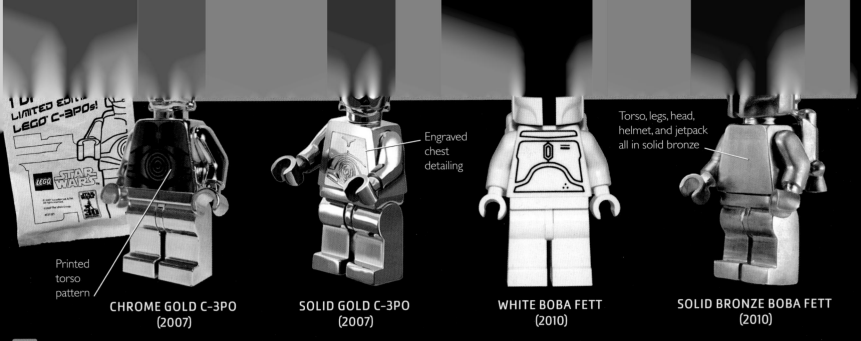

Printed torso pattern

CHROME GOLD C-3PO
(2007)

Engraved chest detailing

SOLID GOLD C-3PO
(2007)

WHITE BOBA FETT
(2010)

Torso, legs, head, helmet, and jetpack all in solid bronze

SOLID BRONZE BOBA FETT
(2010)

▼ Comic-Con Exclusives

Annual Comic-Con events have undergone a massive surge in popularity in recent years. The LEGO Group has a big presence at these gatherings, where they often hand out or sell exclusive promotional sets or minifigures. This range displays some of the recent Microfighter giveaways—revealed before the launch of the 2014 Microfighter line.

Only 1,000 produced, packaged in a special metal cube

SAN DIEGO COMIC-CON
JEK-14 STEALTH STARFIGHTER
(2013)

Movable wings

Exclusive Boba minifigure

***STAR WARS* CELEBRATION VI**
BOBA FETT'S MINI *SLAVE 1*
(2007)

Available to the first 200 customers on each day of the 2012 New York Comic Con

Exclusive Luke Skywalker minifigure

NEW YORK COMIC-CON
LUKE'S LANDSPEEDER
(2012)

▼ *Star Wars* Celebration Exclusives

For Celebration 2017, the LEGO Group released an exclusive set based on Han and Luke's rescue of Princess Leia on the Death Star. Fans had to enter a lottery to granted a chance to get their hands on it.

▼ New York Toy Fair Exclusives

In 2005, at the New York Toy Fair, attendees of the LEGO Group's V.I.P. gala event received a special edition of the Darth Vader transformation set, packaged inside a special slipcase.

Fan Creations

The LEGO® fan community spans generations, reaches across continents, and bridges languages. The beauty of LEGO bricks is that you can make just about anything with them and groups of expert builders, or AFOLs (Adult Fans of LEGO), do just that. Their custom-made designs even have their own specialist term: MOCs (My Own Creations). The simple brick has been transformed into the most creative and versatile construction element in the world.

▶ Mos Eisley

The Brickish Association is a UK-based community of AFOLS. Its members displayed their impressively detailed Mos Eisley diorama at the UK's National Space Centre and at *Star Wars: Celebration Europe* in 2007.

12 people built and contributed buildings, vehicles, and minifigures

A Boba Fett minifigure watches over the scene

Many movie-accurate details (these stormtroopers are searching for missing droids)

▶ Carbon-Freezing Chamber

Markus Aspacher (markus1984) took just five days to create this wonderful MOC of the Carbon-Freezing Chamber in 2013. Measuring 13 x 16 in (34 x 40 cm), it utilizes around 2,000 bricks. A Han Solo minifigure being lowered into the freezing chamber brings the whole grisly scene to life.

Fortified entrance to the core of the Death Star

Rebel X-wing starfighter

Sculpture is life-size!

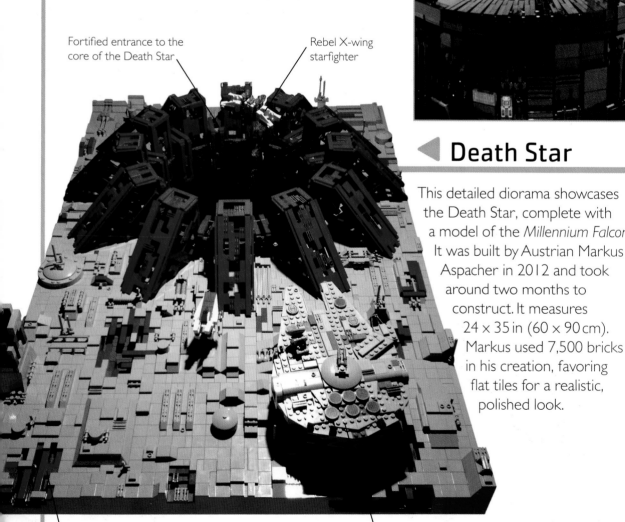

◀ Death Star

This detailed diorama showcases the Death Star, complete with a model of the *Millennium Falcon*. It was built by Austrian Markus Aspacher in 2012 and took around two months to construct. It measures 24 x 35 in (60 x 90 cm). Markus used 7,500 bricks in his creation, favoring flat tiles for a realistic, polished look.

"Unfinished" section of hull represented by red bricks

Detailed model of the *Millennium Falcon*

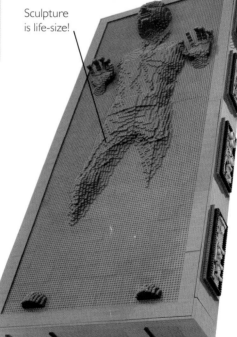

▲ Frozen Han Solo

Artist and brick builder extraordinaire Nathan Sawaya used 10,000 bricks to create this 5½-ft- (1.7-m-) tall sculpture of Han Solo frozen in carbonite.

Model of the crashed starship *Dowager Queen*

Some of the landspeeders are motorized

50 LEDs light the interior

Tan-colored bricks were collected over many years, many from LEGO Adventurers "Egypt" sets

Echo Base

Mark Borlase's recreation of Echo Base took four years to build. It has motorized hangar doors, a *Millennium Falcon* and superbly detailed AT-ATs. Snowtroopers lower themselves from AT-ATs and advance toward the rebel lines, which are complete with laser turrets and tauntauns.

Theed Hangar

Amado C. Pinlac (ACPin) has been building impressive MOCs for over a decade. This wonderfully detailed diorama captures the Theed hangar battle scene and includes four N-1 starfighters and an advancing Trade Federation droid army. The scene took Amado three months to build.

Anakin Skywalker takes off in an N-1 Naboo starfighter

Obi-Wan and Qui-Gon battle Darth Maul

CAMP FIRE ON TATOOINE

THE BATTLE OF HOTH

FAN ART
South Korean photographer Je Hyung Lee (storm TK431) creates imaginative images using his own backgrounds and a variety of LEGO *Star Wars* minifigures. The scenes have a modern, humorous twist, so don't be surprised if you see a stormtrooper-versus-Jedi ice-hockey match or stormtroopers playing the guitar and toasting marshmallows around a campfire!

Set Index

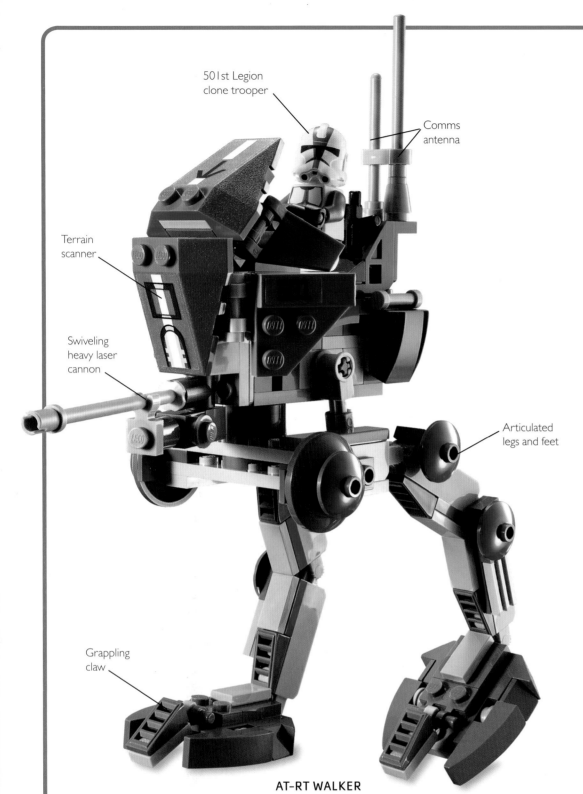

501st Legion
clone trooper

Comms
antenna

Terrain
scanner

Swiveling
heavy laser
cannon

Articulated
legs and feet

Grappling
claw

AT-RT WALKER

Senior Editor Laura Palosuo, Selina Wood
Senior Designer Joe Scott, Lauren Adams
Editors Matt Jones, Helen Murray
Designer Elena Jarmoskaite
Cover Designer Rhys Thomas
Pre-Production Producer Siu Yin Chan
Producer Louise Daly
Managing Editor Paula Regan
Managing Art Editor Jo Connor
Americanizer Megan Douglass
Publisher Julie Ferris
Art Director Lisa Lanzarini
Publishing Director Simon Beecroft

Consultants
Huw Millington and Giles Kemp

This American Edition, 2019
First American Edition, 2009
Published in the United States by DK Publishing
1450 Broadway, 8th Floor, New York, NY 10018

19 20 21 22 23 10 9 8 7 6 5 4 3 2 1
001–311498–Apr/2019

LEGO, the LEGO logo, the Minifigure and the Brick and Knob configurations
are trademarks of the LEGO Group. All rights reserved.
© 2009, 2012, 2014, 2019 The LEGO Group.
Produced by Dorling Kindersley under license from the LEGO Group.

Copyright © 2009, 2012, 2014, 2019 Lucasfilm Ltd. and ™.
All rights reserved.
Used under authorization.

Page design copyright © 2009, 2012, 2014, 2019 Dorling Kindersley Limited
DK, a Division of Penguin Random House LLC

All rights reserved. Without limiting the rights under the copyright reserved
above, no part of this publication may be reproduced, stored in or
introduced into a retrieval system, or transmitted, in any form, or by any
means (electronic, mechanical, photocopying, recording, or otherwise),
without the prior written permission of the copyright owner.
Published in Great Britain by Dorling Kindersley Limited.

A catalog record for this book
is available from the Library of Congress.
ISBN 978-1-4654-7888-7
ISBN 978-1-4654-8161-0 (Library edition)

Printed and bound in China

A WORLD OF IDEAS:
SEE ALL THERE IS TO KNOW
www.dk.com

www.LEGO.com
www.starwars.com

Acknowledgments

DK would like to thank Randi Kirsten Sørensen, Heidi K. Jensen, Paul Hansford, Martin Leighton Lindhardt, Maya Pazvantova, Jens Kronold Frederiksen, César Carvalhosa Soares, Madison Andrew O'Neil, Henrik Andersen, Kurt Kristiansen, Niels Mølgård Frederiksen, Aaron Douglas Anderson, Michael Lee Stockwell, Martin Fink, Hans Burkhard Schlömer, Christian Minick Vonsild, Jan Neergaard Olesen and Tim Trøjborg (photographer) at the LEGO Group; Jennifer Heddle and Mike Siglain at Lucasfilm; Chelsea Alon at Disney.

The publisher would also like to thank Huw Millington and Giles Kemp for lending their expert LEGO Star Wars knowledge and the permission to use their photographs; Gary Ombler for his photography; Jason Fry, Simon Beecroft and Simon Hugo for writing; Elly Dowsett for proofreading. For his contribution to the first edition of the this book, DK would like to thank Jeremy Beckett.

PICTURE CREDITS
Images supplied by the LEGO Group. Additional photography by Gary Ombler, Jeremy Beckett, Sarah Ashun and Brian Poulsen. Page 156: Bottom left and center © Markus Aspacher (markus1984); bottom right, Han Solo in Carbonite sculpture © Nathan Sawaya. Photo courtesy of brickartist.com; Page 157: bottom left © Amado C. Pinlac (ACPin); center right © Mark Borlase/Brickplumber; bottom right © Je Hyung Lee (storm TK431); top right © Ian Greig, 2007.